AFRICAN ETHNOGRAPHIC STUDIES OF THE 20TH CENTURY

Volume 63

SOCIAL AND RITUAL LIFE OF THE AMBO OF NORTHERN RHODESIA

SOCIAL AND RITUAL LIFE OF THE AMBO OF NORTHERN RHODESIA

BRONISLAW STEFANISZYN

LONDON AND NEW YORK

First published in 1964 by Oxford University Press for the International African Institute.

This edition first published in 2018
by Routledge
2 Park Square, Milton Park, Abingdon, Oxon OX14 4RN

and by Routledge
711 Third Avenue, New York, NY 10017

Routledge is an imprint of the Taylor & Francis Group, an informa business

© 1964 International African Institute

All rights reserved. No part of this book may be reprinted or reproduced or utilised in any form or by any electronic, mechanical, or other means, now known or hereafter invented, including photocopying and recording, or in any information storage or retrieval system, without permission in writing from the publishers.

Trademark notice: Product or corporate names may be trademarks or registered trademarks, and are used only for identification and explanation without intent to infringe.

British Library Cataloguing in Publication Data
A catalogue record for this book is available from the British Library

ISBN: 978-0-8153-8713-8 (Set)
ISBN: 978-0-429-48813-9 (Set) (ebk)
ISBN: 978-1-138-59847-8 (Volume 63) (hbk)
ISBN: 978-0-429-48633-3 (Volume 63) (ebk)

Publisher's Note
The publisher has gone to great lengths to ensure the quality of this reprint but points out that some imperfections in the original copies may be apparent.

Disclaimer
The publisher has made every effort to trace copyright holders and would welcome correspondence from those they have been unable to trace.

SOCIAL AND RITUAL LIFE OF THE AMBO OF NORTHERN RHODESIA

BRONISLAW STEFANISZYN

EDITED WITH A FOREWORD BY
RAYMOND APTHORPE

Published for the
INTERNATIONAL AFRICAN INSTITUTE
by the
OXFORD UNIVERSITY PRESS
LONDON   NEW YORK   TORONTO
1964

Oxford University Press, Amen House, London E.C.4
GLASGOW NEW YORK TORONTO MELBOURNE WELLINGTON
BOMBAY CALCUTTA MADRAS KARACHI LAHORE DACCA
CAPE TOWN SALISBURY NAIROBI IBADAN ACCRA
KUALA LUMPUR HONG KONG

© International African Institute 1964

CUM SUPERIORUM PERMISSU

Printed in Great Britain by
Ebenezer Baylis and Son, Ltd.
The Trinity Press, Worcester, and London

FOREWORD

RAYMOND APTHORPE

THE present study of the matrilineal, Bantu-speaking Ambo or Kambonsenga of Northern Rhodesia carries forward Central Bantu studies in the tradition particularly of Smith and Dale, and of Doke.[1] 'Central Bantu' is used here in a wider sense than that preferred by Professor Mitchell.[2] Contrary to his tentative suggestion,[3] inter-clan joking relations are not confined to peoples west of the Luangwa river. Variants of the inter-clan joking described in the present study for the Ambo are, for instance, institutionalized also in Nsenga and Cewa society east of the Luangwa, according to my own field observations in Petauke at intervals from 1958–61. On the whole, this ethnographical account of the Ambo would serve for the most general purposes, as well for the Lala-speaking people to the west[4] and the Nsenga to the east and south-east. And I have suggested elsewhere that there is some reason to consider the Cewa, rather than the Nsenga, as the most westerly of the Maravi peoples.[5]

Ethnological generalization of this kind, however, is at best misleading. Nsenga claim to be exclusively different from Ambo in cultural identity, and certainly the relation between clan and chieftainship posited in Nsenga belief is not a simple replication of that among the Ambo. Also, if Ambo in Lusaka or (say) in the chiefdom of Mwape on occasion claim to be Nsenga, this may be on account of the greater prestige attaching, at the present time in some contexts, to the title 'Nsenga' and not for any historical or ethnographical reason. But obviously Ambo could not possibly claim

---

[1] E. W. Smith and A. Dale: *The Ila-speaking peoples of Northern Rhodesia* (1920). C. M. Doke: *The Lamba of Northern Rhodesia* (1931).

[2] J. Clyde Mitchell: *An outline of the sociological background to African labour* (1961) (Ensign Publishers, Southern Rhodesia), p. 12.

[3] J. Clyde Mitchell: *The Kalela dance.* Rhodes–Livingstone Paper No. 27 (1956) at p. 37.

[4] A bibliography of J. T. Munday's Lala studies is on p. ii of my general introduction to *Central Bantu Historical Texts* I, Rhodes–Livingstone Communication, No. 22 (1961).

[5] Raymond Apthorpe: 'Problems of African political history: the Nsenga of Northern Rhodesia', *Rhodes–Livingstone Journal*, XXVIII (December (1960), pp. 47–67.

FOREWORD

to be 'Nsenga' if the identifying criteria concerned were either unmistakable or at least readily demonstrable.

My own part in preparing this book, which I undertook originally as Research Secretary of the Rhodes–Livingstone Institute in connection with my own studies of the Nsenga of Petauke which I had just started, has been to select and to edit from Father Stefaniszyn's more extensive manuscript. The original of this is deposited in the library of the University of the Witwatersrand. The author himself revised my changes in his text where necessary. His total Ambo material exceeds the scope and length of the study presented here. In addition to already published papers (*see* bibliography) there remains in manuscript a corpus of folklore and further information on medicine and magic, for example. Both the author and I, however, would record that we planned a joint field trip to carry his inquiries yet further, particularly with regard to positional succession and political kinship of which Father Stefaniszyn had made no study while in the field as a missionary, and to certain rites which are described in the present book on the basis of informants' accounts rather than from direct observation. Unfortunately the project became unfeasible for various political reasons and we had to abandon it.

It would also have been particularly valuable to have inquired further into *nkole* (*nkhole* in Nsenga),[1] a legal process which operates without the intervention of the chief being deemed a necessary prerequisite, but with recourse to the authority of a senior member of a lineage (*see* page 52). There are references to this institution both in the journals of early travellers and in Government archives for the area, as well as in the early ethnographies (e.g. Doke *op. cit.*), but not, strangely enough, in the later contributions to Central African studies made by Richards, Gluckman, Colson, Mitchell and others. My own comparative studies into political institutions in Central Africa, so far as they had gone before being curtailed, were leading to the conclusion that the Northern Rhodesia Native Courts' Ordinance of the 1920's (amended in the following decade) not only restored to chiefs some powers lost to them under British South Africa Company rule, but also conferred on them a jurisdiction in some matters of customary law which they had not enjoyed in the days before British occupation. Apparently the Colonial authorities

[1] My colleague at the Rhodes–Livingstone Institute, W. J. Argyle, has also culled data on this institution from these various sources. I gratefully acknowledge exchanges with him on topics raised in this Introduction, but mine is the responsibility for the final argument adduced.

FOREWORD

vii

concerned were acting upon what they supposed to have been 'traditional' rights of chiefs in this regard.

Father Stefaniszyn's Ambo studies were not carried out as part of the research largely planned and guided by Professor Gluckman at the Rhodes–Livingstone Institute until 1947, and at the University of Manchester for some years further. The present study of a pattern of social and ritual life differs considerably from the structuralist social anthropological analyses by 'the Manchester school'. It may be suggestive for future research, as well as evaluatory of the present contribution to Central African studies, to single out two such differences for special comment.

Such social anthropological analyses as have been made of Central African religious systems stem from Durkheim's rather than (say) Weber's epistemological position: in particular they focus on cult rather than on ethic.[1] This means that since there appear to be few cults of high gods in Central Africa, but many of ancestors, very little attention can be paid in these particular anthropological analyses to a significance of high gods which is not manifested in cults. High gods are said to be 'withdrawn' because they are 'neglected' in ritual. But religious significance is not necessarily restricted to ritual or cultic significance. It is, therefore, an insufficient analysis of high gods that inquires only into the presence or absence in a particular society of cults relating to them.

Professor Colson's studies of Plateau Tonga religion,[2] for example, are to all practical intents devoid of constructive analysis on the subject of the high god *Lesa*, to whose existence she alludes however. Their emphasis is more or less exclusively on ancestral shades. The passages on the Ambo supreme being in the last chapter of the present work, brief though they are, point to a significance of a high god which is inaccessible to a Durkheimian analysis of cults such as Colson's. In West Africa also, new studies of religious systems are adumbrating a dimension of belief, the social existence of which one would not have suspected from Durkheimian 'social structural' analyses. One may contrast for example Professor Fortes's studies of West African religion as systems of ancestor worship with Dr. Bolaji Idowu's account of Yoruba religion with its stress on the high god *Olodumare*.[3]

---

[1] Talcott Parsons: *The structure of social action* (1947), p. 676.

[2] E.g. Elizabeth Colson: 'Ancestral spirits and social structure among the Plateau Tonga', *International archives of ethnography*, XLVII, Pt. 1 (1954), pp. 21–68.

[3] E.g. Meyer Fortes: *Oedipus and Job in West African religion* (1959) and his earlier Tallensi studies; E. Bolaji Idowu: *Olodumare: God in Yoruba belief* (1962).

viii FOREWORD

If the emphasis in Durkheim's sociology of religion is on cult and that of Weber's on ethic, Radcliffe-Brown may be regarded as the heir of Durkheim in social anthropology and Malinowski as the heir of Weber. Few studies of African religions from a Malinowskian point of view are available. Of other approaches, a third is derived from the intellectualists Tylor and Frazer and from Lévy-Bruhl, which lays emphasis on ritual and religion as a mode of thought rather than as an organization of offices with various rights and duties attached to them. In this approach, special importance is attributed to symbolism. Perhaps it will be these two latter developments of avenues of inquiry into the sociology of religion that will prove to be the most constructive in respect of a significance of a high god above and beyond cultic representation.

Secondly, recent social anthropological studies in Central Africa have emphasized 'the village' as 'one social group [that] occurs in all the tribes whatever their environment and whatever their other forms of social organization . . . a discrete group of people who reside in usually adjacent huts, who recognize allegiance to a head-man, and who have a corporate identity against other groups'.[1] The emphasis in Father Stefaniszyn's account is on the Ambo village as a 'rallying point' rather than a corporate unit (page 43). He also notes (page 27) that an Ambo village may be said to belong to a particular clan which is usually regarded in Central African studies as a dispersed, non-corporate unit. Both observations are true of villages of the Nsenga of Petauke and, I suspect, of Central Bantu peoples in general.

Professor Colson observes in a characteristic passage describing the matrilineage and clan among the Gwembe Tonga that 'several matrilineages belonging to the same clan may be present [in a neighbourhood] *each one completely independent of the other* [italics added] though they share the same clan name and recognize their common clanship'.[2] Though it may escape positive analysis by the methods typical of 'the Manchester school', there is more in common clanship for Central Bantu peoples than only the name: *only corporately* could those matrilineages be 'completely independent' of one another. Clanship relations in Central Africa may be non-corporate but they are not therefore non-existent. Ethnographic observations such as those of Father Stefaniszyn show clanship to

[1] Max Gluckman, J. C. Mitchell, J. A. Barnes: 'The village headman in Central Africa,' *Africa*, XIX, 2 (April 1949), pp. 89–106, at p. 90.
[2] Cited in my review of Elizabeth Colson: *Social Organization of the Gwembe Tonga* (1961) in *African Studies* Vol. 22, No. 1, 1963, p. 46.

FOREWORD

be of considerable social significance as a concept which is current and acted upon in the population concerned, in the context of 'the village' as well as in others. One would scarcely suspect this from most social anthropological analyses for Central Africa. Yet even for the Plateau Tonga, Colson remarks that 'the clan – not as a body of people but as an institution – is the most permanent element in Tonga social organization'.[1] It is unfortunate that while the methods of analysis used by the Manchester school usefully demonstrate what clanship in Central Africa is not, they do not extend to showing what clanship is. But the point requires fuller examination than is possible here and I have in fact undertaken this elsewhere.[2]

The problem of the relation of one people to another is always partly one of the relations to each other of the various methodologies used in studies of the peoples concerned. This is particularly true in the present case, as already implied. Father Stefaniszyn's account of the social and ritual life of a Central African people lacks the structuralist orientation of the kind associated with most major studies in Central Africa. On the other hand, it has the advantage of its author's long practised fluency in the language and long contact with Ambo society over a period of several years, 1936 to 1953 and 1957 to 1961. Short, sharp, specifically problem-oriented inquiries by visiting specialists have their own rewards, but nonetheless they are likely to reflect the observer's own personal interests and procedures rather than topics which are of recurring general social relevance to the society concerned. To some extent, this is less likely in the case of a series of more random observations made over a long period of close contact. It is to be hoped that institutes of African studies will continue to devote part of their resources to encouraging and making available studies like the present one. Not only are these germinal in themselves of ideas for special studies: they are also useful ethnographic introductions to an area, to be read for their general interest before moving to specialist accounts.

It remains to be noted that in the text *l* rather than *r* is used in the orthography for Ambo words. Occasionally, 'sibling' or 'clan' is inserted before 'sister', for example, to make clear the social context concerned. Also, I have not attempted here to compare Nsenga with Ambo beliefs and practices where I have information on the former from my own and my assistants' observations in Petauke, and from

[1] In 'The Plateau Tonga of Northern Rhodesia' in Colson and Gluckman (editors): *Seven tribes of British Central Africa* (1949), p. 132.
[2] Raymond Apthorpe, 'The methodology of Central African social anthropological studies'. (Mimeographed, 1962)

FOREWORD

those of E. H. Lane Poole, made mainly in the decade preceding 1925, which I am in course of preparing for publication. Dr. Leach in his Malinowski Lecture, *Rethinking Anthropology*,[1] has recently raised some important issues of 'comparison' versus 'generalization' which future work in 'comparative sociology' must examine. But, contrary to one implication of his thesis, 'generalization' requires the use of categories as much as 'comparison' does—if of a different sort. An emerging new dimension of African studies in which, as distinct from social institutions, a people's philosophical concepts are the focus of interest is, in effect, providing relevant categories for sociological generalization in African studies. Here one cannot fail to mention Father Tempels's pioneer study of *Bantu Philosophy* (Eng. transl. 1959). There is a hint of Tempels's terminology in this present account of the Ambo but this is because he is concerned with concepts very closely related to Ambo and also the Nsenga (see page 97 fn.). Central Africa—Zambia in particular—enjoys unparalleled 'ethnographic coverage' and few 'ethnographic gaps' remain[2] but many of these Central African studies are out of phase with this new and promising orientation in African studies.

---

[1] E. R. Leach, *Rethinking Anthropology* (1961), London School of Economics Monographs on Social Anthropology, No. 22.

[2] Taking into consideration research both published and being prepared for publication these are limited chiefly to the Bisa, the Lenje, the Lala and the non-Lozi peoples of Barotseland.

ACKNOWLEDGEMENTS

THIS work is a result of my investigations during my stay among the Ambo as a missionary from September 1938 until April 1943, and again from November 1950 to July 1953. After leaving the Ambo I presented my collected material on their social and ritual life and material culture for the Ph.D. degree at the University of the Witwatersrand. My study at the University was made possible through the generosity of the Catholic Bishops of Johannesburg, Dr. W. Whelan O.M.I. (now Archbishop of Bloemfontein) and Dr. H. Boyle. I owe much also to the Lyndhurst Convent and the Parish Priest, Father M. G. Killoran. My thanks must also go to my ordinary, the Catholic Archbishop of Northern Rhodesia and to my ecclesiastical superiors, Fathers M. Folta and J. Plawecki, for giving me time to study.

At the University my supervisor was Dr. M. D. W. Jeffreys, to whom I am indebted for my introduction to anthropological studies, for the arrangement of my thesis, and the use he allowed me to make of his vast private library. I am grateful to the Rev. J. T. Munday of Broken Hill, Northern Rhodesia, who is conversant with the Ambo people and their language, for reviewing the manuscript of my thesis in 1956 and making many valuable suggestions.

My chief Ambo informants were the late Chikwashya Kakote and Mulaku Kalubangwe, the late Chief Mambwe Mwengu Mboshya, Chief Chisenga Lishyoka Mboloma, the late Chief Nsangwe III Chisomo, the late old *nganga* Lwenda of Malkopo, the late headman Mbilisau, treasury clerk Mr. Anthony Chibuye, teachers Paulo Chibuye, Paulo Munshya (now Chief Mboshya), and many others. They all helped Kateka, 'the peaceful ruler', in his search for knowledge.

I was helped financially by a Rustenholz scholarship, by a grant from Mr. C. A. Denny, and by the Association of Polish Settlers in Johannesburg, for which I am most grateful.

Lastly, I extend my heartfelt thanks to Dr. Raymond Apthorpe who, while senior research officer of the Rhodes–Livingstone

xii ACKNOWLEDGEMENTS

Institute, accepted responsibility for the final editing and presentation which has made possible the publication of this contribution to Ambo studies.

Lusaka, Northern Rhodesia, BRONISLAW STEFANISZYN
March 1961

CONTENTS

FOREWORD — v

ACKNOWLEDGEMENTS — xi

INTRODUCTION — xvii

I. CLAN AND MATRILINEAGE — 1

The clan (*mukoka*); list of clans; list of sister clans; funeral friendship; the matrilineage; siblings; mother and children; grandparents and grandchildren; the family; affinal relatives; the sexes; a note on kinship terminology; preferential marriage between alternate generations

II. THE VILLAGE — 27

The formation of new villages; breaking up of villages; village plans and sizes; marital exile; Mtondo village of the Mwanso clan; clan composition and attitudes in the village; the village headmanship; medicine against lions (*luteta*); doctoring a ford against crocodiles; doctoring against hyenas; other considerations

III. CHIEFTAINSHIP — 52

The chiefdoms and the Nyendwa clan; funeral rites; mourning of the land; the interregnum; selection, succession and instalment; the rights and duties of a chief; prohibitions for the chief; warfare; chiefs' medicines; some modern circumstances

IV. CHILDHOOD AND PUBERTY — 74

Pregnancy; the delivery; difficult delivery; the killing of a child whose upper teeth appear first (*lutala*); birth out of wedlock; first touch of the child by the father; the rite of 'nursing the child on the mat' (*kulela kwa mwana pa mpasa*); aftercare of 'the child of sprouting'; the naming rite (*kuilike 'sina*); the meaning of the naming rites; infancy; weaning; cutting teeth and losing them; childhood; girl's maturation; boy's maturation

V. MARRIAGE — 99

Courtship; the wedding; special avoidances of married couples; final emancipation of the young couple; the making of a hearth; marriage rules; polygamy; divorce; widows

VI. DEATH, SUCCESSION AND INHERITANCE — 121

Death; funerary inversions; death and burial of a leper; death and burial of a pregnant woman; burial of a stillborn child (*kapopo*); funeral of a childless woman; funeral beer; redemption of the bereft; inheritance of the widow; succession to headmanship; final funeral beer

xiv · CONTENTS

VII. RELIGION AND DIVINATION   134

The supreme being; divination; diviners; divination techniques;
divining medicines; beer offerings (*bwalwa bwa mupashi*) in
private contexts; dreams; omens; alien shades; chiefs' shades;
spirit possession; medicines of spirit possession; spirits in
animals and trees

BIBLIOGRAPHY   163

INDEX   165

LIST OF MAPS, DIAGRAMS AND TABLES

Map

The Ambo country   xv

Diagrams

I.	Principal kinship terms in Ambo	24
II.	Kinship terms for wife's kindred	24
III.	Classificatory relationships	25
IV.	Grandparent—grandchild marriage	26
V.	Marital relationship in Mtondo village	32
VI.	Affinal and agnatic matrilineages in Mtondo village	34–5
VII.	Plan of Mtondo village in 1944	39
VIII.	Plan of Mtondo village in 1950	40

Tables

I.	The average number of people in a village	30
II.	Marital residence	33
III.	Disposition of clansmen in the villages	41
IV.	Disposition of clanswomen in the villages	42
V.	Incidence of polygyny	112
VI.	Percentage of polygyny	112
VII.	Divorce rate	114
VIII.	Grounds for divorce	115

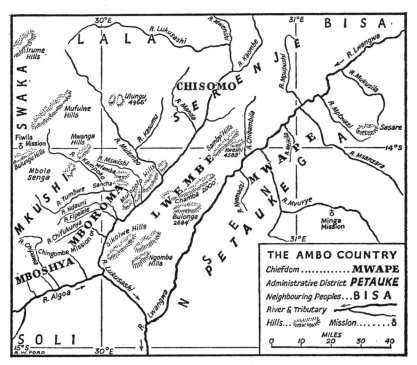

The Ambo Country

INTRODUCTION

The Country

AMBO land is divided between three administrative districts of Northern Rhodesia, those of Mkushi, Serenje and Petauke. In the north, in the Chisomo country in the Serenje district, the Ambo extend to 13° 30″ latitude in the valley of the Lukusashi and its tributaries. They overflow eastwards into the Luangwa and beyond; in the west they have settled on the left bank of the Lunsemfwa from its confluence with the Lukusashi upstream.

The valley floors of the three great rivers, Lukusashi, Lunsemfwa and Luangwa are not of uniform ecological character. The Ambo cultivate only the narrow strips of alluvial soils immediately bordering these rivers, their tributaries and lesser streams. These riverine belts are extremely fertile and their sandy loam soils retain moisture throughout the year, enabling the Ambo to grow maize four times a year, and always have a plentiful supply of fresh greens for relish. In these gardens the Ambo produce their main cash crop, tobacco.

These permanent streams and also superficially dry water courses have their banks overgrown with luxuriant vegetation of which the most important species are *Adina microcephala*, *Kaya nyassica* (*mululu*), excellent mahogany, *Trichilia emetica*, (*musikisi*), *Acacia*, *Ficus* and *Kigelia spinnata* (*mulungula*). (Trapnell, 1943, p. 14.) *Pennisetum purpureum* (*malenje*), buffalo grass and *phragmites communis* (*mitete*) reeds grow close to the water. *Oxynantera abyssinica* (*ntele*) bamboo, thrives in the valleys of small streams. The last two plants play important and characteristic parts in the economy. The staple crop is sorghum. The most important minor crops are pumpkins, sweet potatoes and groundnuts.

The people live along these rivers, streams and water courses, the villages being situated on elevated ground usually not further than half a mile from the water's edge. In fact, the proximity of good water is the main ecological factor determining the site of villages. A cluster of villages along a stream forms an informal social group of neighbours (*mitala*).

xviii INTRODUCTION

The prevalence of tsetse fly rules out the keeping of cattle and pigs. Chickens are reared by most people for ritual, social and economic reasons. Dogs are used for chasing small game especially the warthog, rabbit and cane-rat.

The intervening watershed country between streams is inhospitable, dreary bush, *mpanga*, for the most part either mopane or Brachystegia country. Mopane bush is characterized by mature, heavy brown soil. The typical mopane landscape, *lupani*, is flat with sparse trees and scanty grass with sand glades, *cinguwa*. The mopane lands are dotted with fantastic heavily eroded gullies. There is another type of country, rises surfaced with water-worn stones and pebbles, covered with still more sparsely scattered dwarf mopane trees. These barren shingle-strewn rises are especially common at the foothills of the escarpments. They also support *Terminalia* (*kabesya*) and *Commiphora*.

Brachystegia country is *misamba*. The soil is grey-brown and immature, with a colluvial origin. Large stretches of this country are overgrown with *Isoberlinia* (*sandwe*) *Dyospyrous mespililformis*, (*mucenje*) and *Cordyla africana* (*mtondo*).

Game is represented by elephant, buffalo, eland (not plentiful), roan antelope, ubiquitous kudu, herds of mpala roaming in the mopane, waterbuck and an occasional reedbuck. The smaller variety is confined to bushbuck in the thickets along the streams and duiker in the Brachystegia woodlands; small griesbuck is fairly common. Antelopes living in the valleys are rather limited in variety. The wild pig, difficult to hunt, is a scourge of the maize-growers along the small streams, who must also contend with monkeys and especially with sizeable troops of baboons. Zebra are found in the foothills only. According to old people, hippopotami have increased since they were prohibited beasts, and now frequently destroy maize, particularly in winter gardens along the large rivers. Lions occasionally kill people; leopards are common. The cane-rat is the chief source of meat in winter and spring time.

Ambo distinguish three seasons of the year; the rainy season, *mainsa*, from November till March; the dry cold season, *mwela*, from April till August, and the hot dry season, *tusuba*, from September till the rains. The average rainfall is 36 inches per year. Temperature records have been kept in the neighbouring Petauke district. The mean minimum temperature is 64·5° F., in Feira 58° F. The absolute maximum in Petauke is 109° F., in Feira 118° F. Temperatures in the Lukusashi valley fall somewhere between these

INTRODUCTION xix

two regions. Chingombe Mission, which lies in the heart of the Lukusashi valley, is 1,700 feet above sea level.

The People

The Ambo or, alternatively, the Kambosenga, number about ten thousand.

Population density is in the region of 5 persons per square mile in Chief Mboloma's area, and 7 in Mboshya's country.[1] There is no reason to assume that other chiefdoms differ significantly.

Many Ambo regard Chisomo's people as Ambo but young people in that chiefdom identify themselves with the Lala, a trend originated by the Administration. The language of the Chisomo people, however, is influenced by Bisa and they have many connections with the neighbouring Lala on the plateau; historically the ruling Chisomo matrilineage descended from that of the neighbouring Lala Chief Chibale and was not genealogically connected with that of the founder of the Ambo, Kunda Mpanda. Both chiefs, however, are of the matriclan Nyendwa.

Chisomo country extends on both banks of the middle of the Lukusashi and in the east reaches the Luangwa. In the west it is hemmed in by the escarpment hills. In the south it borders the Lwembe chiefdom, north of the Mulembo.

The lands of chief Lwembe spread out on the left bank of the Lukusashi and cross the Lwangwa in the east. Along both banks of the Luangwa, however, the majority of the people are Nsenga.

The chiefdom of Mwape is on the eastern side of the Luangwa. It is only nominally an Ambo chiefdom, for historical and dynastic reasons. I have found only three villages there of Ambo ancestry, and the younger generation in these villages, though proud of their Ambo origin, speak not Ambo, but Nsenga.

Mboloma's chiefdom extends from the Mulembo in the north to the Lunsemfwa in the south. To the west it is confined by the Chifukunya range. In the east its border with the Lwembe chiefdom is the Lukusashi river. In the times before the coming of the British Administration both banks of the Lukusashi were included in Mboloma's chiefdom, the Muchinga range east of the Lukusashi separating it from the lands of Chieftainness Mwape.

Mboshya's people maintain close social contact with the people of the Lukusashi valley.

[1] Information from the District Commissioner.

xx INTRODUCTION

History

According to their own tradition the Ambo emigrated from Luba country. This agrees well with the traditions of other peoples of this region. Scarcity of land and density of population are indicated as the reasons for emigration.

Lungo, of the Fish clan, a son of the Aushi chief Makumba Chawala, settled first on the Mulembo river, fleeing and hiding from his half-brother Kunda who sought to marry Lungo's daughter Kaluba. Among other first settlers was another half-brother of Lungo, namely Mambwe Chisaka of the Mpande shell clan. Mambwe dispossessed the local Nsenga chief, Mumba Chundu. The Ambo call their conquered territory *kuNsenga* and probably took possession of it between 1830 and 1840.

Mambwe Chisaka was soon followed by Kunda Mpanda who found Lungo, killed him and married Lungo's daughter. Their union was regarded as incestuous. Kunda fought the Nsenga but in his third expedition lost his life in a battle with a Nsenga chief, Nkana Yalobe.

Mambwe Chisaka mobilized the Mpande clan and the related Tembo clan of the Lenje chief Chipepo, and avenged the death of Kunda by killing Nkana Yalobe. The skin of Kunda was recovered and buried on the Mulembo on the village site of Mambwe Chisaka and Kunda Mpanda. This burial was the beginning of the grave-yard of the Nyendwa chiefs, the successors of Kunda Mpanda. Matrilineal descendants of Mambwe Chisaka are in charge of the place to this day.

Kunda Mpanda became a legendary hero of the Ambo, with the honorific title of *Kankomba*, 'scraper of pots'.

After the death of Kunda, Chilimba Nondo, his sister's son, succeeded him. According to tradition his was a peaceful reign, which means that he ruled before the coming of the Ngoni. The most important event ascribed to his reign was the founding of two other chiefdoms carved out from Kunda's heritage. Chilimba installed his sister Mwape in the eastern regions and this chieftain-ship is always inherited by females in Mwape's matrilineage. Chilimba also posted his sister's son Lwembe at an exposed position to defend Mwape against the Nsenga. He also gave to one of his relatives a country in the west under the name of Mboshya's chiefdom.

After Chilimba's death Mubanga occupied the seat of the Kan-

INTRODUCTION xxi

komba, but little is known of him. He was succeeded by three brothers, Bwashi, Chibuye and Lwembe (II), his sister's sons.

Bwashi resided among the Swaka at the hill of Katukutuku, where he felt safer against the raids of the Ngoni who appeared in his time. In the Lukusashi valley, Chibuye ruled for many years, seemingly in deference to his elder brother Bwashi. Chibuye, 'the peacemaker', allied himself with a new power, the Chikunda, thus protecting himself from Ngoni attacks. After Bwashi's death at the hands of the Ngoni, Chibuye became the Kankomba, but only for five years. He moved to the Mulembo, lived to a ripe old age and died about 1890. He was succeeded by his younger brother, Lwembe II Mukombola, who reigned for one year as the great chief.

After the death of Lwembe Mukombola, Mboloma I Chinda Chontabunga, came to power, being Bwashi's sister's son. Mboloma had been previously for many years a right-hand man of Bwashi, executing his orders which sometimes included death sentences. This did not make him popular, and he was in any case a man of quarrelsome nature. At the outset of his reign he met with much opposition on all sides and soon he was fighting an Ambo chief, Namupala, in Bukanda, in what is now the Congo, with Chief Mboshya and with the sons of Lwembe, Chembe and Munsunki. Having little success in war, he retired to the Lala plateau and settled on the Chisela stream near the Ilume hill. There the Ngoni raided him and burnt the regalia, *mata*, the bows of the preceding Kankombas.

In the meantime in the Lukusashi valley the most prominent headman was Nkumpa, the son of Chibuye, but the whole region was under the sway of the Chikunda.

After Chinda Mboloma's death Mubanga Kalutwa was installed and during his period British administration was introduced. He was succeeded by his sister's son, Lubula Komanga, who was followed by his sister's son, Chisenga Lishyoka, who rules the country at the present time.

Mwape I Namukwanga died about 1880; she was succeeded by her daughter Mwape II of Chibambila, a ruthless and intelligent woman who did not shirk from assassinating many other political rivals.[1] She caused the death of the renowned headman Mushyalila and later of his son Milonga. This latter involved her in hostilities on the left bank of the Luangwa with a Chikunda leader, Matekenya, and she had to flee the country to Bembaland.

Mwape also fought Chikwashya, the feudal priest-prince on the

[1] Lane Poole, 1934, p. 69.

xxii INTRODUCTION

Mulembo, the heir of Mambwe Chisaka. When in addition Mwape caused the assassination of Mkwemba, the successor of Lwembe I, another Chikunda warlord Kayetano Chimtanda, who was active on the right bank of the Lwangwa, turned against her until the coming of the British Administration put an end to these encounters.

Mwape was a polyandrist and is said to have killed her sons. She died in 1910.[1]

The chiefdom of Mboshya suffered three raids from the Ngoni. Later on, Mboshya Mambwe Lumpukanya fought the Chikunda leader Kayetano. The cause of their hostilities was the accidental killing of Mboshya's wife by the Chikunda during a raid.

Something has already been said as regards the beginnings of the chiefdom of Chisomo. The most famous Chisomo chief was Nesangwe II Chitmwalwo ('the fighter'). He repelled three Ngoni raids, fought the Bemba (called here the Bayongo) and the Chikunda. He died in 1941 in ripe old age.

[1] Stephenson, 1937, p. 84.

I. CLAN AND MATRILINEAGE

The clan (mukoka)

EVERY Ambo man, woman and child belongs to a clan by birthright bestowed by his or her mother. Should an Ambo claim his father's clan as his own, he is promptly asked whether it is his own clan he is referring to or his father's. The Ambo firmly believe, in spite of all assurances to the contrary, that the writer of this book has a clan membership but that he conceals it in order to avoid obligations of giving assistance to any supposed clansmen.

Clans are known by names signifying animals, plants and other material objects such as fire, rain, lead, clay. Many clan names found among the Ambo are commonly found also among other tribes of the Bemba group, and also among the Nsenga. There are only small differences between the list of Lamba clans according to Doke (1931) and those among the Ambo. These peoples are closely related linguistically and culturally. The *bene Misisi*, the Pubic hair clan, *bene Kabundi*, the Galago clan, *bene Nkalamu*, the Lion clan, *bene Cowa*, the Mushroom clan, *bene Kalowa*, the Clay clan, are absent in the Ambo valleys though they are listed for the Lamba. Clans found among the Ambo and not among the Lamba include the *bene Mubinda*, the Loin cloth clan, *bene Bi*, the Anus clan, *bene Mwanso*, the Penis clan, and *bene Nkalambo*, the Lead clan. In Ambo country there are a few individuals of *bene Nsanje*, the Blue monkey clan, who are said to be Lwano immigrants. There are also a few *bene Nsye*, the Locust clan, who claim to be of Nsenga extraction and who had in recent times a village of their own, Kanchebele. The *bene Mbeba*, the Mouse clan, are Swaka rather than Ambo, according to general belief.

Many clan names differ from those of the clan objects used in common speech. For example, the Wasp clan is *bene Tembo*, but 'wasp' in common speech is *lisasango*. Some clan names are diminutives of those in common speech such as the Sorghum clan, *bene Kasaka*, common *masaka* (sing. *lisaka*). Other clan names are used in common speech, e.g. the Rain clan, *bene Mfula*. Sometimes an

SOCIAL AND RITUAL LIFE OF THE AMBO

archaic word supplies a clan name, sometimes a word from another language.

Ambo give the same kind of explanation of the origin of clans as do the other tribes of their group. For instance, parties of mourners returning from a burial infringed a prohibition: they went to look for honey and were named accordingly the Honey guide clan.

Clanspeople claim ultimate common matrilineal descent, but the genealogical links are forgotten and genealogical distance is not reckoned. Even the clan ancestress is not remembered. Clanspeople call each other 'sibling' (*mukwabo*); they maintain strict exogamy, extend mutual hospitality and often material assistance, and should avoid taking each other to the Native Court. People not of one's own clan one terms 'strangers', *bana ba bene*, 'children of (their) owners'.

Clan exogamy is the strongest, though negative, mark of clan identification. There is a tendency among the older generation to extend exogamy to 'sister clans' (*see* page 5) whose clan objects stand in conceptual proximity. And general opinion does not favour marriages between funeral friends, as discussed later in this chapter. In practice, however, marriages of both these kinds occur. It is said that illicit intercourse takes place between the more distant clan members, perhaps after beer drinks. I know two instances of apparently endogamic marriage in the Wasp clan which are socially approved because the parents of the husbands came from a distant tribe on the Zambezi. (*See* Diagram V. Te (x) married Te (7) and Te(y) married Te (9).)

Reciprocal hospitality within the clan is another strongly emphasized centripetal feature. It has a very practical consequence in a country with a sparse population, where there are no hotels, rest-houses or restaurants. Mutual assistance is practised mostly in time of food shortage. Usually clansmen in disputes within the clan are conciliatory and forgiving but in extreme cases this clan privilege is not observed. Nevertheless a man should not take legal action against a fellow clansman. This rule of not disputing with a fellow clansman meant, in former times, a virtual prohibition of enslavement within the clan. In the contemporary context, much bad feeling over the payment of fines and compensations is avoided: such payments are regarded as incompatible with the notion of brotherhood. This behaviour stands out in striking contrast to that towards 'strangers' to whom one might easily become liable for heavy compensation—in former times—enslavement possibly being involved.

CLAN AND MATRILINEAGE

Relations with a stranger are marked by meticulous correctness, particularly when he is ill or dying, to avoid danger of dispute. The same propriety should be observed towards one's own wife and all her children.

To throw an imprecatory curse upon a clansman or a clanswoman is a serious matter. It must be ritually withdrawn, or it is regarded as an unnatural offence much like incest. Usually the curse is of the form that one will not have relations with, or will not talk to, a clansman for the rest of his life. Such a curse is withdrawn through drinking a potent medicine, *coni*, in the presence of a clan elder such as a headman.

Medicine of swearing, coni.

If two *bakwabo* (members of a clan irrespective of sex or matrilineage) swear that they will not meet each other till death, the head of the matrilineage exorcizes them by means of 'medicine'. Otherwise it is feared that the curse may come true and one of the disputants may die. It is the only instance where matrilineal solidarity in Ambo society is safeguarded through the use of magic.

Ingredients: A tree struck by lightning. This is mixed in the compound as a sign that if the culprit should again commit the offence of swearing at a clansman, he will meet with a strange accident or misfortune.

Coni, the root. This tree has the same name as the name of the compound medicine of swearing. I have no data on its natural properties which lead to its use here.

A piece of cloth with the menstrual blood of a clanswoman, a symbol of the clan and especially of the matrilineage, and of common descent. Lastly, urine of a clansman and clanswoman as the symbol of a common mother and common womb.

The parties which cursed each other drink this compound and are 'publicly' admonished and reconciled. The headman, as the head of the matrilineage, addresses the culprits: 'You have drunk *coni*; let your hearts be calm, because of the medicine you have drunk, you have all come back to the womb of your mother. You must not repeat the oath again'.

Here is an instance of magic and ceremonial being used to bolster up clan—and particularly matrilineal—solidarity. Though in individual cases clanspeople may not get on well together and persons of different clans may develop devoted and trusted friendships,

4 SOCIAL AND RITUAL LIFE OF THE AMBO

nevertheless the common tie of clan membership predisposes individuals to an increasing measure of intimacy.

A group of school boys of 10 to 12 years of age were observed standing embracing one another. Asked whether they ever fought between themselves, they explained that they were 'brothers', and therefore could strike one another only lightly. They pointed to other boys of the same village, of different clans, whom they might not touch, lest their mothers should bewitch them out of revenge. Clan consciousness in attitudes towards 'strangers' may thus be shown at an early age.

Common clanship transcends tribe. Machisa, of the Gourd clan, was sick of a protracted disease. He was Soli by tribe but had married uxorilocally in Ambo country. A Gourd clansman, the headman of a village a day's walk away from where Machisa lived, and not only a member of another major matrilineage but also of another tribe, anxiously inquired into the condition of Machisa his clan 'brother'.

List of clans

English	Ambo clan name	Common word	Remarks
Fish	bene Nswi	*nsabi*	Lenje, *Nswi*: Tonga, *bena* or some say *bene* plur. of *mwina*, more common *mwine*.
Crocodile	Ŋandu	*ŋwena*	
Finger millet	Besa	*mao*	
Wasp	Tembo	*lisasango*	
Anus	Bi	*munyo*	
Whirlwind	Luwo	*cipunga*	Tonga, *Luwo*: wind. Doke (1931: 196) gives *Luwo* as a small elephant.
Honey bird	Nguni	*mwebe*	Nguni, *cuni* bird
Lead	Nkalambo	*mtofwe*	
Fowl	Ŋanga	*nsumbi*	
Musamba tree	Musamba	*musamba*	
Wild pig	Ngulube	*ngulube*	
Goat	Mbusi	*mbusi*	
Cattle	Ŋombe	*ŋombe*	
Drum	Ngoma	*ngoma*	
Rain	Mfula	*mfula*	

CLAN AND MATRILINEAGE

English	Ambo clan name	Common word	Remarks
Snake	Nsoka	*nsoka*	
Elephant	Nsofu	*nsofu*	
Wild rubber	Bungo	*bungo*	
Mpande shell	Mpande	*mpande*	
Dog	Mbwa	*mbwa*	
Gourd	Lungu	*lungu*	
Loin cloth	Mubinda	*mubinda*	
Grass	Kani	*cani*	*kani*, diminutive
Bee	Kasimu	*nsimu* pl.	*kasimu*, dim.
Bead	Kalungu	*bulungu*	*kalungu*, dim.
Sorghum	Kasaka	*masaka* pl.	*kasaka*, dim.
Penis	Mwanso	*bukala*	
Vulva	Nyendwa	*ndofu*	Doke (1931: 195) gives *nyendwa* as needle. The Ambo at first give also this euphemistic meaning
Pigeon	Kunda	*nkwilimba* or *kunda*	
Clay	Mumba	*bulongo*	
Iron	Mbulo	*cela*	Tonga: *mbulo*
Wild dog	Mpumpi	*mumbulu*	Chikunda: *mpumpi*

There are some other clans which appear to be infiltrations, and are either numerically small or else comprise simply single matri-lineages.

English	Ambo clan name	Common word	Remarks
Mouse	Mbeba	*mbeba*	Swaka immigrants
Ant hill	Culu	*culu*	
Leopard	Ngo	*mbalali*	
Fire	Mulilo	*mulilo*	
Bean	Nyangu	*nyangu*	clan common among the Nsenga
Blue monkey	Nsanje	*nsanje*	Lwano clan
Locust	Nsye	*nsombe* pl.	

List of sister clans

'Sister-clans', *pa bwanankasi*, are those whose clan objects are of similar nature. Other clans are associated in the idiom of the grandparent-grandchild relation.

6   SOCIAL AND RITUAL LIFE OF THE AMBO

Whirlwind and Elephant clans, because *luwo* means also small elephant as well as whirlwind, are sister clans. Also the Loincloth and Vulva clans, because the loincloth covers the vulva; the Bead and Mpande shell clans, because both clan objects are similar ornaments.

The Penis and Vulva clans are not considered as interdependent which would argue funeral friendship (*see* below) but are viewed as sister clans. In the Mboshya country, however, these clans are aligned in funeral friendship.

Other sister clans are Sorghum and Finger millet clans, because both objects are grain. The Fowl and Pigeon clans, because both objects are birds. The Elephant and Wild pig clans, because the clan objects are both game meat. The Musamba tree and Drum clans, because their objects are both timber. The Wild rubber and Musamba tree clans, because both clan objects are trees. Also the Vulva and Bean clans, but for a reason I could not discover. The Iron and Lead clans, because both objects are metals.

Snake and Bee clans are in grandparent-grandchild relationship because the snake protects the hollow where the bees nest. The linking of Snake and Bee clans in this manner is based on the analogy of a grandparent taking care of a grandchild.

Funeral friendship

As a rule persons calling each other 'sibling' do not bury each other. The reason Ambo give for this rule is that the nearest of kin, the siblings, are overwhelmed with sorrow. I prefer to translate the institution *bunungwe* descriptively as 'funeral friendship'. As I have already described this in detail[1] it will be sufficient here to describe it only summarily.

Funeral friendship has as its basis a permanent alliance between certain clans. All clans are allied one to another in groups according to definite rules. The grouping is based on the characteristics of clan objects which stand to each other in a relation of hostility or of interdependence. Thus the Pigeon clan is allied to the Grass clan, because the pigeon is dependent on grass for making a nest. The Pigeon clan is also allied to the Snake clan, because the clan objects are hostile; snakes kill pigeons. The Pigeon clan is also allied to the Sorghum clan, because of the dependence of the pigeon on sorghum for food. However, Grass clansmen have other alliances also as, for instance, with the Rain clan, since grass is dependent on rain. Grass

[1] Stefaniszyn, 1950, pp. 290–306.

CLAN AND MATRILINEAGE

is eaten by goats, cut by iron, burnt by fire. Thus the Grass clan is allied to the Goat, Iron and Fire clans, apart from many other clans with which grass has some connection—at least in Ambo eyes—such as the Penis, Cattle, Whirlwind, Leopard, Sorghum, Fish and Bee clans.

This theoretical alliance of certain clans in practice offers possibilities and gives rights to their members to form particular friendships. Thus, a man may have a few male or female funeral friends drawn from clans socially approved for that purpose. The relationship between such friends is that of ordinary friendship, but it carries with it the duty of organizing mortuary rites. Funeral rites may, however, be performed by any members of a clan allied to the clan of the deceased. Funeral friendship is characterized by a joking relationship. Funeral friends may even curse one another without giving offence. The subjects of jests are mostly clan objects. Funeral friendship affords clan-strangers the most intimate privilege of being admitted to the rituals of the shades within the matrilineage.

The Wild dog clan, *bene Mpumpi*, draw their funeral friends from the Clay clan, (*bene Mumba*), Iron clan, (*bene Mbulo*) and the Wild pig clan, (*bene Ngulube*). A member of the Clay clan speaks to a Wild dog clansman: 'You are stupid, you are a slave, I am a chief, you are living in my house [a reference to African wolves living in burrows].' The Wild dog answers: 'You are our mother, we are slaves.' The Iron clan to the Wild dog clan: 'We are brave [men]. If you are too fierce, we take iron, we would wound you.' The Wild dog agrees: 'We are afraid.' The Wild dog clan to the Wild pig clan: 'You are slaves, we catch you like anything.' The Wild pig clan answers: 'We are afraid.'

The function of funeral friendship is the social integration of potentially hostile and actually mistrustful 'strangers', a technical Ambo term for non-clansmen as discussed above. On the positive side it is admittance of 'strangers' into the clan-matrilineage; on the negative side the function of funeral friendship is the prevention of feuds and tension.

The matrilineage

The Ambo clan comprises in the first instance major matrilineages. Members of a major matrilineage claim descent from one founder ancestor, a prominent headman, called *cisinte* or *cikolwe*. Though the common ancestress is remembered and is usually a

8 SOCIAL AND RITUAL LIFE OF THE AMBO

sister of the founder, her name is very seldom referred to in ordinary life. Besides the name of the founder, that of his village or stream where he lived is usually remembered also, even though his descendants are widely dispersed.

Genealogical seniority is reckoned between the members of a major matrilineage. Such a major matrilineage with a definite traditional kinship, is called *cikoto*, often stressed with *cimo*, 'one'. It must be made clear that a major matrilineage does not exist as a residential unit. It is rather a figure of speech, expressing and comprising the closer genealogical relations which exist between a number of minor matrilineages. The relations between the older members of such a major matrilineage, especially between the heads of the minor matrilineages, are more cordial than those between clansmen who are not of one *cikoto*. This is shown in visiting each other and in mutual assistance in times of food shortage.

There is a group of minor matrilineages of the Musamba tree clan, all of which hived off from the matrilineage of Mwape Katuta whom they acknowledge as their ancestor, *cikolwe*. Mwape Katuta was the last prestigious headman before the scattering of this large matrilineage which comprised one large village, the minor matrilineages founding villages of their own.

After Mwape Katuta died his village dispersed, it is said, because he had no obvious successor, though some of the matrilineages claiming to have hived off after his death may well have done so earlier. Some may have emigrated even before his installation. So important was Mwape Katuta in his day, that history is recounted by those related to him as if it revolved entirely around him.

A 'minor' matrilineage is also called *cikoto*. It is composed of segments descended from various 'mothers', usually three or four generations ago. However, even among commoners and non-aristocratic families some individuals claim to know the names of ancestresses five and even six generations back.

Each of the segments of a minor matrilineage is known by the word *kapafu*, 'womb'. *Banyina*, 'mother', is used synonymously for 'womb'. Thus the clansmen or clanswomen of the same matrilineage may be of the same segment, if their mothers are of 'one womb' or of 'one mother', or of different segments, if their mothers were of 'another womb' *kapafu kambi*, or if they were of 'another mother', *banyina bambi*. These designations refer also to the present generation, with appropriate adjustment then signifying siblings or non-siblings. Sometimes, however, the 'one womb' refers to a

CLAN AND MATRILINEAGE 9

common grandmother without any specification. Importance is attached to the seniority of segments, which plays its part in the claims for the office of the headman or the chief. Segment seniority carries with it certain rights of respect of the elder 'brother' or 'sister' especially in in-law relations.

Each matrilineage greatly values a village of its own. To have an independent and autonomous matrilineal home, a village, represents one of the great social values of the Ambo. Such a village is identified with the minor matrilineage and in Ambo parlance it is 'owned' by the matrilineage. Such a village is the home of an Ambo, *kwabo*, a rallying point for matrikin when they live dispersed in other villages. Many matrilineages live for generations thus scattered. Their members keep in touch one with another, but they are not organized corporately, lacking a leader and a sufficient number of close matrikin.

The actual residence of all the matrikin in their own village is not, of course, compatible with the rule of clan exogamy. The composition of the local community will be considered in the next chapter.

Siblings

Though a minor matrilineage is based on common cognatic descent from one progenitress, the strongest ties of emotional attachment and of identity of economic interests are to be found among siblings.

Siblings tend to live in their own village, and to return to it whenever free to do so under the rules of marital residence. Men try to avoid matrilocal marriage: women do their best to oppose the virilocal stage of marriage. It is siblings who hold together in a village even if they do not own it, but then they tend to found one of their own as soon as they can muster enough members. Siblings not residing together compensate for their dispersion by visiting each other a great deal, and therefore tend to marry either within the village or in the close neighbourhood.

The identity of interests of a sibling group manifests itself in various ways. In olden times a brother could hand over a sister or a sister's daughter into slavery as payment or as a pawn for his adultery or homicide. He is the guardian of his sister, after her mother's brother, and will pay compensation for his sister's divorce or adultery, and he will assist her in paying death dues for her

10 SOCIAL AND RITUAL LIFE OF THE AMBO

husband. These latter commitments in particular devolve on a woman's eldest brother rather than on her mother's brother.

The eldest brother or the eldest sister is *mukulu bantu*, 'the elder of the people'. The eldest sister will be respected by her brothers-in-law as a mother-in-law after the death of her mother. She will assume responsibility for the rearing of the children of her deceased sister. After the death of her mother all her younger siblings will look to her for care, if she is grown up.

The eldest brother will act as a guardian of all siblings, particularly if they have lost their genitor. He will assist them financially, when the 'father' or the mother's brother is unable to do so owing to age, infirmity or sheer indifference. As to the authority of the eldest son over his siblings, even the 'father' himself on occasion will ask him to harangue them as their matrilineal guardian, as of the same 'womb' and not, as he is himself, as a clan stranger.

Siblings succeed one after another as chiefs and headmen or tribal officials, and they may inherit wives from one another and also possessions, such as guns, spears or axes. In inheritance and succession they enjoy priority over other classificatory brothers. Siblings, of either sex, may be seen travelling together or chatting alone in a hut without arousing even a suspicion of incest.

Mother and children

A girl is the constant companion of her mother from the time when she is being weaned till she grows middle-aged, when she may go to live virilocally. Her amusements when young are mostly imitations of her mother's work.

Little girls of five or six years old like to draw water in small tins, accompanying adults. A girl six years old and more sometimes has a small mortar and a pestle of her own to pound grain. She begins to look after the cooking of vegetables; she is sent with her companions to collect vegetables in the fields and the bush.

The older the daughter is, the more she becomes the companion and help of her mother. She works either with her mother, almost as her equal, or instead of her, and accompanies her on visits. Even while still a minor, a girl is trusted to take her mother's place at the fire, minding the cooking pot or a baby brother or sister. When the girl reaches puberty she is more obedient towards her mother, and even more under her mother's control. As to marriage, the mother has the last word and the most to say.

CLAN AND MATRILINEAGE

Daughters are so much attached to, and dependent on, their mothers that it appears they very seldom dream of eloping and readily discard suitors and even husbands on the advice of their mothers. This dependence, lifelong co-operation and the ensuing attachment explains much of the marital status, attitude and behaviour of the girl. She will be married matrilocally, and this matrilocality must be viewed in the above context. As individuals of course, mothers differ. I have one case of a mother following her daughter in the latter's initial virilocal marriage. Similarly, daughters differ in their individual behaviour.

Sons are as devoted to their mothers as daughters. An old widow may attach herself equally to her married daughter or son if she has no village of her own where she may also choose to live. The attachment of sons to mothers is all the more remarkable and real inasmuch as boys are little in contact with their mothers from 5–6 years onwards (*see* Chapter IV). Mothers have first claim on the financial help of their sons, in most cases in the form of clothes.

Externally behaviour between a mother and her children appears cool, indifferent and dignified. Greetings between them are casual and not marked either with much respect or familiarity. The mother always sits, the son will squat, *kusonkama*, and clap hands, *kulisya mapi*.[1] Nowadays, mother and son will shake hands. Mother and daughter exchange greetings sitting down.

Deep affection between mother and children is brought into the open only when one of them is gravely ill. A mother will lie on the bed with the corpse of her child. I think other relatives do not do this. A linguistic expression of filial sentiment is the common Ambo exclamation *mama, mama–ee*. It is used as an exclamation of surprise and also in mourning.

Grandparents and grandchildren

Whereas between adjacent generations there is on one side deferential respect and on the other side authority, there is none of this

[1] *Kulisya mapi*, clapping of hands for greeting is different from clapping of hands for chiefs and shades. The latter is described in the chapter on religion. In the former the left palm is straightened and the fingers of the right hand strike the centre of the left hand. *Kusonkama* is a manner of sitting which has two variations. In one, common at meal times, the buttocks touch the heels and the knees are kept apart. In another a buttock is rested on its corresponding heel while the other leg, though sharply bent at the knee, is thrust forward in front of the crouching body. Thus the shin of the last leg is vertical to the ground. In both cases the knees are kept apart. The latter *kusonkama* position is used for a short time particularly when greeting or asking for something.

12 SOCIAL AND RITUAL LIFE OF THE AMBO

between persons of alternate generations. The utmost familiarity reigns between the persons of such generations so that they are looked upon as equals. A mother sending a young son to his maternal grandmother says: 'Go to your grandmother and play with her, she is your equal.' Young children, too big to sleep in their parents' hut and too small to go to the respective dormitories of boys and girls, sleep with their grandparents, either paternal or maternal. This familiarity is linked with the possibility of marriage between individuals of two generations apart. Children are often sent to their grandmothers, usually maternal ones, after weaning and as orphans, especially if there are no mother's sisters. Orphans are usually better looked after by their grandmother than by a mother's sister who may have a number of her own children to care for.

The custom of begging from a grandparent (*kusenga mapi*) illustrates the relationship between the alternate generations as one of generosity, kindness, and accessibility, on the part of the grandparent. When the new moon appears, a grandchild comes to the door of its maternal grandparent, claps hands, and is given either a fowl or an axe. Customarily this took place only once a year and grandparents gave only to the first of their grandchildren who approached them.

The easy relationship between alternate generations is connected with the possibility of intermarriage between a grandparent and grandchild. Such marriage is, however, not allowed between descendants in direct line even though their clan affiliation is different. One matrilineage may come to stand in grandparent-grandchild relationship towards another matrilineage. One whole matrilineage stands to all the members of another in the classificatory grandparent-grandchild relationship.

A special relationship exists between the maternal uncle and grand-nephew. In Ambo terminology mother's mother's brother is *bambuya*, as are all other grandparents and classificatory grandparents. However, the mother's mother's brother and sister can be specified as 'grandparents of brotherhood', *bambuya pa bukwabo*. The maternal grand-uncle is consulted about the affairs of grand-nephews and particularly grand-nieces, but allows their maternal uncles to act. Grand-nephews often consider themselves as successors of their grand-uncles. Such nephews may expect to take over a village headmanship or a chiefship from their uncles. They are more respectful and more obliging towards their grand-uncles. The old chiefs and headmen are more authoritarian towards their grand-

CLAN AND MATRILINEAGE   13

nephews and nieces as heads of the segments, but they never assume
the authority of the maternal uncle; they remain more approachable
to their wards and much of the grandparent–grandchild familiarity
still remains.

The family

It is significant that the Ambo have not developed a term for the
elementary family—viz. husband, wife and their unmarried
children. But there is a term *simaŋanda*, 'owner of a house', which
means a house in which a wife and possibly children dwell. To have
a house means to have a family. The expression refers only to the
man and does not adequately correspond with the concept of the
elementary family. It will be recalled that the Ambo have an unam-
biguous term for a clan, which may also mean the whole tribe, and
another word for matrilineage whether minor or major (*cikoto*). It
should be emphasized that all the mother's sisters of a person are
his or her 'mothers' and all their children 'brothers' and 'sisters'.
All the classificatory brothers of the mother are 'mother's brothers'.

This amalgamation of various kin into classes in terms of Ego's
own elementary family shows the Ambo elementary family to be
basically an integral part of a matrilineage.

In particular at the beginning of a marriage, the elementary
family is scarcely differentiated from what is often termed an expanded family. This initial elementary family has its own house but
hardly any economic autonomy, lacking its own grain bin, garden
and kitchen. And the token marriage payment has bypassed the
father, having been given to the bride's senior maternal uncle. The
mother's brother is the 'owner' of the members of the elementary
family, the father is not, though each has his own 'jurisdiction'. The
father is in terms of social structure a stranger, who has acquired
definite customary rights over the mother of the elementary family.
He has few direct rights over their offspring. The powers he has are
merely directive and tutorial, together with heavy responsibilities
in respect of the supply of food and the provision of clothing.

A mother's brother is not the 'owner of the wife', *mwine wa mkasi*,
he is only the 'owner of the person', *mwine wa muntu*.

The elementary family gradually comes to enjoy an economic
autonomy. Divorce or the death of the mother brings autonomy and
independence to an end. When the mother dies her offspring are
entrusted to her sisters or her mother. The widower–father is

14 SOCIAL AND RITUAL LIFE OF THE AMBO

relieved of all responsibility towards his children. Their mother's brother takes charge of them through his sisters. When the father dies or is divorced, the truncated elementary family survives and may be fully reconstituted through a remarriage of the mother. The only exception to this would be in the case of the levirate or of the sororate, but both these forms of marriage are extremely rare.

It is convenient to describe under the heading of 'the family' some of the relations of husbands and wives. Husbands and wives have supernatural responsibilities towards each other. Should the husband have extramarital relations while his wife is pregnant, it is believed that he threatens her life. The wife must also observe prohibitions connected with fire during her menses lest she afflict her husband with a chest disease. The marital bond survives the death of the spouse, until the survivor is released from the spirit of the dead spouse through ritual payment of death dues. During the prohibited period the man, too, is ritually barred from any sexual freedom in which he might otherwise indulge.

It is often maintained that in Africa traditionally the husband has an exclusive sexual right over his wife but that the wife cannot claim the same right for herself. For the Ambo this statement needs qualification. Certainly the husband has the exclusive and inalienable right of sexual access to his wife. An infringement of this results in an action in the Native Court and the liability of the adulterer to pay heavy compensation. Compensation on the part of the adulterous wife's minor matrilineage, payable to the injured husband, was only recently introduced.

By customary law the wife cannot sue her husband for an act of adultery. In cases, however, of characteristically dissolute conduct, the wife, backed by her minor matrilineage, can divorce him. Another sexual freedom the husband enjoys is the right to polygamy, but customarily he should seek permission from his first wife before taking another. The wife is *muka muntu*, 'a wife of a man', and *muka bacite*, 'the wife of So-and-so'. Her husband is also sometimes described in the same way. The concept *muka muntu* implies that a person is not free to dispose of sexual favours as he or she pleases. Such sexual rights belong to somebody else. As the husband is referred to as the 'owner of the wife', so also is the wife spoken of as the 'owner of the husband'. Thus the Ambo wife enjoys certain reciprocal, exclusive rights to her husband but they are not absolute and are not customarily enforced to the same extent as they are in the case of the husband.

CLAN AND MATRILINEAGE

At this point it must be remarked that the Ambo have in common with other Central Bantu peoples a special term for marital jealousy, *bukwa*, which may be used in respect of both men and women. Marital jealousy is at the root of the practice of keeping a second wife at another village, which is usual in the initial stage of polygynous marriage. It is a concept which accounts also for the prohibition against cohabiting with two sisters, even clan sisters, at the same time, since it is considered that to do so would cause friction and marital jealousy which would work against the solidarity of the clan and matrilineage. In particular, cohabiting with two sisters at the same time would militate against the identity of interests among siblings and thus destroy their equivalence. This jealousy also accounts for the custom that maintains the respectability of a married, childbearing woman, in that she is expected not to walk far from the village alone, but to be accompanied at least by a child.

Though the husband, after the initial, uxorilocal stage of the marriage, has the choice of domicile, he will sometimes yield to the entreaties of his wife and after a period of virilocal residence goes back to live again among her people.

It is true that men do not seek the company of their wives, for example, in beer drinking, the chief recreation of the men. However, husband and wife work together for more than half the year in their fields, and stay together in a garden shelter during the day where they share meals. After the evening meal the whole family chats at the fire in front of the hut, every day throughout the year. In the village, men eat with boys, and women with girls. In the village husbands and wives may eat together only secretly.

Husbands and wives are expected by social convention to behave together with reserve to the outside world. They will not greet each other in public.

Travelling parties may make an impression on a casual observer that the robust men overload the youngsters and women. But Ambo behaviour in this matter is governed by two principles, by respect for age and sex, and the responsibility of brave men for their weaker dependants. One may see a wife and children, all with loads on their heads, leading the way, while the man will march at the end of the file with his weapons. Ambo say that the man should not be encumbered with loads, as he may be called upon at a moment's warning to ward off an attack. A man encumbered by a load would find his weapons almost useless. However, men returning with women from

16 SOCIAL AND RITUAL LIFE OF THE AMBO

towns are loaded with their belongings to the limits of their strength, and when fetching grain from distant villages, men carry far heavier loads than women and children. A small boy may be seen carrying a goat-skin bag, filled with meal, whereas his father or an elder brother will go free except for his weapons. This arrangement has a practical value even now for the man may thus more easily surprise and kill game met on the path. The place at the back of the file is the most suitable for the purpose of defence. When something unexpected happens in front of the man, he will be less surprised and startled and more ready to come to the rescue than if an accident took place behind him. These precautions originally had in view not so much wild beasts as the raiding parties of olden times. Usually a lion attacks a group of people not from the front but from the rear. Another reason for the man to walk at the end of the file is his responsibility for his dependants in the eyes of their matrilineage. A man can easily describe an accident which happens in front of him to the inquisitive and exacting clansmen of his dependants. Any ignorance as to what had befallen his wife, who was behind him, would be unpardonable.

Affinal relatives

Ambo distinguish among affinal relatives the same generation differences as among own and father's matrikin. To people of the first ascending generation lifelong avoidance rules have to be observed. Though this avoidance may be mitigated substantially throughout the years, it never ceases; a specially respectful distance, aloofness and shyness endure throughout life.

A husband, especially a young one living uxorilocally, makes friends with similar *bako*, sons-in-law, to himself. However, his real supports in the strange environment are his brothers-in-law and, to a lesser extent, his sisters-in-law. When a girl accepts his proposal of marriage, he will send his future brothers-in-law to his prospective parents-in-law, particularly to the girl's mother. He accepts meals from his sisters-in-law, before he is finally invited to a meal by the mother-in-law. In later life his brothers-in-law will be his steady companions in work and in recreation. Often he goes to and returns from work in towns with his brother-in-law. Roughly one third of a man's life is spent in the labour centres.

Most important is the fact that these brothers- and sisters-in-law are judges and intermediaries in case of difficulties with his wife.

CLAN AND MATRILINEAGE

Should these in-laws turn against him, his case is lost; they will advise their sister to proceed with divorce. If the man is liked and esteemed by his in-laws and they are of the opinion that their sister is at fault, he will even be helped by them in the settlement of the dispute. They will intercede with his wife and her mother that she, their sister, should return to her husband.

It illustrates the nature of this kinship that close associates and intimate friends in casual speech address one another as 'brother-in-law', *mulamu*, though they may be complete strangers so far as affinity is concerned.

A woman is less dependent than a man on her brothers- and sisters-in-law. She will not ask them to intercede for her with her husband, and, as we have seen, she does not start her marital life virilocally. Also she will address another woman friend as 'the mother of so-and-so' instead of *mulamu*.

Between sisters- and brothers-in-law the utmost propriety in word and deed is observed. No sister of the principal wife would be married polygamously to the same husband in the first wife's lifetime. For a man, the wife of his brother-in-law is a 'false sister', *nkasi ya bufi*. For the woman, the husband of her sister-in-law is also a 'false brother', *ndume ya bufi*. Thus these affinal relatives have to behave in sexual matters as if they were siblings.

Any sexual lapse between brothers- and sisters-in-law would be incest, but it would not be termed sorcery. Only incest between members of one elementary family deserved formerly the punishment for sorcery, death, or until lately, being sold into slavery.

When a man is visiting in his mother-in-law's village, he goes first to all his brothers-in-law and sisters-in-law. His mother-in-law will then come to greet him, kneeling down and clapping hands, while he is seated. When the son-in-law greets his parents-in-law he crouches *kusonkama* (see above, page 11) and claps his hands. Some men, however, particularly the father-in-law, omit the clapping of hands on this occasion, saying the greeting only.

When a man and his mother-in-law journey together, he precedes her. This is a variation on the order of the sexes usually observed when travelling. A man must avoid his mother-in-law should they find themselves walking towards each other on the same path. If they have been ritually introduced to each other they will step off the path only about a foot: if they have not been so introduced, they will step off about a yard. If a woman is ill, her son-in-law may not come to her himself to inquire after her, but must send

18 SOCIAL AND RITUAL LIFE OF THE AMBO

his wife. A mother-in-law may come to the veranda of a sick son-in-law and ask him herself about his health.

A parent-in-law visiting a daughter-in-law will go first to her parents. The daughter-in-law then comes to them, kneels down and claps hands. If the woman goes to visit where her parents-in-law live, she will go straight away to her brothers- and sisters-in-law. The father-in-law comes, sits, and says 'Peace, mother', *mitende mama*. The mother-in-law will come and kneel down and say the same greeting.

The sexes

It is, first of all, indicative of the attitude of the Ambo towards women that the birth of a girl is announced by a double ululating, that of a boy by a single one. One 'explanation' given is that two shrieks are given for the girl, because the girl will have two ululations in her life, one at birth and the other at puberty. Boys' puberty is not ceremonially commemorated. Others say that two sounds are given for the girl as she is like a chief, because she will remain in the village when married. The boy will go away to marry elsewhere. But whatever the precise significance, it is abundantly clear that a girl is accorded more honour at her entry into Ambo society than is a boy. Women, by their children, increase the matrilineage. They thus deserve more care, protection and assistance than boys. Even as small girls they are provided by father or matrikin with more clothes than their young brothers.

It is to provide further protection for the potential bearer of a minor matrilineage, that she lives the first years of her marital life under the aegis of her mother and matrikin to which her bridegroom 'enslaves' himself (as his mother may call it), when negotiating his marriage. Not until her matrilineage is satisfied as to the character and conduct of the husband does it entrust her to him in virilocal marriage.

The care given to the upbringing and guidance of the girl is in striking contrast with the freedom of action and movement allowed to the boy. As the boy was left to himself to acquire his clothes so also is he free in matrimonial matters. Even such behaviour as when the woman walks in front, when on a journey, while her husband, armed, walks in the rear, is practised for the protection of the woman. However, she lacks the same reciprocal, exclusive marital rights over her husband, socially enforced, as her husband has over

CLAN AND MATRILINEAGE 19

her. And though at the beginning of her married life she is protected by living (from her point of view) matrilocally, thereafter she has no direct choice of residence. Again, though she is accorded double ululation on her birth, she must kneel down while giving or receiving an object from her husband who, standing, assumes a lordly posture. She may even be corporally chastised by her husband in a socially approved manner.

This status of the woman is based on the assumption that in the economic sphere she is not fit to do certain kinds of work. In the sphere of social control, she is held to be too shy and easily swayed to hold her own. Her marital status reflects what is thought to be appropriate to womanhood.

Nowadays, one of the man's most important duties is to provide clothes for his womenfolk. All building activities fall to men. The labour of tillage men share with women: only very few agricultural activities are reserved for one sex. The period of uxorilocal marriage is a test period for the man, to discover whether he is willing and able to till the land vigorously. He works under the guidance of his father-in-law. Should the father-in-law give an unfavourable verdict the mother-in-law will pass the judgement: 'What is the use of begetting children, if he cannot feed them?' Many hold that the garden belongs to the man who prepared the land by cutting the trees, but many maintain that it is only fair to leave it for the woman who cannot start a new field by herself.

The attitude of Ambo society towards the man in marital life is expressed in the instructions given to a girl at her puberty rites. She is advised to bear with the deficiencies of her man, hoping that he will make up for them with other qualities. In the household the woman is responsible for the basic meal, the porridge and the vegetable relish. But her husband is expected to provide her with the better kinds of relish, meat and fish.

Today, the money-earning young man has risen in popular esteem as the source of coveted clothes. The youth spends his years in the towns, returning to his home village every few months or years to rest. He prefers to come back at harvest-time when he will not find famine or the drudgery of hoeing. He roams the countryside in his brand-new clothes looking for beer parties and dances. However, he soon tires of life in the village and goes back to work in the towns. As a pretext he may give the reason that he must clothe himself.

On one of these such 'rests' a boy will look for a wife. Most boys

20   SOCIAL AND RITUAL LIFE OF THE AMBO

come to the home country to marry. Unless he is lucky enough to find a girl in his own village, he will have to work for his mother-in-law in a strange village. Apart from his hoeing and working tests he is watched over for his behaviour towards the elders of his wife's matrikin, and for his dealings with his wife. The final passing of these initial marital tests is the birth of his child.

After some initial work required by the guardians of the girl, he soon vanishes to the towns. He dreads that his young wife may die in childbirth with the subsequent ordeal for himself. In a strange village, in marital exile (*see* below, page 31) he is in a precarious position. He consorts with others like himself and tries to make friends with his brothers-in-law. Irksome marital exile is by no means the least reason for a man wishing to take his wife to live in the town.

A boy before his marriage sends clothes to his mother, father and sisters: sometimes he may also clothe his brothers. When he courts a girl, he sends her clothes and possibly her mother too and continues to do so after the marriage. He cannot often afford to please his own family of orientation as well as his in-laws. But to supply his wife with clothes is his first duty. To supply his elementary family is a matter of ethics, from which he may excuse himself.

A man has exclusive sexual rights over his wife, and is also entitled to wifely economic services. His duties towards her are economic (as laid down above) and social, the keeping of the avoidance rules, and the paying of respect to the whole generation of his wife's matrikin senior to him, and their spouses. This entails also his co-operation in many ways with the village community, usually with the men under the leadership of the headman, and in private under the leadership of his father-in-law. He has to conform with the rule of uxorilocal domicile; the length of this period is primarily according to the discretion of the mother-in-law.

The birth of a child ends this period of probation. The outward sign of this is the relaxing of avoidance rules. He is hailed as a pro-creator of a minor matrilineage. His sexual rights over his wife are now firmly established on the cultural level. Any infringement of them renders him liable to very heavy compensation from the adulterer. He receives similar compensation at divorce, if he can prove the guilt of his wife or if it is the wife who starts the divorce proceedings.

He claims the right to inflict physical punishment on his wife to a degree circumscribed by custom. Thus beating of wives is prac-

CLAN AND MATRILINEAGE

21

tised and tolerated even by the wife's matrikin, if they are persuaded that the husband is in the right. If he harms her, he has to pay compensation to her; and he may not beat her with a stick, and when she is undressed for the night.

In this matrilineal society, children do not succeed, or inherit from, their fathers. The father can bequeath his most valuable possession (until lately a gun) to a son, but this is not usual. He may do so only when he has another gun to leave for his sister's son, for example, and when his matrilineage agrees to such an arrangement. Nevertheless, his wife's minor matrilineage highly respects him for the breeding of its children, as is reflected in the custom of introducing the son-in-law (*see* below, page 106). As long as the man's children live, they show special gratitude by means of hospitality towards their father's close matrikin. In comparison with the Bemba, however, Ambo do not always inform a father about his daughter's marriage. If he is estranged from his wife and takes no interest in his children, he is not informed at all of the pending marriage. Fathers, in Ambo culture, are primarily 'begetters'. It is as such that a man has disciplinary rights over his immature children. He may for example, chastise a daughter until she reaches the age when her breasts develop.

It is maintained that a man never teaches his children sorcery because, being of a different clan, they might turn against him or his matrikin.

A man has the right to give the birth names of his father and of certain of his matrikin to his children except when he is a consort of a Nyendwa clanswoman. At the present time a man claims the right to name his first-born child after his, rather than his wife's, ancestors.

Of the customary relationships of the father to his child it is said that 'he [the father] just begot it only', *walimufyele likoso*. This position of the father was graphically described by an Ambo friend, who said that a father could at a moment's notice take his gun and spear and walk out of the house, deserting his wife and children. The mother's brother, on the other hand, is the 'owner of the people', *mwine wa bantu*, 'people' being his sister's children. First and foremost this expression refers to the full mother's brother; to classificatory mother's brothers the term applies in a less effective way.

It is affirmed that the mother's brother would be foolish to interfere with the task of the 'father', while the children are young.

22 SOCIAL AND RITUAL LIFE OF THE AMBO

The mother's brother acts on behalf of his minor matrilineage only when the father fails in his task through death or divorce, or sometimes, absence, disease or sheer neglect. When a child dies or is ill and a diviner has to be consulted, both the father and the mother's brother together approach the diviner. This illustrates well the relations between them. The mother's brother goes with the father lest the latter hides the diviner's pronouncement if it is against him.

The mother's brother is spokesman for his sisters' children in court cases, and must provide compensation for a niece's divorce. In olden times the mother's senior full brother had the right to hand over his daughters into slavery as payments on his own behalf, though he was expected to redeem them eventually. On the basis of such authority there arose an attitude of fear towards him: his nephews might not even converse with him, or approach him closely. On the other hand, though children must respect their fathers, this does not exclude some familiarity between them. A boy on being asked whom he favoured more, father or mother's brother, preferred his father because, as he put it, the mother's brother has his own children to care for. However, this clash of interest is not widespread or general. The mother's brother is a brother-in-law to the father, and their relationship is one of friendship, familiarity and common interests.

A note on kinship terminology

Ambo	English	Symbol	Remarks
usi	(his, her) father	SI	*tata*, my father
nyina	(his, her) mother	NY	*mama*, my mother
mwana	child (son or daughter)	MW	
(*ba*)–*mbuya*	grandparent	BU	
musikulu	grandchild	SK	
mukwesu	sibling	KW	
ndume	my sibling brother		
nkasi	my sibling sister		
munsyo	mother's brother	SY	
mwipwa	sister's child	MP	
mufyala	cross-cousin	FY	
mulume	husband		
mukasi	wife	KA	
mulamu	sibling-in-law	LA	
usifyala	father-in-law	SF	

CLAN AND MATRILINEAGE

Ambo	*English*	*Symbol*	*Remarks*
nyinafyala	mother-in-law	NF	
mukweni	son-in-law		
mulokasi	daughter-in-law		
usinkasi	father's sister	SI	Addressed *tata*
nkasi ya bufi	wife's brother's wife		'false sister'
ndume ya bufi	husband's sister's husband		'false brother'

All classificatory and real parents of the parents-in-law are termed grandparents, and avoidance rules do not apply to them. The term for sibling sister, *nkasi*, used by her brother only, is ordinarily non-classificatory; the same holds for the term *ndume* (*yanji*—my) used by the sibling sister about her brother. Neither the term for husband nor that for wife is used in the classificatory sense. Otherwise all the terms are used in both primary and classificatory senses.

Classificatory sister's children are not necessarily of the mother's brother's clan; they may be father's brother's daughter's children. The Ambo do not differentiate between the two types of cross-cousins. Male Ego is classificatory mother's brother to the children (A2, A3) of his mother's brother's son (A1), because their father, A1, is preferential husband of Ego's sister, regardless of whether A1 actually married Ego's sister or not. However, in his turn, Ego is classificatory father to the children, B2 and B3, of his mother's brother's daughter, because Ego expected to have married her, even though he may in fact have married another woman. As to the children of father's sister's son and daughter, Ego is classificatory mother's brother to the children of X1, Ego's father's sister's son, because X1 is preferential husband of Ego's sister, even though X1 might in fact have married a stranger (*see* Diagram III, page 25).

Ego is classificatory father to the children of Y1, because he is potentially preferential husband of his father's sister's daughter, Y1, even though he married another woman.

Ego (male) is called mother's brother of the children of his wife's brother, because Ego's wife's brother's wife is 'false sister' (*nkasi ya bufi*) to Ego; thus her children call Ego their mother's brother, *munsyo*. Again Ego (female) stands in the relationship of father's sister to the children of her husband's sister, because the husband of her husband's sister is Ego's 'false brother' (*ndume ya bufi*).

The striking fact about this kind of classificatory mother's brother is that in a matrilineal society, through a 'legal fiction' he is not of the same clan affiliation as his sister's children.

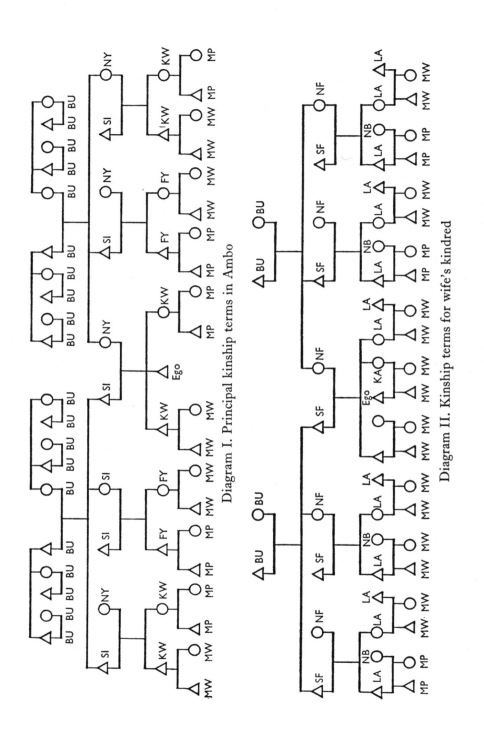

Diagram I. Principal kinship terms in Ambo

Diagram II. Kinship terms for wife's kindred

CLAN AND MATRILINEAGE

I did not specifically inquire into positional succession and perpetual kinship but I have recently discovered that some matrilineages stand in a grandchild relation of perpetual kinship to the chiefly matrilineage, because an ancestor in the commoners' matrilineage happened to be a son of the chief. The perpetual grandchildhood is passed matrilineally from the sisters of the chief's son.

A grandchild may ritually inherit the name and kinship position of the dead grandparent of the same sex. The siblings of the heir also share in the inherited position. Then the children of the

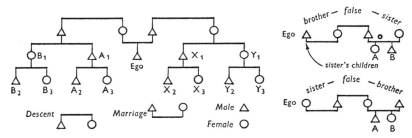

Diagram III. Classificatory relationships

grandparents stand in the relation of children to the heir. However this may be the case only matrilineally—a man may be succeeded only by his sister's daughter's son, and a woman by her daughter's daughter.

Preferential marriage between alternate generations

Preferential marriages are allowed theoretically between most classificatory grandparents and grandchildren. However, preferential marriages between the alternate generations are between persons whose respective matrilineages are allied in the relationship of alternate generations. Thus a man A marries a woman B whose mother was begotten by a clansman of A's matrilineage. Less common is the marriage of a man A with his 'grandmother' B. He calls her 'grandmother' because her (male) matrikin had begotten his real or classificatory mother. Although marriage as shown in Diagram IV is valid according to Ambo customary law and may have been practised in the past, nowadays the girl has enough freedom and her mother's backing to insist that the age of her fiancé should not differ greatly from her own.

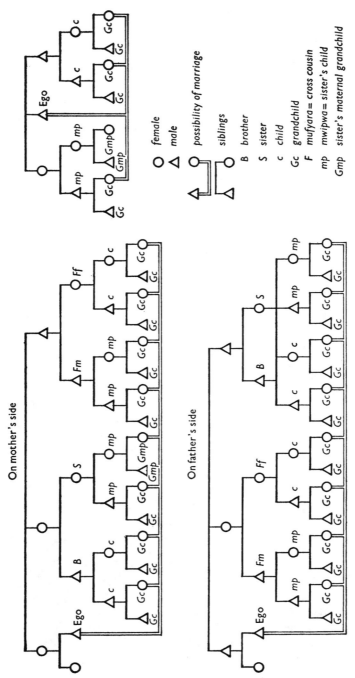

Diagram IV. Grandparent-grandchild marriage

II. THE VILLAGE

The formation of new villages

THE Ambo village is formed and maintained by a minor matrilineage; in Ambo parlance a village belongs to such-and-such a clan, meaning a minor matrilineage of such a clan. The establishment of a village of matrikin is the outcome of the interplay of two tendencies observable in the matrilineage, of solidarity and of segmentation. The first tendency springs from the sentiment of the sibling group and its extension. The second is born of the tension between siblings and their distant matrikin. The distance of the kinship bond is the negative element working towards the formation of the village, whereas the closeness of kinship bonds is a positive element.

Every woman, particularly if she bears many children and especially daughters, is the potential ancestress of a matrilineage. If she is married in her matrilineal home village and avoids life-long marital exile (*see* page 31) her offspring, by force of common habitation, may for more than four generations stay within the parent matrilineage and its village. Ambo deplore and try to guard against losing their sisters in virilocal marriage, realizing that such foreign residence, if prolonged through two or three generations and given sufficiently numerous offspring, leads to the formation of a separate minor matrilineage with a village of its own. There are instances of many a far-seeing elder, as a matrilineage head, hurrying to distant regions to bring back widows and often their progeny stranded in their late husbands' villages.

A new village may be built by the simple withdrawal of a core of matrikin, usually a group of siblings. For example, before the coming of Europeans, Lupanda, a grandson of a chief, had a palisaded village in which his own classificatory sister's son, Kanyo, had his own section (*cikole*). The raids of the Ngoni and Chikunda scattered the village. When it was reconstructed, in fact, two villages were formed, one by Mainda, the youngest brother of Lupanda and his successor, the other by Musinuka, a brother of Kanyo, who took over Kanyo's segment. Later, one Kawamba having nine 'sisters'

28 SOCIAL AND RITUAL LIFE OF THE AMBO

seceded from Musinuka out of nostalgia for the old village area, but being also harassed by famine.

Another way in which a village may be formed is by the coming together of scattered individuals of one's own clan segment who live in various villages in marital exile. Men seeking to organize their minor matrilineage into a village, canvass not only their nearest clansmen—in the first place their real brothers, their sisters' sons and grandsons—but also brothers-in-law, husbands of their sisters' daughters and granddaughters. A founder of a village canvasses only men connected with his minor matrilineage, such as real brothers, mother's sisters sons and nephews. A founder also depends on the womenfolk of his matrilineage, but women have no decisive right and initiative in selecting domicile, therefore the founder directly asks his 'brothers'—and 'sons-in-law' to join his projected community.

The ambition of establishing a village of one's own is particularly widespread among middle-aged men. Such a leader seldom breaks up an established village-owning minor matrilineage. More often than not his ambition to start a new village is because he failed to attain the headmanship of the old. In some cases observed the headmanship of a village was a bone of contention. However, to build an entirely new village, a leader needs as a prerequisite a well developed matrilineal segment. The starting of a new village is taken as a sign that a segment has matured into a minor matrilineage.

An entire village may have to move for an economic reason, such as a failure of crops. A signal for a move may be the death of an old headman, or a panic caused by a number of deaths, especially if they were sudden or followed short illness, of young people, with the accompanying suspicion of sorcery. Sorcery may even cause the scattering of the inhabitants of the village, at least temporarily.

At bottom, the attitude behind the foundation of new villages and the moving of old ones is expressed in the rite of the new fire kindled on the new site. The new fire is a symbol of a better future; the old fires are left behind, symbols of the past and of past misfortunes associated with the old site, such as famine, death and disease, as well as sorcery, quarrels and jealousies. This explanation was given by the people themselves. Apart from this, people dwell on the possibility of better luck and an altogether rosy future on a new site, with more game, better soil, fewer weeds to hoe, more winter gardens, more fish, more relish.

New trends are noticeable in village organization. Nowadays a

THE VILLAGE 29

would-be headman may canvass friends and various kinds of relatives before starting a new village. Thus in new ones there is not necessarily a hard core of a closely-knit owning minor matrilineage.

Breaking up of villages

Villages last only a few decades, except those which have ritual functions such as Chikwashya (*see* page 56). They cease to exist in two ways. Their inhabitants may withdraw in affinal and agnatic matrilineal segments from the village-owning matrilineage to establish new settlements, as described above. Sometimes single families leave one by one, joining other villages. Then the village, reduced to a few individuals, continues a precarious existence until the District Commissioner orders them to join a village with the required number of tax-payers. In other instances the village breaks up spontaneously, and the villagers scatter and join relatives elsewhere.

The reasons for the break-up of villages are various. When the majority of the villagers are non-owners of the village, after the death of the headman the village is unlikely to continue as such. The villagers have no common bond and each man returns to his own minor matrilineage group or that of his wife. An unpopular headman is simply left alone with one or two of his closer relatives, such as a brother, or maternal nephew or a brother-in-law. Mwape Katuta broke up owing to the lack of a suitable leader and successor after the death of the headman. A suspicion of sorcery may account for the scattering of a village.

Village plans and sizes

There is no particular ground plan for villages. Huts are scattered in a rather haphazard way a few yards distant from one another and tend to be more congested at the outskirts of the village. Towards the centre of the village there is a more open space.

In front of the headman's hut there is a shelter, *citenge*, a conical grass roof on usually a double row of forked poles, with an elevated, mud plastered floor. I shall refer to this as the 'village shelter'.

Clan brothers, who will usually be of the minor matrilineage owning the village, build far from one another lest they quarrel. This holds true especially of the brothers of the headman. His brothers-in-law will build next door to the headman, and near him

30 SOCIAL AND RITUAL LIFE OF THE AMBO

his widowed sister will have her hut. Such an arrangement of dwellings facilitates daily social intercourse, especially the evening chat after supper, when the whole family and neighbours gather at the fires in front of their houses.

The *bako*, the sons-in-law of the headman and of his brothers and sisters, will build near one another and will keep together, converse together, and formerly ate together. All uterine nephews of the headman and of his brothers will join with his sons-in-law. These nephews have to show special respect to their uterine uncles, behaviour which is not unlike that of the sons-in-law to their fathers-in-law. Thus the spatial distribution of the village tends to reflect social groupings formed according to different generations.

As the size of the village at the present time is on the decrease, the former spatial as well as social sections of the village (*fikole*, (plural), which were built according to clan distinctions, are no longer kept up.

TABLE I

The average number of people in a village

Village	Men	Women	Unmarried children	Total	Men away	Women away
Chitubula	9	13	19	41	3	
Mulayshyo	7	12	17	36	2	
Mumpampa	16	19	41	76	3	1
Saka	12	21	27	60	3	1
Nshyolama	12	19	32	63	2	2
Kalolo	4	8	20	32	1	1
Machisa	8	10	19	37	1	
Manchiti	8	25	31	64	3	5
Muntanga	9	14	20	39	4	1
Katetaula	12	20	29	61	3	3
Kaumbo	12	19	21	52		
Chininka	10	19	27	56		
Chiliti	8	14	19	41		
Mainda	12	25	20	57	2	
	139	238	342	715	29	14

As shown in Table I the average number of people in a village is 51. In my village counts I have included migrant labourers if they

THE VILLAGE

still have huts in the village. Government statistics do not distinguish between migrant labourers and those who are domiciled in towns and have no intention of going back to their villages.

As to the numerical strength of matrilineages, at least of those which possess a village, the number varies between ten and twenty adults. Among them is a number of people with varying degrees of loyalty to the matrilineage. Some people of course are born and bred in marital exile. When asked about their matrilineage, they know it and can say whence they had originally come, but in fact they would be loath to return to their matrilineal homes. Nonetheless, probably the majority of the Ambo at any one time are living in their matrilineal centres.

Marital exile

If a married Ambo man or woman lives away from his matrilineal home village, *kwabo*, he says that he lives in *cendo*[1] which I can best translate in this context as 'marital exile'. Unmarried people living away from their matrilineal home are also said to be in *cendo*, because they attach themselves to others who are in marital exile. Thus the residents of a village are sharply divided into 'the owners of the village', *bene ba musi* and those in *cendo*, people who immigrated for marriage. This division corresponds closely with that into the 'clan relatives', *bakwabo*, and 'strangers' (to the clan), *bana ba bene*. The agnates of a headman, whether he is dead or living, and of his clansmen, are all in *cendo*, though they are already married in the village of their fathers and grandfathers, and though they may assert that they have no other home, having lost all connection with their distant minor matrilineage.

I once heard two elders deploring marital exile: 'Marital exile scatters people', *cendo cikolufya bantu*. Reference was made to a classificatory sister of the spokesman whose mother emigrated following her husband. The sister lived with her married son after the death of her husband in her adopted village. Another headman declared that he never ceased to tell the young people, particularly boys, to marry within their village. Yet another when asked why cross-cousin marriage is favoured answered that but for such marriages the village would be broken up, *bangatoba musi* 'lest they break up the village'.

---

[1] *Cendo* derives from *kwenda*, to walk, to travel.

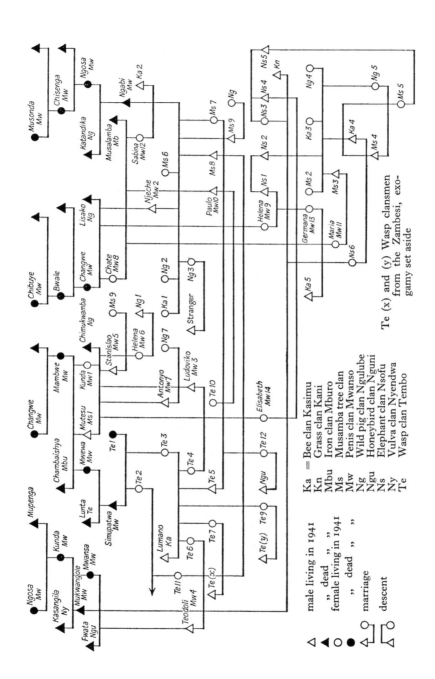

Diagram V. Marital relationships in Mtondo village

THE VILLAGE

Every headman, as the guardian and leader of the matrilineage, tries to keep his female dependents in the village. A woman living in marital exile is potentially able to form a separate minor matrilineage, though she will not necessarily do so. Furthermore many women return to the village of their minor matrilineage on the death of their husbands together with their married daughters and even married sons, irrespective of where the sons married. The same may happen after divorce.

Men are more free than women to choose their marital residence except in the initial stage of their marriage, and in some exceptional circumstances. Some go to marry far away where they would not be allowed to take their wives to live virilocally. These men may be of independent character. Others do not care to live with their matrikin because they have no siblings there or close relatives such as mother's sisters' children. Many men avoid the matrilocal stage of marriage by intra-village marriage. The rule is, however, that marriage is initially matrilocal for some years, and then virilocal with the permission of the husband's in-laws, 'so that his matrilineage (*bakwabo*) may take care of him'.

It is convenient here to give Table II which shows percentages of different kinds of residence after marriage, in my sample of 294 cases. *Matrilocal A* are cases where the husbands as well as wives are Ambo. *Matrilocal B* are those in which husbands are strangers from distant countries. This latter is the most advantageous form of marriage for matrilineal unity. 'Matrilocal' rather than 'uxorilocal' is the term used in Table II to emphasize that it is residence at the wife's mother's village that is the essential consideration.

TABLE II

Marital residence

Type of marriage	No:	Percentages
Preferential:	40	13·61
Matrilocal A:	97	32·99
Matrilocal B:	19	6·46
Virilocal:	70	23·81
Intra-village:	68	23·13
	294	100·00

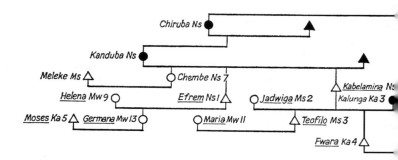

The matrilineage of the Elephant clan

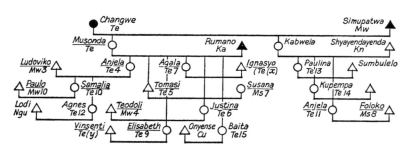

The matrilineage of the Wasp clan

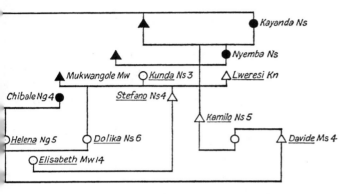

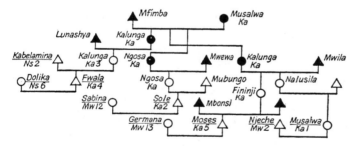

The matrilineage of the Bee clan

Diagram VI. Affinal and agnatic matrilineages in Mtondo village.
Persons with names underlined were living in Mtondo village in 1941

36 SOCIAL AND RITUAL LIFE OF THE AMBO

Table II shows the great extent to which matrilineal interests are looked after and safeguarded. Virilocal marriages comprise less than a quarter of all marriages (23·81%), but the centrifugal effects of this form of marriage are often moderated by only short inter-village distances being involved. All other categories of marriages fall essentially within the matrilocal types and the majority of these last for life.

An appreciation of marital exile is important because fragmentation of the Ambo matrilineage is bound up with marital residence.

Mtondo village of the Mwanso clan

I have chosen Mtondo village (*see* Diagrams V and VI) as an example to discuss in detail. It was typical of the general Ambo pattern especially in that it was composed of several matrilineages of different clans which hived off from the village-owning Mwanso clan-matrilineage to form villages of their own. However, as many as four new villages were formed in this way, Mtondo is exceptional. It is more usual for only one or two new village headmen to emerge in this way.

Mtondo village was rather larger in 1944 when I knew it than the average village, having (*see* plan page 39) 23 families (polygamist headman Njeche being counted as two families according to his two wives). Mtondo village then had over 100 inhabitants. Table I gives 51 persons as an average number for a village but that count was made in 1950 when a regulation permitting a village of five taxpayers had been in operation for a few years. My census of Mtondo village was taken at a period when a minimum of ten taxpayers was required to form a village.

The core minor matrilineage of Mtondo is composed of four segments with the ancestresses: Musonda, Changwe, Chibuye and Ngosa. These segments claim to be of one minor matrilineage but the members cannot trace all the links between their common ancestresses. They remember their founder, a male, Mubanga, a son of the renowned chief Chibuye. The second headman was Kanjiri, honoured by those of his descendants who are hunters. Mukwangole was the third headman. (I have no data on the genealogical connexions between these heads.) After his death, Njece was chosen in his place from another segment, Teodoli being passed over, probably because Njece was older. When Njece became old, Ludoviko Chamalashya was deputy headman.

THE VILLAGE

Practically no Mwanso matrikin had been lost to Mtondo in marital exile in 1944. Marriages were all within the village. Thus Teodoli (Mw 4) married into the Wasp matrilineage, Antonyo (Mw 7) brought an outsider to the village from the neighbouring village of the Wild Pig clan but there were other Wild Pig people residing in the village. Ludoviko (Mw 3) married into the same group as Teodoli.

Stanislao (Mw 5) married a Musamba woman, whose clan was widely represented in the village. Paulo Musalamba (Mw 10) again married into the Wasp clan. He and his wife belonged to succeeding generations of sisters' sons and sisters' daughters, sons and daughters-in-law.

Then Njeche, the headman, was united by marriage to Wild Pig Musamba and Bee clans.

The women of the Mwanso matrilineage also married mostly within the village. Chate (Mw 8) however married a Swaka stranger of the Mouse clan; she was a widow at the time of census; her daughter Maria (Mw 11) married a Musamba man. Elizabeth (Mw 14) married one of the Elephant clan, who formed a matrilineage in the village. Helena (Mw 6) married another Wild Pig man. Another Helena married (Mw 9) an Elephant man. Sabina, another daughter of Chate, married a Bee man of the Musinuka matrilineage, close neighbours.

A second clan was represented in Mtondo by the minor matrilineage of the Wasp clan descended from Changwe. Changwe was married to a Mwanso, Simupatwa who was a clan-brother to headman Njeche. Changwe was the progenitress of a new matrilineage. She had two daughters, Msonda and Kabwera. Msonda had five daughters and a son, Thomasi. Two of the daughters, Anjela (Te 4) and Justina (Te 6), married Mwanso men and they lived in the village. Only the youngest daughter, Baita (Te 15), lived outside the village in virilocal marriage. Kabwera lived for a long time virilocally.

The third matrilineage was of the Elephant Clan, which came from the Lwano in two groups of siblings as shown on the chart. They also could not trace their common ancestress, though they knew relationships through three generations. This matrilineage had two segments (Diagram VI) descending from two clan-sisters Kanduba and Nyemba. These segments were each composed of two brothers and a sister. However, one of the sisters, Chembe (Ns 7), did not live at Mtondo. Efrem (Ns 1) married a

38 SOCIAL AND RITUAL LIFE OF THE AMBO

Mwanso woman as did another of his clan-brothers Stephano (Ns 4).

The fourth clan represented in Mtondo village was Musamba tree clan. Its members did not belong to one minor matrilineage. There was one group of two siblings, brother (Ms 4) and his sister (Ms 5). One Musamba woman (Ms 9) was married to a Mwanso man, other Musamba women married men of other clans within the village.

The fifth was the Bee clan, three men and one woman. Of the men one was of the Mainda matrilineage: two men and the woman were of the Musinuka matrilineage. They kept in contact with their closely matrilineally associated villages in the neighbourhood, and after the death of the woman all her children emigrated, joining their matrilineal village of Musinuka.

The sixth section comprised three women of the Wild Pig clan, Namukose (Ng 2), a wife of headman Njeche, her daughter (Ng 3) married to a stranger from the Sena country (Portuguese East Africa), and Helena (Ng 5). One man, Damiano (Ng 1), was from the Lala country, and a member of a different major matrilineage. Damiano was united with the Mwanso through a marriage bond with their woman (Mw 6).

The seventh section was composed of a brother and his sister, of the Mouse clan, which is practically unrepresented among the Ambo. The brother, Musalamba, begot many children for the Mwanso clan. His sister, Stelia, was the principal wife of headman Mukwangole, and also had numerous offspring. She was from Swaka country. A few years after her husband's and brother's deaths she took most of her children back to Swaka country. She is not shown on Diagram V, as she left the village before the census.

Two strangers married uxorilocally in the village. One was mentioned above, of unknown clan membership. The other was a Grass clansman, Lwereshi a widower, marrying an Elephant woman (Ns 3).

Thus the village was 'owned' by the Mwanso matrilineage. The Wasp and Elephant clan-matrilineages had developed into numerically strong matrilineages, with a growing consciousness of their identity as different from their matrilineages of origin. The other clans represented in the village were genealogically heterogeneous and still belonged to their matrilineages organized in other villages, such as the Bee or Musamba or Wild Pig clansmen.

THE VILLAGE

Mouse clansmen faded away from the village as their linkage with it was severed through death of the husband and the brother of the progenetrix Stelia.

Mtondo village broke up into four villages along the lines of clan affiliation. The occasion for the split was the change of the village site and the making of new gardens. Some leaders, such as Kamilo of the Elephant clan-matrilineage and Thomasi of the Wasp group, exploited the situation, relying on their well developed kin groups.

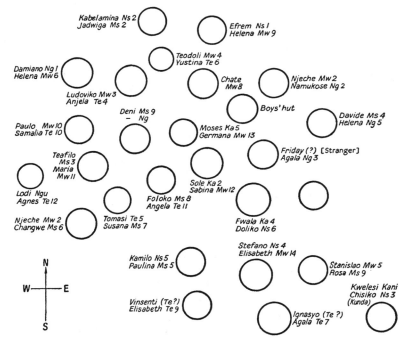

Diagram VII. Plan of Mtondo village in 1944 (before the break up)
Not to scale

Out of original Mtondo, the headman (Mw 2) remained and one of his clan brothers Ludoviko (Mw 3). Other men were all brothers-in-law: Efrem (Ns 1), Stefano (Ns 4) and Damiano (Ng 1). Two sons-in-law also remained, the 'stranger' and Moses of the Bee clan (Ka 5). (Moses, after the death of his Mwanso wife rejoined his village of Musinuka in 1957.)

Thomasi of the Wasp clan matrilineage succeeded in persuading all his brothers-in-law to follow him. He also enlisted the support of his two sons-in-law. One of them was Paulo (Mw 10), a Mwanso who left Mtondo only to help Thomasi to found the village, as he put it. (He returned to Mtondo in 1960 to take over the headmanship.) Another Mwanso man joining Thomasi was Teodoli (Mw 5).

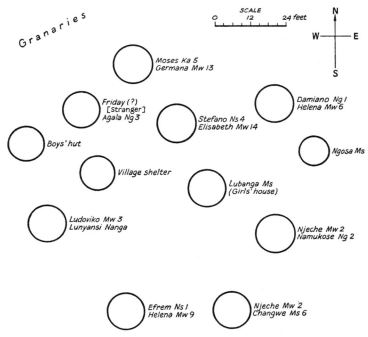

Diagram VIII. Plan of Mtondo village in 1950 (after the break up). Ludoviko Mw 3 divorced Anjela Te 4 and married Lunyansi. Lubanga is the daughter of Changwe Ms 6, whose mother is Ngosa.

He resented being by-passed in the selection of the headman. As the years passed, three married clan sisters of Thomasi, of the segment of Kabwera, one of them with her husband, returned from their virilocal marriage after the divorces and death of their husbands. They were Paulina (Te 13), Kupempa (Te 14) and Anjela (Te 11).

Kamilo (Ns 5) fared worse than Thomasi in founding his village.

THE VILLAGE

None of his uterine and clan brothers followed him, resenting his junior age. Two of them, married to Mwanso women, Stefano (Ns 4) and Efrem (Ns 1) remained in their old village as was stated above. Kabelamina (Ns 2) followed into the village of his son, Teofilo (Ms 3). Kamilo received support from only his sister's daughter's husband Fwara (Ka 4).

The fourth village was that of Teofilo, of the Musamba clan. The feature of this village was that it had no matrilineal core, his numerous matrikin being domiciled on the line of rail. He had the support of two Musamba clansmen one of them being Davide (Ms 4), but they did not belong to his minor matrilineage. Therefore his village proved unstable and by 1958 he was ordered by the chief to return to Mtondo.

Clan composition and clan attitudes in the village

The minor matrilineage 'owns' the village in the sense that it supplies its headman and considers it as its home. What has been said of the inner workings of a minor matrilineage refers equally to the village, for the former does not live theoretically but actually in the framework of its village.

The minor matrilineage is not a self-sufficient unit, but exogamous. Spouses and the children of the spouses of the male matrikin owning the village are of alien clans and thus socially are strangers in the village. Table III shows the disposition of clansmen in the village. The difference between this sample and that of Table II is accounted for by three widowers. Table IV shows the disposition of clanswomen.

TABLE III

Disposition of clansmen in the villages

Number in sample of men wedded	Number of wedded men in their matrilineal villages	Number of men in marital exile	Percentage of wedded men in their matrikin villages
297	86	211	28·9

SOCIAL AND RITUAL LIFE OF THE AMBO

TABLE IV

Disposition of clanswomen in the villages

Number of wedded clanswomen (Including widows and divorcées)	Number of wedded women living in their matrilineal villages	Number of wedded women in marital exile	Percentage of wedded women in their matrilineal village
428	159	269	37·4

The sample was taken from 29 villages which were distributed as follows: 18 villages from Mboloma's country, 9 villages from Lwembe's country and 2 from Mboshya's country.

As to the composition of a village according to clans, there is a marked tendency for groups of clansmen of different clans to constitute a village. The internal composition of each matrilineal group in a village varies. Some are minor matrilineages developed in marital exile. Other groups of clansmen are completely unrelated by kinship, having in common only the common clan name. A third category is of clansmen of one matrilineage which owns a village in the neighbourhood or in a distant part of the country. A fourth is similar to the second, villages comprising a few clansmen or even one or two clansmen who have severed all connection with their parent matrilineage and are reared abroad, yet usually know the matrilineal village of origin, and the place where the village was situated. Their 'original' matrilineal village itself may even have scattered.

Such an arrangement according to clan is the effect of the tendency of multiple intermarriage between particular matrilineages either within the village or with a neighbouring village. In Ambo opinion it is commendable to marry into a group where another clansman has married and has made a success of it. Frequent visiting between affines contributes to further matching. Once the distrust between strange groups has been broken through by one successful marriage, the road is open to further marriages. Intermarrying may persist through generations, so that alien clanspeople in the village become agnates of the matrikin owning the village.

The village as a home of the matrikin is a place of refuge in time

THE VILLAGE

of crises particularly for those matrikin who live in marital exile. For those scattered individuals who do not belong to a matrilineage possessing a village, their place of refuge is a sibling's home. Most Ambo hope to the last to end their days amongst matrikin. Widowers and widows bereft of their spouses return to their matrilineal home village, the mothers bringing with them children, especially unmarried ones. Divorced persons also go back to their matrilineal home.

With these practical considerations there goes an emotional attachment to one's home villages, particularly if siblings or mother also live there. This affection is starved by upbringing in marital exile or through tension with some matrilineal clansmen. On the whole, the owning minor matrilineage shows some pride in its village—owning of a village represents a social value. Contrasts between owners and 'strangers' emerge in time of conflict. 'The strangers' are at once insulted and reminded that they live in this village only as strangers or guests. This is the most common insult used: it is termed *kutopa musi*.

Village-strangers in marital exile find themselves in subordinate positions where they serve to maintain the village-owning matrilineage. As men, they beget children for other matrilineages and rear them as well as contribute to the numerical strength of the village manhood and its economy. They are the *bako* (sing. *muko*), the sons-in-law, sent on errands, ready for any work and service, sent most often on compulsory Government labour, ready at the call of their mothers-in-law. They are strangers on trial and have to be well behaved. When they grow older, however, as the 'fathers' of the village-owning matrilineage they enjoy increased respect and gratitude from the minor matrilineage they served.

Women strangers are not on such trial. They help the men of the minor matrilineage to stay in their villages, but on the other hand they bear children matrilineally foreign to the village. If they or their husbands die or they are divorced, their children often withdraw from the village as well as themselves. If alien children are already locally married, and their mother is not anxious to return to her matrilineal village, she may stay on with her children. Such a group of siblings forms a segment on its own, aspiring to independence both from its own parent minor matrilineage and from the village-owning matrilineage, their hosts. Even intravillage marriages, though they may be stable during the lifetime of the spouses, do not contribute to village continuity. If the children of these

44 SOCIAL AND RITUAL LIFE OF THE AMBO

marriages are numerous and of a clan other than that of the village-owning matrilineage, the tendency is for them to establish their own village.

Though in an average Ambo village of some twenty years ago perhaps five to six clans were represented, usually only one kinship group other than the village-owning one created a section of the village, *cikole*, under its own leader, *mukulu wa cikole*. It is related that in Lupanda's village his own sister's son, Kanyo, had his own *cikole*, which branched off to form the present village of Musinuka. There are other reports of big villages and the larger matrilineages of older times being divided into sections. At the present time here and there are still vestiges of *fikole* (plur.), but nothing more. The warden of a section was an intermediary between his matrilineage and the headman and headman's matrilineage. Formerly the fear of raids seemed to have held population together in big villages.

The village headmanship

As in many other Central African societies, among the Ambo the village is primarily a discrete group of kinsmen related in different ways to the village headman. But it must be emphasized that genealogical links with the headman cannot always be traced. The position he holds must be viewed against the background of the village as an organized matrilineage, but with that proviso. To the description already given it may be added that a village is an autonomous unit in such matters as the choosing of a new site, and in the rituals of requests for rain, first fruits' dedication and fish-weir construction. The village holds its own beer parties to which people living in other villages may not be invited. Male villagers may hunt together.

The village headman refers to his village as 'at my home', *kwanji*, whereas other villagers say 'at our home', *kwesu*. He is the representative of the village both in internal and external affairs. At the distribution of game meat, one hind leg is due to him. Together with members of a deceased chief's matrilineage, a village headman takes part in the selection of a successor. A headman should be greeted by a respectful clapping of hands, and at beer parties he has the privilege of sitting on a stool. He receives a special gift of beer at the larger parties, and is informed of and invited to smaller ones in other villages about which other people might not come to know.

The headman plays an important ritual role at the building of

THE VILLAGE 45

a new village or the moving of an existing one to a new site. Many headmen, but not all, know how to protect their villages against lions, and their village fords, bathing places and water-drawing places against crocodiles. Headmen should also doctor their villages against the baneful influence of hyena (*see* also pages 151-2).

Medicine against lions (luteta)

The ingredients of *luteta* medicine are: (i) *Mwafi*, the roots. This tree was used in sorcery trials; here it is used to bewitch the lion. (ii) *Nkalamu-ya-pansi*, the roots. The name of this tree means 'lion of the earth' or 'lion of the underground'. It is so named because the roots are reddish brown in colour, resembling the colour of lion's hair. This tree provides a representation of the lion for the medicine to act upon. (iii) *Chaff of sorghum.* This is like the hair of the lion. (iv) *Mweyama*, the roots. This tree represents water for it grows in water. It is said that when a lion has drunk water, he loses his fierceness. (v) *Mfubatwa*, the branches. Being like the claws of the lion, this ingredient introduces another representation of the lion. (vi) *Lusato*, python fat. The python represents strength. (vii) The egg of the crocodile. The lion does not eat crocodiles, therefore this ingredient symbolizes immunity against lions. Furthermore, the gall of the crocodile is believed to be a powerful poison. (viii) Teeth of a lion, which afford another representation of the lion for the medicine to act upon.

These ingredients are classified by the Ambo into *fiti*, 'trees' and *fisimba*, 'animal parts'. Another mode of subdivision overlaps from another point of view. First there are the representations of the lion, then vehicles of forces let loose to act upon the lion. The second group consists of *mwafi*, to bewitch the lion, and *mweyama*, to rob him of his fierceness. Python counteracts the strength of the lion, the crocodile introduces immunity against the lion.

The leaves of the above trees are thrown on a fire kindled in the middle of the village to fumigate it. While throwing the leaves, the spell is said: 'I do not want a lion to come here.' At first the diviner drives a horn with the medicine into the ground at a spot on the outskirts of the village. Then he tramples round the village breaking down the grass as he goes along, finally rolling on the ground. The breaking of grass round the village demarcates the boundary where the lion should stop. Hence *luteta* from *kuteta*, to cut, to blaze the trail. When a lion rolls on the ground, he is content.

46 SOCIAL AND RITUAL LIFE OF THE AMBO

Prohibitions associated with this doctoring are (a) That water should not be brought into the village in an open pot. The women drawing water leave baskets on the outskirts of the village, which they use to cover their pots on their return. The water, coming from the bush, represents it and is identified with the bush. The lion is also identified with the bush, even being referred to as 'the bush', *mpanga*. To bring an open pot with water into the village would be tantamount to bringing in 'the bush' with an open mouth. (b) Fresh bark rope, tied in a bundle, must not be brought into the village. Such rope is reddish in colour, reminiscent of the colour of the lion. Bark rope is described as *kusweta*, to be red, just as the lion is spoken of as *kusweta*. Coming from the bush, the bark represents it as well as the lion. The bush was 'tied up' through the application of medicines. Therefore this 'tied up' or neutralized bush may not be brought into the village. The tying up would be interfered with and undone. (c) Bound firewood may not be brought in as it also represents 'the bush' as above. (d) It is forbidden to pound grain at night lest the bush be aroused. Let sleeping dogs lie. (e) For the same reason, wood should not be chopped at night. (f) A big log of firewood should not be pulled through the village lest a human being be so pulled by a lion. (g) The word 'lion' may not be pronounced in the village after sunset lest it summon the animal. A lion is referred to as 'hyena', 'the bush' or *ciswango*, the wild beast.[1]

Doctoring a ford against crocodiles

The ingredients for this medicine are: (i) *Musolo* (*Pseudolachnystylis maprounaefolia*), the roots. *Musolo* resembles *kusolola*, 'to rearrange fire sticks', also 'to chase elsewhere'. Hence this ingredient is to chase the crocodiles elsewhere. (ii) *Kabosya*, the roots. This name resembles *kubosya*, to make rotten. Both trees on account of their significant names are much used in magical medicines. (iii) *Kaputu*, bark rope. *Kaputu* resembles *kuputula*, to snap. It is used so that the teeth of the crocodile may also break or become loose when it bites someone.

The roots of *kabosya* and *musolo* are bound with bark twine of *kaputu* and thrown into the water at the place where the village has

---

[1] My informant, a chief, gave only the prohibitions Nos. a, b, c, and g. The rest were supplied by his brother and maternal grandson, potential heirs to the chieftainship. I think they may have added prohibitions from other prescriptions, as this list looks rather too full to observe.

THE VILLAGE 47

access to the river. When throwing in the medicine a spell is recited: 'This is our safe ford, a person is not bitten here, no. Lesa himself may help, Lesa may help truly with his power. It is not ourselves who have created the trees, no.' *Fwe cito cesu ca makosa, tapali kusuma muntu, iyo, Lesa yanka eungafwa, eungafwilisya nkosa syakwe Lesa, tefwe twalengele fiti, iyo.*[1]

Now the spot in the river is fumigated with leaves of *musolo* and *musokolobe. Kusokola* means to chase away, e.g. the baboons from the fields.

Prohibitions: A pot which had been on the fire, *nongo ya mifito,* may not be washed in the river, but only on the bank. In such a pot food is cooked, so it is argued that the crocodile, smelling the pot, may feel hungry. Again, such a pot is set on the fire and a torch must be lighted if one is to see inside it. A crocodile also would see better; if the pot were dipped in the river it would light up the river. Children when bathing must not catch one another by the leg, an action imitative of the crocodile.

Doctoring against hyena

If an hyena excretes in the village, the village must be doctored. It is feared that otherwise the village would scatter because the hyena, 'the cattle of the sorcerers', has an evil influence. The excreting of the hyena in the village means that the village has been doomed by sorcerers.

The medicine is composed of *kafungu,* the bark. The name resembles the word *kufungula,* 'to open'. The village should be opened again. Excrements of any edible animal are mixed together to neutralize that of the hyena, to bury the excrements of the hyena. The village is fumigated with this compound. No spell is uttered.

Other considerations

Headmen usually do not go to towns for work. They are expected to stay in their villages. A headman who keeps a second wife in another village and visits her there, is often referred to as a fool, for he should remain in his own 'to look after the village', *kusopa*

---

[1] The appeal to Lesa is exceptional here, and is probably because of the influence of Christian teaching. The common belief is to ascribe all efficiency of medicine to the power inherent in it. The spell is composed for the occasion on the model of a prayer at an offering to the shades. It may be that reference to God was made as a gesture for the benefit of the writer, a missionary.

48 SOCIAL AND RITUAL LIFE OF THE AMBO

musi. He plays a principal social role in the countryside along with other influential persons such as renowned hunters, diviners, gunsmiths and, nowadays, teachers and shopkeepers. He must receive guests and travellers and take care of them, providing a hut for them to sleep in, *kusonta ŋanda*, ('to point out a hut'), a mat and possibly also a meal. I know of one instance of a headman living matrilocally in a village not his own, as his wife was unwilling to move to her husband's home. The headman had no suitable deputy. The chief insisted that he should reside in his own village, mainly because, he said, there was nobody but the headman to receive travellers. The duty of keeping up social contacts between the segments of a major matrilineage devolves mostly on the headman, as the social representative of his minor matrilineage.

It is the ambition of most if not all men to become headmen, not least for the perquisites of the post. If a person refuses a headmanship it is because he fears being bewitched by his close matrikin. In choosing a headman account is taken of the seniority of the individual before that of his segment, out of respect for age, but also coupled with fear of retaliation through sorcery. The personal character of the candidate is an over-riding qualification, however, so a junior in age and segment may be selected. Nowadays, when a headman grows old and finds it hard to attend the official meetings of headmen at the chief's court, a deputy headman is selected, who has the right of succession. However, many headmen die young, without having a deputy-successor, and then canvassing for a suitable candidate comes into play. First choice by kinship is a sibling, but if none is available nor a classificatory brother the office must pass to the next descending generation. A woman may succeed but only if there is no suitable clansman and only until such time as a suitable male in the village-owning matrilineage reaches sufficient age.

A headman's duties towards the members of his village vary in proportion to the nature of the kinship linking him to particular persons. His duties and rights first refer to his siblings and their matrilineal descendants, not as a headman, but as the senior relative or a head of a segment. His second range of duties, which include limited economic assistance, is towards all the other members of his minor matrilineage. These duties include limited economic assistance. Of old, he could not hand into slavery members of this group for his own advantage, and at the present time he is not obliged to assist them financially. He has the duty, as headman, to assist them in less onerous matters, such as providing them with

THE VILLAGE

accommodation and with a garden. In one village the women wanted to change their headman for a more helpful clansman because the former was unwilling to construct grain bins for them. It was evident that only the women who lacked near male kin or husbands were agitating. It was not expected that the headman should do these tasks alone but that he should organize the work, persuading the men of the village to do it.

As has been said, the relations between various segments of a minor matrilineage are marked with studied politeness, in contrast to the nonchalant behaviour towards the siblings. This polite behaviour refers particularly to the headman.

The headman claims a wardenship and control of his 'sisters', this sorority group being called *ibumba*. Among his 'brothers' he acts as *primus inter pares*.

The wardenship of the headman, as the head of the minor matrilineage, extends not only to his actual matrilineal relatives in the village, but also to all the other clansmen and clanswomen and their matrilineal descendants and the members of his minor matrilineage living in marital exile. He will take care of them in cases of trouble such as sickness or a law suit and he will assist them to return to his and their village.

The headman is not socially responsible for the inhabitants of his village who are affines or agnates of the minor matrilineage owning the village; they are the responsibility of their own minor matrilineages. The village headman may play only an intermediary role between them and his matrilineage or between their matrilineage and his, in times of trouble. Otherwise he has only a general care over persons in this category in so far as they are members of his village, an economic and social unit.

I know of a headman who complained again and again to the chief about villagers not of his own clan, that they were living at their fields. He was afraid of being accused of negligence should these 'strangers' meet with misfortune or an accident.

Thus far the internal position of the headman has been discussed. What of his external position?

As the chief was not subject to any central authority of the state, so also were the socio-administrative units of the chiefdom, the matrilineal villages, almost autonomous with very limited dependence on chief's authority. This autonomy is best evidenced in the free selection of the headman by his village-owning matrilineage without any right of intervention on the part of the chief.

50   SOCIAL AND RITUAL LIFE OF THE AMBO

Apart from the village autonomy described above the headman of the village played an essential part in the administration of the country, which was divided administratively into villages. However heterogeneous may have been the composition of a village, it was treated as an administrative unit. The chief dealt administratively not with the heads of matrilineages but with the headmen of villages. The chief may be said to rule his people indirectly through his headman.

In this capacity a headman had to organize the delivery of tribute to the chief on behalf of the village, whether in kind or in labour. He was called as official witness in any dispute or incident involving one of his villagers. He arranged offerings to the chief's shades on behalf of his village by providing an approved officiant. The headman had to inform the chief about the shifting of his village: a visiting chief was received by him. As representatives of administrative components of the land, headmen had the right to help select the chief.

All headmen were not socially equal. In Mboshya's country there were two hereditary headmen, court officials, *bamubala*, Mutanta and Lisebele, who were privileged much as sons of a chief were elsewhere. The sons of a chief had greater prestige and a higher social standing than the ordinary commoner headmen. Then there were the headmen of Nyendwa villages, who also enjoyed a privileged status. Nowadays relationships are much more egalitarian than in the past, certainly between headmen. Even the privileged position of such ritual officials as Chikwashya is a thing of the past. The suppression of slavery has levelled many social differences.

At the present time the headman finds himself on the lowest and unpaid rung of the administrative ladder under the Native Authority system. Periodically he has to make long journeys to meetings of headmen at the chief's capital to hear instructions and new rules and orders to be conveyed to his people. In many cases he is held responsible for the carrying out of these regulations, and is liable to be fined himself if they are not. It is improper for an official or a missionary to deal with a village community except through its headman. Another heavy responsibility which falls on him is in the supply of men for compulsory labour, who are most unwilling to undertake this type of work owing to low wages, its compulsory character and the difficulty of getting food on the job. Sometimes the headman must offer himself for such labour.

The administrative status of the headman in present times is

THE VILLAGE

reflected in the practice of appointing a younger man as official headman, if the old head is too frail to walk to the headmen's meetings at the chief's capital. The old man still remains the 'social' headman, the head of the matrilineage, and is respected as such by his village. In the social framework a young deputy headman has little standing even though the old headman is no longer acknowledged officially.

To sum up, the headman has manifold duties and plays various roles. He is the head of his own segment within his matrilineage, and the leader and guardian of his minor matrilineage. However, he has to direct the whole village community which includes stranger groups of other clans. Over this category of villagers he has very limited rights of administrative character. He is the main officer and intermediary between the chief and the villagers.

III. CHIEFTAINSHIP

THE Ambo hold an intermediate position between a political society of the Zulu–Bemba type and stateless tribes of the Nuer–Tallensi type.

Socially approved self-help in Ambo society is evident in the institution of the seizing of hostages, *nkole*. To recover a debt a man could seize a woman or a child from the territory of the debtor's chief. Having seized such a hostage he would go to a neighbouring village and announce there what he had done, and why he had done it. Thus he incited the matrilineage of the hostage against his debtor. The injured matrikin then brought the case before the chief and the debtor had to hasten to pay his debt and so redeem the hostage. Debts of this kind were incurred by such incidents as addressing a person by a wrong name or by soiling someone with excrement or urine at a beer party during the night. Customarily the redress required was enslavement but a wrong-doer was always allowed to substitute the payment of a slave for his own enslavement.

Consonant with the ideas behind *nkole* were those of running amok, of outlaws, *tupondo*. The seizer of hostages, however, did not kill; the *kapondo* might kill anyone on sight. A man became an outlaw or an avenger if, say, his sibling brother had been killed but he could not prove the guilt of the culprit he suspected. If an outlaw killed, he would announce the deed and its motive in the next village he came to before running away to a distant country where the local chief would receive him as a follower after an appropriate ritual. The innocent matrilineage of the latest victim demanded wergild from the one responsible for the original manslaughter.

Certainly it appears that the *nkole* institution could have worked without the chief's intervention, but it is not clear to what extent the chief intervened in the case of *tupondo*.

The chiefdoms and the Nyendwa clan

There are five Ambo chiefdoms: Mboloma, Mboshya, Mwape,

CHIEFTAINSHIP

Lwembe and Chisomo. All these are ruled by matrilineages of the Nyendwa clan. The first four chiefdoms originated through division of Kunda Mpanda's heritage; the matrilineages today holding these chiefdoms originated from Kunda Mpanda's matrilineage. Mboloma, as the successor of Kunda Mpanda, has always been the senior Ambo chief. However, in present times these five chiefdoms are situated in and divided between three Administrative districts, and thus Mboloma is unable to emphasize his position over the chiefs living in other districts. Chief Lwembe also claims to be a senior chief of the Ambo in Petauke district. The two chiefdoms of Mwape and Lwembe in Petauke district form a closely knit political unit, based on close positional kinship relations between the two chieftainships. Mwape's seat, inherited in the female line, supplies a son for the Lwembe seat.

Chief Chisomo of Serenje district devolved from the Lala chief Chibale, also a Nyendwa. He is inclined to gravitate towards the Lala. Mboloma also claims seniority over some neighbouring Lala chiefs.

I omitted to inquire into positional relationships linking Ambo chiefs. Positional succession certainly exists between the present chiefs and the agnatic descendants of chiefs. Between Mulaku's matrilineage and Mboloma the relationship of grandparent—grandchild has been stabilized, Mulaku being a grandson of Chief Chibuye.

District	Chiefdom	Population	Year
Petauke	Mwape	$(5,247)$[1]	1938
"	Lwembe	———————	"
		1,000?	
Mkushi	Mboloma	2,980	1948
	Mboshya	1,918[2]	"
Serenje	Chisomo	3,955[3]	1946
		Total 9,853	

[1] Tew, 1950, p. 33. The majority of the population in these districts is Nsenga.

[2] Information supplied by the District Commissioners.

[3] Peters, 1950, p. 2. Estimated population according to my own data: 1,600 people were in 26 villages, not counting dependent children in 13 villages; thus the average was 61 people per village.

The chiefdom of Chisomo was not listed among the Ambo in the Ethnographic Survey of Africa, *Bemba and Related Peoples of Northern Rhodesia*, p. 48, but Ambo in Chisomo's country are mentioned on p. 41 as probable. I have made further inquiries since which suggest that all Chisomo's people should be considered as Ambo. The reasons are given later in this book.

54   SOCIAL AND RITUAL LIFE OF THE AMBO

The density of the population was given for chief Mboloma's country as 5 per square mile for the 680 square miles of that territory. Mboshya's country with 280 square miles had a density of 7 per square mile. The other three Ambo chiefdoms hardly differ in density of population from these but in any one chiefdom population distribution is very uneven.

Ambo believe that the Nyendwa clan has ruled the Lala-speaking peoples, the Swaka, bena Bukanda and the Ambo but not the Lwano, since time immemorial, either as chiefs or village heads.

All Nyendwa clanspeople were privileged whether or not they occupied either of those positions. These privileged clansmen and clanswomen were addressed as chiefs or mothers of chiefs. At all social gatherings such as beer-drinks the Nyendwa are specially honoured. Nyendwa matrilineages had their own graveyards apart from those of commoners and of the ruling chiefs, and the children of Nyendwa men are buried with their fathers, though such agnates are not of noble clan. Spouses of Nyendwa men and women, however, were not buried in Nyendwa graveyards. On the model of ruling chiefs no Nyendwa ever went to a graveyard. Nyendwa matrilineages appointed slaves who buried the Nyendwa dead.[1] At the present time some Nyendwa, especially the younger ones, do not observe these prohibitions.

Another set of privileges is concerned with the naming of children. A Nyendwa husband has the right to name all his children, giving them the names of the guardian shades of his own clan and of his *lumbwe* father. *Lumbwe* is a commoner who has married a Nyendwa woman. A Nyendwa woman, *nyinamfumu*, 'the mother of chief', also gives names to all her children, which are taken from her clan and also from her father. Thus the spouses of the Nyendwa have no right to name their children.

Marital residence, which is so crucial in the social life of a people, operates in favour of the Nyendwa. A Nyendwa woman does not go into marital exile. The *lumbwe* comes to live with her. Formerly a Nyendwa woman would send messengers to bring her a husband who caught her fancy. She would give a male slave to his matrilineage and calico to the chosen man. If the man were married, he had to leave his wife, who was not compensated. The consort, *lumbwe*, could not have two wives simultaneously, neither had he the right of divorcing his Nyendwa wife. She, however, could divorce

[1] All Nyendwa in the Chisomo country are buried by Chikwe of the Pumpkin clan.

CHIEFTAINSHIP

AMBO CHIEFS

Chiefdom: Mboloma	Mwape	Mboshya	Lwembe	Chisomo
1 Kunda Mpanda 1830?				
2 Chilimba Nondo 1850?	Mwape Namukwanga 1880[1]	Mambwe we Tumba	Lwembe I	Nsangwe I
3 Mubanga 1860?		Kunkuma		
4 Bwashi 1860–1880?	Mwape II wa Chibambila 1880–1910	Chitemba Chishinga	Mkwemba Lwembe II Mukombola	Nsangwe II Chitemwalwo
5 Chibuye		Kalume Kepunde Mwape		
6 Lwembe Mukombola		Mwambwe Lukakanya		
7 Mboloma I Chinda Chontabunga		Mwape Kashimwamba	Lwembe III Chimkoko 1915	
8 Mubanga Shyenge 1921	Mwape III	Chibuye Lupiri		
9 Lubula Komanga 1932	Mwape IV		Ntimba regent 1924	Nsangwe III
10 Chisenga Lishyoka	Mwape V 1928	Mambwe Lwengu 1950	Lwembe IV 1930	
	Mwape VI	Shitima	Lwembe V Taulo 1943 Lwembe VI White	Nsangwe IV

[1] According to the chronicle of Richard Chimkoko, now deposited in the historical manuscripts collection at the Rhodes–Livingstone Museum, Livingstone, the second chieftainess was Chibuye Mtondo.—R.A.

56 SOCIAL AND RITUAL LIFE OF THE AMBO

him. The *lumbwe* was executed, if his wife died in childbirth, for he was held responsible for her death. If he begot frail children, another man was invited in his place to sleep with his wife for a night or so.

A Nyendwa man never went to work for his mother-in-law but sent slaves to do the work instead. Even now he would send a bag of salt to the mother-in-law in substitution for the labour. Thus the Nyendwa man never married uxorilocally. When he chose to marry he sent a woman slave to the matrilineal relatives of the bride to exchange for her. If she were already married, the husband had to release her, but was compensated with a slave.

Now many of these privileges are discontinued, because the chief has no power to enforce them.

Funeral rites

The Ambo chief becomes 'divine' only through and after death, as a shade with far greater power than shades of commoners.

Among the Ambo, as among their neighbours, the amount of splendour and ceremonial in the funeral accorded to the dead was commensurate with the dignity of the deceased. The leper, the sorcerer, the still-born child were not worthy of any funeral. Chiefs merited especially elaborate funerals. The most illustrious of all Ambo chiefs with the hereditary name of Mboloma, the successor of the legendary hero Kunda Mpanda, the conqueror of new lands, was accorded the most honourable rites. It is not known whether Kunda Mpanda was turned magically into a lion after his death, but his successor and heirs were made into lions, as will be described.

Since the coming of the British Administration the elaborate ritual of the burial of Kankomba chiefs has been upset. Chikwashya, the hereditary burier of chiefs, told me that since the coming of the Administration the last two chiefs, Shyenge and Komanga, were not turned into lions, but this statement cannot be vouched for.

I will discuss first the funeral rites of Chief Mboloma.

The chief's corpse was tended by his funeral friends of the Drum and the Goat clans after the same pattern as that for commoners. A funeral friend of the Goat clan was custodian of the chief's corpse, with the title *Kasembe*, while it was decomposing. Another official concerned with the funeral was Chikwashya, of the Mpande shell clan, called 'the burier', *kansanda*. This office is inherited within the Mpande shell clan from Mambwe Chisaka, the half

CHIEFTAINSHIP

brother of Kunda Mpanda who buried him, or at least his skin. Chikwashya's duty is to bury the bones of the dead Mboloma, to feed and to let out the chief changed into a lion, and to perform sacrifices on chiefs' graves. The Pumpkin clan also assisted in burying the bones of Mboloma. Mumba Chundu, the original Nsenga chief on the Mulembo, was of the Pumpkin clan, and it is his matrilineage which is represented. Another official was Chilemba of the Wild Dog clan. Chilemba was the magician who actually transformed the dead chief into a lion. That office is hereditary in a matrilineage of the Wild Dog clan because of its importance in its original country, among the Aushi. All these offices were hereditary.

When the chief dies, there is a short wailing lasting for some two hours. In the meantime his body is attended by his funeral friends. In former times they folded the body into the foetal position. It wore only a loin cloth. It was seated on a platform some eighteen inches high and two feet broad, constructed in the hut where the chief had died. Under the platform a small pit was dug, perhaps eighteen inches in diameter and about two feet deep. Into this pit a washing basin, *cibate*, was sunk, which collected the rotting matter. Some accounts speak of four pots being placed in the pit for that purpose. A screen of cloth across the hut ensured that the body was not visible. *Kasembe* sat at the door. He was also called *kapyanga*, 'the sweeper', because he swept the decaying matter into the basin or basins. *Kasembe* accompanied everybody who wanted to see the corpse, lest anyone should try to take away a part of the body for purposes of sorcery. People who saw the body were called *kampenga*. There was a nauseating stench in the chief's hut, but one was not allowed to spit or even to clear one's nose. The custodian burned fowls' feathers in an attempt to stifle the stench.

The place where the chief rotted was called *kabungwe*; the village where the chief died was *cipembwe*. At such a village *miyamba* trees were planted to commemorate his death.

After two or three months, Chikwashya was notified officially of the death and decomposition of the chief's body. A man adorned with red feathers of the lourie was sent with the message. He carried a goat or, lately, a pound, as a present for Chikwashya. Other accounts mention a gun as the present on this occasion. The herald approached the village of Chikwashya and shouted: 'That in which you trusted, dogs have eaten', *cimuteketele mbwa syalya*. Then the herald ran away for fear of being molested. Chikwashya sent word to Chilemba; both met and went to the capital. As mourners

58   SOCIAL AND RITUAL LIFE OF THE AMBO

they fired guns on arrival and enquired officially into the chief's death.

Chilemba entered the mortuary with the representatives of three other clans, of the Wasp, Gourd and Rain clans. He took the rotten matter to mould a lion (in the account: *likatesi* 'a monster'). Though the word 'to mould', *kubumba*, as also used in the context to mould a pot, figures in most accounts, other descriptions suggest that the lion-chief was an actual tamed lion cub. As the making of the lion was a most esoteric act, information on it cannot but be scanty and confusing. 'To make a lion-chief' is *kusangula nkalamu*, which means to turn or to change into a lion. Chilemba used for that purpose 'the medicine of transformation', *ya nsangu*, which had to be fetched from the original home of the Ambo with the Aushi. Other accounts say that with the rotten remains of the chief's body he smeared 'the lion' for three days so that it might grow. On the third day he said: 'Today, the chief has grown.' On the fifth day he announced: 'it has grown up, let us bury the corpse.'

The actual burial took place in dry weather, when the river Mulembo had subsided, because the chief's remains were not to be taken across the water in a canoe. The burial grounds of the Mboloma chiefs lie on the Mulembo, where the village of Kunda Mpanda was situated. The place is referred to as Kalyango, 'the little door'; the graveyard is also spoken of as *milende*, 'a sacred spot'; the old Chikwashya spoke of the graveyard as *kuipanga*, which is usually used of the capital of the reigning chief.

When setting out to fetch the bones of the chief's body, Chikwashya drew water from the Mulembo and gave it to drink to the buriers who were the chief's funeral friends, *banungwe*, of the Drum and Goat clans, and also in the later stages on the Mulembo, to those of the Gourd and Mpande shell clans who joined the procession then. The chief's bones were tied into a bundle for burial. A few slaves, male and female, and a few chief's wives were then killed, if they had been objectionable to the chief or unfaithful. The corpses were laid one beside the other and those carrying the chief's remains, as they came out of the hut, crossed the row of corpses. Such an arrangement of corpses is called *musansiko*. The idea of *kusansika* is to roll out a sleeping mat; thus *musansiko* is best translated by 'mattress'. Many people accompanied the funeral procession which moved slowly, to the accompaniment of a double bell, *lusonsolo*, and drums. Wherever the funeral procession stopped, the buriers scraped the spot clear of grass, and spilled meal and red

CHIEFTAINSHIP 59

powder. Then they laid down the chief's bones. While leaving the place after a rest, each mourner threw a stone on the spot, where the chief's remains were laid down without speaking: passers-by for some two months also added stones to the pile. The remains of the chief were laid for the last night in the hut of the son of Chikwashya, where the lion-cub was also kept. In the morning the remains were carried across the Mulembo and laid to rest. A round hole was dug some nine feet deep in which the bones were put. On the top much cloth was laid, but no soil.

Over the grave of the chief a hut was built of round poles, with a flat roof also made of poles. The hut was without any entrance. There the lion was placed after the funeral. The lion-chief when still in confinement was given at night separately sorghum meal and a red powder (of the *nkula* tree). If the lion scattered the flour, the comment was that the lion-chief would be meek. If he scattered the red powder, it was taken as a sign that he would attack people. In that case the lion-chief may even have been killed. When on the point of releasing the lion from the hut, Chikwashya came to the lion with a gun, and pointing the gun towards him said: 'Look, chief, if you meet people on the path, do not trouble them. They will kill you. Look at the gun.' Then he showed a spear and again said: 'Do not annoy people.'

Some lions roaming the country are believed to be the old chiefs. When a lion roars near a village, the headman shouts: 'If you are a chief, stop roaring. If you are not a chief, go on roaring. If you are a chief, seize game for us.' When a lion is a chief, he is believed to consent to the request by growling. The shades of the chiefs were thanked for the harvest in the thanksgiving ritual of first fruits. Whoever ate the first fruits before this ritual would be mauled by a lion, for he trespassed on the chief's right as the owner of the land by not thanking him for the crops. Such a trespasser was punished by the chief's shade sending a lion against him, or by the chief himself coming as a lion to maul the culprit.

A lion was roaming around a chief's village one night in 1953. The chief put out some gruel of uncooked meal and water in a dish. The lion tasted the gruel and walked off. People believed therefore that the lion was not an ordinary lion but a chief of old. In the same year, at another village, for some days a pride of some twenty lions roamed and roared at night. The lions came to the outskirts of the village. The chief's messenger wanted to climb a tree and shoot them at night, but the elders restrained him for fear he injured

60 SOCIAL AND RITUAL LIFE OF THE AMBO

some former chief. As the lions did no harm to anybody, the elders suspected that at least some of them might have been deceased chiefs.

Mourning of the land

After the death of the chief the funeral friends announced 'the mourning of the land'. People had to come to wail at the capital. They were told to bring foodstuffs such as flour, goats and fowls. Boys and girls had to come to dance. The war drum, *mandu*, was sounded, the chiefly double bell, *lusonsolo*, was rung, the gourd drums were beaten. There seems to have been a degree of licence. One account relates an exhortation of an elder: 'Listen, now you have gathered. Listen, you may not show marital jealousy, no, all are to catch at the breasts of others' wives, because a great lord has died.' Another report is to the same effect.

When parties of mourners came to the capital, they let off guns at random. People already in the village came forward to meet new arrivals, to restrain them.

So commemoration went on for some two or three months until the corpse had rotted away. In the meantime, the whole country was mourning. All subjects of the dead chief, except his funeral friends, had their heads shaven. All cocks in the whole country had to be killed lest they crowed. The crowing of a cock is a symbol of fame and renown. As it is heard far away from a village, so is the fame of a man widely known. Now a chief has died, there should be silence in the villages. To save a cock, its neck had to be tied up secretly to prevent it crowing. The killing of the cocks was done by the *bakali*, the chief's bodyguards, who with red feathers on their heads, toured the villages for the purpose. There is a persistent tradition that they killed people as a sign of mourning. Chikwashya gave me a very reasonable explanation of this custom. He said it was not a random killing but a calculated, if disguised, punishment of a village for having neglected or shirked the tributes due to the chief. Another sign of mourning was that during the whole period all the drums in the country except in the capital were silenced. Spears were wrapped in cloth, until the funeral beer-drink.

The funeral rites for a chief other than Mboloma scarcely differed from those described above. There were some differences, however. Outstretched, the corpse of an ordinary chief was laid on a platform. He was buried on the fifth day, but another account has

CHIEFTAINSHIP

it that an ordinary chief rotted for two months in former times. Ordinary chiefs were never changed into lions.

The following incident shows the spirit of mourning even in recent times at the funeral of an ordinary chief. A woman of the Nyendwa clan, while sitting in the place of mourning, rested the calf of her leg on a log so that it should not be dirtied by the ground. But people at funerals, especially women, may not go about finely dressed but should look neglected. She was upbraided by a Mpande man. Her relative, Chief Mboshya, had to pay a fine on her behalf.

The wives of the dead chief led exceptionally austere lives during the period of mourning until the burial. They did not wash or walk about. To come out of their huts, they had to creep on their knees, covering themselves like initiate girls. They were hiding from the sight of men. They slept on the bare floor and had little food.

The close matrikin of the deceased chief went to the diviner to ascertain who had caused the chief's death. The diviner might pronounce that so-and-so had committed adultery with one of the chief's wives. The chief's men set out on a punitive expedition. They adorned themselves with ringing bells, *indibu*, hung round their belts, and with tufts of red feathers on their heads as they went into action. They went for the doomed man and a fight ensued. The relatives of the suspected man defended him. After the encounter the warriors went home, carrying the heads of the slain, which were stuck on pointed poles some nine feet high. After the fight the warriors danced a war dance, *kwanga*, to mark their triumph. Eventually the hut of the rotting chief became surrounded with such gruesome poles.

At the present time this ritual and killing is obviously curtailed. The *mandu* drum exists no more, and a *lusonsolo* is lacking in some chief's capitals.

The interregnum

The moment the chief dies, his son sends for another chief to take care of the country, until the new chief has been chosen. The chief-in-charge hurried with his armed force to prevent any rival from seizing the country. When another chief drew near the capital, the chief-in-charge sent him flour and bullets. If the approaching chief chose bullets, it meant a combat; if he chose flour, it meant

62 SOCIAL AND RITUAL LIFE OF THE AMBO

peace. The chief-in-charge sent the *bakali* round the country to invite the headmen to come to the capital to mourn the chief.

Selection, succession and instalment

The selection, succession and instalment of a chief hardly differ in pattern from that of a village headman. Like the headman, a chief is selected from the closest surviving matrikin of the deceased, and, as with the headman, the most eligible candidate from a genealogical point of view may be rejected by the selectors. Nonetheless, a candidate from any minor matrilineage other than that of the deceased is inconceivable. However, some differences must be recorded. A chief is selected by headmen of the land as well as by his close matrikin. And candidates for a chieftainship must be male except in the case of the stool of Mwape, which is occupied only by women.

The selection of a chief is primarily by people of the land since village headmen acting as councillors, *mpemba*, either accept the proposed heir, or else he is passed over in favour of a man of more equitable temperament and greater ability.

The chosen candidate is caught by a headman, rubbed with red powder and addressed: 'Look, you, you have been rubbed with the red powder of the chieftainship. Everything that you have been doing, you must stop now. Keep the words of dignity, of ruling the country and all people.' Then he is set free until the funeral beer party for the deceased chief.

On the second day of the funeral beer-drink the headmen meet in the chief's village. In another group are gathered the women of the ruling Nyendwa matrilineage and in a third group are assembled the Nyendwa men. One of the headmen, their spokesman, proposes the candidate. The candidate's mother is asked if she agrees to the selection, as chiefs are especially exposed to the dangers of sorcery. If the chosen man accepts candidature a mat is spread out and a stool set upon it. He is seated thereon; at his sides sit a grandson and a granddaughter. A Nyendwa chief has been invited to install the heir. All the personal possessions of the late chief to be inherited are laid on the mat; wives are inherited, or released, in a separate ceremony. The chief-elect has a white cloth wrapped round his head. The installing chief throws meal on all objects to be inherited and on the head of the chief-elect, and says: 'Now we make you an inheritor, you are Mboloma (i.e. the name of the chieftainship);

CHIEFTAINSHIP 63

we throw the flour; this is the spirit', *lomba twamupyanika, emwe Mboloma; tukoposa bunga emupasi uyo*. The white calico on the head is explained as a sign that the new chief has received the old chief as his guardian. The same meaning is expressed in the throwing of the flour; white stands for a good spirit, for luck and good omens.

In front of the seated chief a small eating basket, *kasele*, is placed. The chief's clansmen and headman come up and place presents (*kutaila*) in the basket. When laying down a present each giver instructs the chief: 'You lord, rule us well, not with anger—just as your late brother has ruled us,' *we mfumu, mutusuuge bwino, bukali tebo, mgafilya batusungile bakwanu bakale*. 'Stop adultery. Do not fight with the people if you go round the country,' *bupulusi muleke, kutalwa ne bantu kani mwaya mu calo*. At the end of the ceremony the chief is carried to his hut on the back of a close matrikinsman (*mukwabo*).

If the new chief is succeeding Mboloma, he now goes to the Mulembo river, where together with his sibling sister he is splashed with water by Chikwashya. The chief then tours the country. Beer is brewed everywhere in his honour, and he is invited to drink.

The rights and duties of a chief

In the sphere of marriage, the rights of chiefs are no different from those of other Nyendwa clansmen and clanswomen. But one chiefly sexual privilege used to be practised even into recent times. A chief on tour, when stopping for a night at a village, is supplied with an unmarried woman. This used to be considered a great honour conferred on the woman, but times have changed. A few years ago a woman complained and the chief's official who tried to compel her to visit the chief was gaoled by the District Commissioner.

Each Ambo chief had a right-hand man variously called, *kaulu* or *cilolo*, a kind of chief herald who was sent to execute the chief's orders. Such a man was Chief Bwashi's sister's son, Chinda Mboloma Chontabunga. He is said to have brought the heads of those he executed to the chief. The chief also had other henchmen, his police or bodyguard, the *bakali* who were sent under the command of the *cilolo*. It is said that the *bakali* were recruited from refugees. There used to be one, and only one, case where a private individual had the right to kill another person without being authorized to do so by the chief. An adulterer was killed should he

64 SOCIAL AND RITUAL LIFE OF THE AMBO

resist the husband who had found him and should he not plead guilty. It is difficult now to discover exactly in what circumstances the adulterer was slain. According to Doke (1931, p. 68) the neighbouring Lamba killed the adulterer and the adulteress wife, when caught red-handed. My Ambo informants did not stress the last circumstance, but it is probable that they followed the same custom. In many cases, however, the adulterer could be allowed to pay compensation to the injured husband, handing over his sister, his sister's daughter, a slave or a gun. Then he could take the adulteress for his wife. The method of seeking refuge was as follows. The slayer hurried to the chief's capital and took refuge in the sanctuary of the chief's ancestor-shrine, *kasaba*. There he sat until his presence was reported to the chief. Then he was called before the chief to account for his deed. Next day the chief ordered the matter to be investigated. Provided the slayer's explanation was verified he then danced before the chief to the accompaniment of a war drum and a double bell, and was decorated with a red lourie feather. He was in fact honoured as a hero, a brave man, *mwanalume*. The slayer would be given a slave or a relative of the chief's for a wife. For safety's sake, he settled in the chief's capital. The chief's men had the right to seize the mother and the sibling sister of the adulterer and the adulteress, to become slaves of the chief. The injured husband received one of them as compensation. It is said that married sisters were not captured. Their husbands had to redeem them.

Although most of the chief's armed force was recruited from *bakali*, not all of them were. It is reported that when Mboloma Chontabunga attacked the sons of Lwembe, Chembe and Munsunki, Mboloma's brother-in-law, Shisamba, was killed. It may be inferred from this that he took part in that armed expedition.

The chief gained greatly from the enslavement of female relatives of adulterers who had been killed. Some informants maintain that a similar procedure of enslavement followed in the case of an execution of a sorcerer or a sorceress. In the absence of any other comparable form of property, slaves constituted an important asset, and were used more or less as currency, together with ivory and guns. The chief had more ivory and slaves than any other important man, so he could obtain more guns, which increased the armed power of the chief's warriors and made for the greater resistance of stockaded villages, as in the hostilities of Mboshya-Kayetano, Mwape-Chikunda and Chisomo against the Bemba. The chief had a monopoly of ivory. When an elephant was killed or found dead,

CHIEFTAINSHIP

the tusk which lay on the ground was the chief's, as owner of the land. The other tusk went to the hunter. A hunting 'licence' cost three elands, which had to be delivered to the chief as a fee. The chief gave back some of their meat to the hunter as a present. After such a payment a hunter had hunting rights in an area usually delimited by the name of a particular stream. It seems that a hunting so obtained was exclusive to the hunter.

Now, when game is killed some dried meat, usually of one hind leg, is brought to the chief, especially if the hunter's village is near to that of the chief. The skins of lions and leopards belong to the chief. Feathers of the lourie, *ndubaluba*, also belong to the chief, who may give them to the killers of men and lions.

Calico was another object of property. The chief possessed more calico than anyone else in his country. It is significant that Chipwitima, when he received a gift of calico from Bwashi, began to call himself chief, and by this brought upon himself the wrath of Bwashi.

The rule of the chief in olden times must have been paternal, equitable and based on reciprocity. The hunter received one elephant tusk; he received also a portion of the eland he paid to the chief. The killer of the adulterer and the executioner of the sorcerer both received slaves from the chief. The chief addresses his people as 'my children', but the subject addresses the chief as 'lord', *sikulu*, or simply 'chief' in the respectful plural form, *bamfumu*.

The chief had the right to call for tribute labour of some two or three days' work by a few men from each village every year. Tribute labour was sought when, for example, the chief wished to make a new field, or to build a new granary or a house. When in need the chief might ask for grain, usually two goatskins of flour from each village carried by three men. If women brought meal or grain they carried it in two baskets: if the grain were unthreshed, then double the amount had to be brought.

The Ambo chief, unlike a Bemba chief, has no rights of appointing headmen. An Ambo chief is informed only of the names of successors. This lack of controlling power on the part of chiefs also extends to the military sphere. Unlike his Bemba counterpart he cannot mobilise the entire manhood of his land at any time. Mboshya established representatives of two matrilineages of different clans in the positions of hereditary court officials as a reward for the support he received from them in his wars.

66 SOCIAL AND RITUAL LIFE OF THE AMBO

In the judicial sphere cases 'of shedding blood in the land of the chief', *kuitila mulopa mu calo ca mfumu*, i.e. homicide, merited the chief's intervention. The chief is 'the owner of the land' or 'of the bush'. That is why the shades of the chiefs are approached to save the country from drought. Also the chief is figuratively called 'the land', *calo*, as in the acclamations in greeting the chief on arrival: 'the country has arrived', *calo cabwela*. As with other goods the chief gives land to the people, who are his 'children'. But when an Ambo says that his chief is the owner of the land, the meaning of this expression is that the chief could to some extent direct the use of the land. He could for example apportion land along a stream to a matrilineage, which could then exclude other people from using it whether for cultivation or for hunting. To the chief as controller of the use of the land, headmen have to report land requests, but for him to refuse one would be resented as an irresponsible and tyrannical act. Every Ambo has a right to a garden in his chief's country. It is the village which occupies a tract of land with the approval of the chief. The individual chooses land under the direction of the headman, and in consultation with the other members of the village.[1] If a garden, still usable, becomes vacant it is the headman who disposes of it to a newcomer. If an individual or a community wishes to cultivate in another chief's land, the petitioners have to ask permission of the chief to be allowed to use the land.

Ambo attitudes are liberal towards the use of the land for every inhabitant of the country. This rule is reflected in the proverb, 'they do not fight for the land', *musili tabalwila* (cf. Richards, 1939, p. 269, on the Bemba). In the distribution of garden sites the rule of equity is followed which is supplementary to the liberal use of land. Old people and old widows are granted land near the villages.

Prohibitions for the chief

The reigning chief had to observe certain prohibitions, and still does. He may not eat zebra or bushbuck as these animals resemble

[1] An interesting case occurred when a headman refused a garden to an outlaw, who was a chief's 'brother', accused of poisoning the chief. The guilt was not proven in the Administration's court, but the dying chief accused his 'brother' of the crime and public opinion accepted the accusation. The man was banished to Ambo country in the Congo, to Bukanda. This sentence of banishment was passed by a council of chiefs, who were all Nyendwa by clan like the outlaw. He defied the sentence and remained in the same area but was tolerated because the Administration took no action against the outlaw. Though the outlaw lives in a village of his own country, the headman fears the risk of formally accepting him into his village by allotting him a garden.

CHIEFTAINSHIP 67

lepers. The spots and stripes are like leprous spots, and the hoofs are like lepers' limbs. It is feared that through contact with them the chief may be affected with these marks of a leper, which would be a great humiliation. The chief may not eat rhinoceros, because this animal behaves like a madman, attacking people on sight. It would be very undesirable for a chief to behave like a rhinoceros. The chief may not sit on the skin of a reedbuck. The reason for this prohibition is obscure and the explanations given are conflicting. One chief explained to me that reedbuck is an ingredient in magical medicine for turning a chief into a lion. Therefore the use of the skin is forbidden to him as incompatible with the medicine. However only one chief, Mboloma, is changed into a lion. Chief Mboloma himself may not cross the Mulembo river, because he will be carried across it as a corpse during his funeral rites. By crossing this river alive he may attract death. Mboloma could never go to Chikwashya's village, neither to Chilemba's, because Chikwashya is Mboloma's burier-priest and Chilemba is another funeral official. A chief must not come into contact with death or with those concerned with burials.

It is a characteristic feature of Ambo chieftainship that it lacks priestly character. The chief does not make offerings to the shades. The explanation given is that the chief is forbidden to approach chiefly graves. Offerings are made by the sons and grandsons of a chief, on his behalf.

Warfare

Methods of Ambo warfare have varied. In the years before European contact the main features of strategy were stockades (*malinga*, plur.). Before the appearance of the Ngoni, called *Mapunde* by the Ambo, stockades were either not built or had been discontinued for some time. This tradition may readily be accepted considering that after the final victory over Nkana Yarobe there was peace for a long time during Chilimba Nondo's, Mubanga's and, largely, Bwashi's reigns.

Stockades were constructed from logs, some twelve or more feet in length, sunk into the ground. This wall was strengthened by another wall of horizontally placed logs on the inner side of the stockade between the outer wall and uprights. The poles of the outer wall were fastened with bark rope to circular bonds after the pattern of the hut walls of poles. In front of the stockade was a

68 SOCIAL AND RITUAL LIFE OF THE AMBO

ditch, the excavated earth being heaped against the walls of the stockade. The ditch was not wider than five feet judging from the traces one can still see. In front of the stockade the ground was cleared of bush and grass so as to expose any stealthily approaching enemy. Here and there, some ten yards apart, there were platforms (*citewa*) erected behind the stockade for the defenders, especially the archers. At a man's height there were square openings of roughly one square foot for warriors' guns.

The huts inside the stockade were crowded together without any apparent order, the spaces between them being perhaps only a foot wide. A site of an old stockade on the Muswishi of the village of Lupanda has a circuit of 300 yards, and contained some 80 huts and grain bins in addition. That stockade had two gates leading to the river which flowed a few yards from the edge of the wall. During a siege water was drawn under the protection and escort of warriors. The gates were closed in the same way as are those of goat and hen houses. Logs are inserted between the door posts and two uprights fixed close to the door posts.

Some smaller villages had much simpler stockades of upright poles fastened with bark rope to withies. Only important villages, generally those of chiefs, Nyendwa clansmen, or sons of chiefs, had the resources to build stockades. People of villages or hamlets which could not afford a stockade, flocked to those which could in time of danger. When a raid was feared, scouts were sent to reconnoitre the countryside. From the accounts I have heard the Ambo have never boasted a centralized military organization. Each stockaded village was left to fend for itself as best it could. Poole (1934, p. 72) records that when Mwape of Chibambila was besieged by the Chikunda, she sent a message to Ntimba for help which raised the siege. But this illustrates co-operation between close relatives.

The only organized military co-operation was the giving of signals over the countryside of an approaching raid. The signal was given through sounding a war drum. It is stated that the war drum was heard much further than the ordinary drum. Its diameter was one and a half feet at the head and it was two and three quarter feet long. At base it was seven inches in diameter but in the middle, it was broader. The skin for sounding was that of a zebra or a hartebeeste as these were held to be the strongest. It was stretched on the drum head as well as on the bottom opening. Pegs were not used for fastening the skin, as in the ordinary drum; it was stretched taut by means of straps drawn alternately from the edge of each skin,

CHIEFTAINSHIP

running over the body of the drum from one skin to another. The drum was suspended from a cross-piece, supported by two forked poles, while two men beat it each with two sticks.

The war bell, or double bell, *lusonsolo*, was a flat bell, really two bells joined at the tops. It was clapperless, some eight inches long and three inches by one and a half at the bottom. The bells were forged each from two concave pieces of thick iron sheet. One bell of the pair was thicker than the other, thus producing a different sound. The bells were stopped with leaves when going to battle. They were struck only after a victory, at rain sacrifices, at the chief's funeral, and probably also at the chief's installation. The possession of *lusonsolo* was a prerogative of chiefly rank. The sons of a chief were allowed to own one.

The heads of slain enemies were kept in the shade huts, on a little platform covered with red cloth. When going to battle, the owner of the heads prayed: 'Thou, as thou diedst, we want to kill that one, that you may be two', *Webo, mfi wafwilile, tukofwaya tukepaye ulya, mube babili*. Then flour was spilt on the floor of the shrine. The end of a battle was celebrated with a war dance by warriors, walking and swinging the body to the right and to the left while singing war songs.

Bows laid on the iron bow-stands of the Bemba type (described by Brelsford, 1940, and Richards, 1935) were kept in the shade shrines. The bow-stand (*tupanda*) was also a chiefly prerogative. The author saw one with Chikwashya in 1942, but by 1950 it had disappeared.

Chiefs' medicines

Chiefs administer medicines necessary for the well-being of their people. One of these is *yalwela*, which protected warriors and stockades in times of war. The ingredients are a burnt stump from the bush, so that warriors may be overlooked by the enemy as if they were merely burnt tree stumps: the leaves of the *nsomwe* tree; and *kaundu*, quail, because though a man may be near this bird, he may fail to see it, so skilfully does it hide itself. The medicine is burnt on a fire. The effect of the smoke given off by the leaves is that the stockade will disappear from the sight of raiders as smoke disappears into the air. After the fire has burnt out, the medicine is put into incisions made on the warriors, two each on the forehead, the chest, the arms and the feet.

70 SOCIAL AND RITUAL LIFE OF THE AMBO

In another prescription, there is *mulembe*, the wild spinach, which is slimy and thus represents blood. The *mutobe* (*Ficus thonngii*) tree, whose name resembles the word *kutoba*, to break, is an ingredient to destroy iron weapons. *Mutobe* is also parasitic, destroying all the neighbouring trees until it alone is left. *Mutyoka*, also a tree, resembles the word *kutyoka* which means in the Nsenga language, to break, to snap. So weapons will snap; the enemy will break under attack. The *nkama* tree is a medicine for immunity, the leaves being slimy; hunters, however, in appropriate prescriptions, use the roots of *nkama* so that the bullets may not glance off the game. *Mululu* (*Khaya nyassica*) is one of the biggest and most imposing trees for its size and height and is used in medicines for strength. '*Mululu* is of importance in *bwanga*', *Mululu mukulu ku bwanga*. The inclusion of *mululu* strengthens the medicine to such an extent that it cannot be overcome by another stronger medicine. *Mofwe* resembles the word *kufwa*, to die. The non-vegetable components are: the brain of the hyena, for the hyena is supposed to dream about, or 'feel', far away meat, and in the same way warriors will feel an enemy far away; *cibuli*, a small animal about which it is said that weapons recoil from its skin so that the warrior will fare in the same way; *nkaka*, the pangolin (cf. *kukaka*, 'to bind'), which will 'bind' or paralyse the strength of the enemy; the egg of the vulture, for the vulture sees meat far away; and salt, for two effects. On the one hand the war for the enemy will be 'bitter', *kulula*, and on the other, the war for the doctored warriors will be agreeable just as salt makes food palatable.

This compound may be drunk with water, or added to food, or one may wash oneself in it and put it on one's arrows.

If it is to work, young animals must not be killed or the warrior will not be able to kill the strong enemy. For a similar reason neither must the old be killed. One must not strip a woman, because the warrior would lose strength. He will be able to fight women only.

Good conscience medicine, *cintemwa*, 'quietens' a man's heart. The ingredients are: *mukomfwa*, the roots; the name resembles *kuumfwa*, to hear, to agree, to obey, so that anyone looking at the chief will lose his anger. *Mwenje*, the roots; the name means also torch, enlightening the hearts of men that they may cease to be angry. The non-vegetable components are: *insoni*, the golden mole. *Nsoni* means shame and shyness. This ingredient makes people shy. *Nkaka*, the pangolin, explained above, binds the hearts of men. The roots of both trees are ground and the *fisimba* are added. Some

CHIEFTAINSHIP

of this medicine is put in incisions in the forehead, the chief smearing himself all over with the rest.

If a chief finds he is not popular he takes earth from the top of an anthill and at night goes to a cross-roads, puts the earth into water, washes his face and says: 'Myself I am an ant-hill. I do not move. These people who pass here, it is they, may they carry my sins', *Nebo ndi culu. Nsikukapo, aba bantu bapita muno ebabula kubipa kwanji.*

Chiefs know a 'medicine of famine', *busibungu*, of which the purpose is to affect the whole country or a village with famine. The ingredients are: *ntetemesi* the inside of the elephant's tusk; a tree which rubs against another tree in the bush; a tree fallen during the rain; one grain of sorghum; soil from the locality to be affected with famine; ashes; and menstrual blood.

These components are put in a hole in the ground in the locality to be affected with famine, which is covered with a flat stone. *Ntetemesi* is soft, without consistency: it will make the crops feeble. Crossed trees rub against each other, so that the locality will always be worried with the shortage of food. Sorghum will be laid flat like fallen trees through heavy rains. A woman in menses affects men with a wasting disease through contact, and so it will curse the countryside. Ashes symbolize drought and dryness; the sorghum will dry out like ashes. The flat stone lays flat the crops and seals the country's doom.

Some modern circumstances

It must not be supposed from the foregoing that the limitations at the present day on the power of Ambo chiefs make their position equivalent to that of chiefs among the Plateau Tonga, for example. A Tonga chief was superimposed by the British Administration on a stateless, apolitical society. On the other hand the Ambo chief is even now an autocrat, commanding obeisance, reverence and submission from his subjects. The grounds for this prestige were not instilled by the British Administration but arise from the attitude of the people towards their chief which is conditioned by tradition. Much of the chiefly authority of the present time dates from the past. If anything the British Administration tends to reduce the standing of the chief rather than to enhance it.

Though the links with the past are vital they are signs only of outward continuity, disguising real changes in the chief's position.

72   SOCIAL AND RITUAL LIFE OF THE AMBO

The old chief was an independent ruler. He engaged freely in diplomacy with his neighbours, foreign tribes, other Nyendwa chiefs, and the independent war lords. Modern changes have severely restricted his political freedom. He is subordinated to the Provincial Commissioner. He has to be recognized, and can be suspended or removed under the Native Authorities Ordinance. He has lost his independent action in external relations with his neighbours.

The economic position of the chief has undergone radical changes. As described, he was in the past always richer than his subjects through slaves, monopolies and tributes. Commoners could also own slaves but the chief had more extensive rights of obtaining them. His riches and monopolies were far greater before in relation to the property of his subjects than is the position at the present time. His independent, customary wealth, monopolies and tributes are gone; he has forfeited all his control over game to the Administration and thus has lost his monopoly of ivory and of elands.

His judiciary powers are greatly curtailed. He judges even minor cases which would never have come within his sphere in former times, since they were the province of the elders of the village and the leaders of matrilineages. His customary jurisdiction in the 'cases of blood' has been taken away from him. He has forfeited the court fees in slaves. All in all, he has ceased to be an independent ruler and has become an official of the Native Administration.

It is not within the scope of this chapter to describe the working of the Native Authority administration. However, some points of contact between the British Administration and the Ambo chiefs cannot be ignored. I have mentioned some powers and rights which the Ambo chief has forfeited. What powers and rights have been given to him at the present time?

The Ambo chief is officially designated as the Native Authority. In this capacity he has two paid councillors and two messengers, and, since the Native Authority also acts as the Native Court, the chief employs a court clerk. With the help of these officials, the chief has to enforce the many regulations brought into existence by the Administration.

The Ambo Superior Native Authority, however, has the power to make rules and orders. It is a Tribal Council, an informal meeting of chiefs and their councillors within their district. Some chiefs are Senior Chiefs, enjoy a higher status and preside over the chiefs' meetings. Mboloma and Lwembe are Senior Chiefs; Chisomo,

CHIEFTAINSHIP

Mboshya and Mwape are Subordinate Native Authorities. Although the Tribal Council issues rules and orders, these are usually initiated by European Administrative Officers. The Superior Native Authority has its own Native Treasury. The revenues of the Native Treasuries are drawn from a percentage of Native Poll Tax, court revenues and grants-in-aid. Expenditure, for example, is on administration of Native Authorities, on education, the upkeep of school buildings, the payment of school attendance officers and agricultural assistants.

IV. CHILDHOOD AND PUBERTY

Pregnancy

THE physiological role of the father in the conception of the child is fully acknowledged in this strongly matrilineal tribe. This is evident from common utterances, for example: 'This is not my person. I begot him only'. In this statement, the first part refers to the social rights; the second refers to the physical role the father played in conception. Something has already been said of the prestige, respect and gratitude which a matrilineage owes to its 'fathers'.

Persons of either sex, who have not yet become parents, are equally bound by prohibitions, lest they procreate children of ill omen, who cut their upper teeth first. It may be inferred from this that the Ambo seem to think that both parents play equal parts in procreation. People who are not parents may not warm themselves under a platform used for drying meat, *lutala*. The same word is used for a child cutting the upper teeth first, who would be destroyed. A childless person is prohibited from bending to drink water from a calabash standing on the ground. In such a position the upper teeth are the first to touch the water.

If there is failure to conceive, a quarrel ensues between the couple, often incited by the wife's mother. Then the couple each go their own way to try other partners so as to prove which of them is to blame. Impotence is sometimes a cause of suicide, when a man cannot bear the ridicule of his companions at his failure.

If children die in infancy or are still-born, the work of a revengeful shade is suspected and its identity discovered through divination.

There are very few prohibitions a pregnant woman should observe. The most important is the prohibition of adultery, which binds both spouses equally.

When it is noticed that a young woman is pregnant, her sister-in-law addresses her: 'Now you are grown up, you will not go to another man, you will guard yourself and your child, which is in your womb, just like you guard your eye.' After some five months, the sister-in-law of the woman again warns her: 'The child has

CHILDHOOD AND PUBERTY

grown in the womb; do not pound grain, do not hoe, do not fetch firewood, do not carry heavy loads.' It is said that when a woman becomes pregnant for the first time, she shows the utmost laziness, is quarrelsome, refuses her husband, and shows aversion even to such food as meat and fish.

The only prohibition based on magical grounds is that she should not sit down for a long time without moving, because in a similar way the womb will be slothful and slow to deliver. But many do not observe this prohibition.

The delivery

Some women go to the bush to have their child. They do not like the noise and the bustle of the village. Normally, however, child-bearing is in the hut and women go outside the village only if their former deliveries have been difficult.

Three women, and only those who have borne children themselves, assist at the delivery. One woman holds the pregnant mother under the armpits. Another stands behind her, holding her tightly in a cloth which covers the belly and reaches up to the breasts. This is done to facilitate the delivery and to direct it. The woman sits on the *nkata*, the pad-ring, (generally used as a cushion on the head under a load), it is said, to prevent the birth of the child through the anus.

One woman, *nacimbela*, the midwife, is in the front of the bearing woman. The child comes down on a piece of cloth. The midwife waits until the afterbirth arrives and then picks up the child. The umbilical cord is first tied with bark string and then cut with a piece of sorghum stalk. It is said that knives came with the Europeans: the cutting of the umbilical cord is done in the traditional way.[1] The midwife then washes the child in cold water. The water is poured away inside the hut, where the afterbirth will be buried at the base of the wall opposite the door.

After burying the afterbirth the midwife ululates once for a boy and twice for a girl. Then a birth song, *cankumbete cankumbatuka*, is started, with numerous repetitions. The meaning is: 'What has embraced me, has left me free.' The song expresses the joy with which the child while yet unborn was embracing the pregnant mother. Now she is set free without misfortune. The village women-folk join in the song outside the hut and clap hands.

[1] Doke, 1931, p. 132.

76 SOCIAL AND RITUAL LIFE OF THE AMBO

The father and the whole village anxiously await the ululation, the men sitting in the village shelter.

After the birth the mother takes porridge with the roots of the tree *wafyalakalimukanda* that she may feel well. The meaning of the name of the tree is 'You have borne what is in the skin', *cipele wa ku taye cisasile*. The mother also takes a thin porridge of sour (fermented) bran, for four days, to have much milk—*kusansa mabele*, 'to shake the breasts'. She also takes sour water, *muteteka*, in which groats have lain for three days. When the milk is not plentiful in the breasts, groundnuts are pounded, shaken and strained with water. This liquid is given to the child to drink. On the first day the child is given gruel made of water, a little meal and soaked roots of *lwabia* and *lwanda* to soften the stomach so that it may excrete well.

Difficult delivery

A difficult labour, it is believed, may be caused in two ways: either one of the spouses strayed sexually while the wife was pregnant, or else an ancestral shade or shades have entered the womb and by making an obstruction claim that the child must be named after one of them. In the first eventuality, there is no necessity to resort to divination; the case is clear because 'the womb goes up'. Adultery whether of one spouse or both is taken for granted. Then the guilty one is persuaded to name the lover. Confession is made by the husband to his clan sisters and by the wife to her clan sisters. Thus the other spouse and his or her matrilineage will never know the name of the culprit. After confessing, the medicines of *ncilu* are applied to the woman and the delivery is supposed to pass smoothly.[1] Should she die, the husband is usually held responsible for her death and penalized. The action taken in such a situation is described in Chapter VI.

A troubling shade is the cause when the 'womb goes down'. Then the diviner is consulted as to the identity of the shade responsible. When this has been ascertained, a sister of the woman in labour spurts water on the woman's chest and on the floor while she

---

[1] *Ncilu* is the ideophone from *kuciluka* to jump over, to trespass, here to trespass over the pregnant womb by having connection with a third party. The prohibition applies equally to both spouses. The belief seems to be based on dynamism. The reproductive power while released into action in pregnancy should not be interfered with through the release of further energy, because then there would be a clash of reproductive forces.

CHILDHOOD AND PUBERTY 77

says: 'Come, be given a name, we call upon you, if it is you, So-and-so, come to be reborn.' In this way a promise is made to the shade that its name will be given to the child immediately after birth.

There are some prohibitions concerning the new-born child. The mother may not touch things which have associations with fire (fire sticks). Otherwise she would cause chest trouble in the husband. She may not touch honey, fermented liquids and salt which others would eat. If she is careless about these prohibitions, she may afflict her husband or other men with chest trouble, *kukowela*, akin to tuberculosis. Marital relations are suspended on account of *bunani*, aversion. The mother may not pound, stir porridge, or draw water until four days to one week have passed and the navel cord has dropped off. At that time she comes out of confinement. Now she may use fire sticks. Should the mother disregard these prohibitions she 'would break the child in the chest', *kukonona mwana mu ntibi*, and contract a chest disease. This is the time also when she ritually washes herself and the sleeping mat she has used.

The midwife may not have sexual intercourse until the rite of 'nursing the child on the mat' is performed. Disregard of this prohibition would have the same disastrous effect as if the parents failed to observe their prohibitions.

The Ambo distinguish different types of birth: *lunyena* is the child which excretes immediately after the birth. Medicine is taken by both the father and the mother to ward off a headache resulting from this condition of the child. The child is also given the medicine. *Lupapi* leaves are smoked in a cigarette or stuck into the nostrils as a precaution against catarrh, according to another version. *Lupapi* resembles *kupapa*, 'to carry a child on the back'.

Mwika is a child born with a leg presentation. Usually at birth the head comes first. Nothing is done, but the singular feature of the birth is noted.

Cikutu is a child born with a caul or membranous covering. The membrane is taken off, the baby is washed with warm water and smeared with castor oil for a week. Otherwise it is feared that the skin may come off.

Busofu is a prematurely born child. After two weeks it develops quickly. Nothing is done about such a child.

Cilema means cripple, whether a child or adult. A child born a cripple is believed to have been bewitched in the womb.

Kapopo is a still-born child. The Ambo consider and treat as still-born any child which dies even within two or three weeks after

78 SOCIAL AND RITUAL LIFE OF THE AMBO

its birth. *Kapopo* is a child which its father has not yet touched ritually and therefore such a child is 'unripe'. Such a child is buried in a special manner.

Twins of the same sex are called *bampundu*, of different sex, *bamapasa*. Twins are thought dangerous, *bakali*, as if loaded with magical dynamic potency because an extraordinary power has manifested itself in them. It is believed that the life of their parents is endangered, unless the potent and harmful forces are neutralized by medicines. Another view is that twins are frail and easily die unless they are strengthened with medicines. *Kasongole* roots are dug out. When digging the spell is uttered: 'Thou tree, be strong enough, be good and may God help me': *We citi, ukume bwino, ciwame na Lesa unjikasyeko*. The roots are soaked in water which the twins then drink. Other medicaments given to twins are *ntindisa*, *lulambatila mulundu* and *coni*. The twins are carried round the village in a basket. Two stalks of grass are picked from each roof and laid in the basket. A kind of spell is said: 'People of Lesa go in the whirlwind, the child may not be despised, it may become angry and die', *Bantu ba ku Lesa bakoya mu cipupu, tekumusyola mwana angakalipa ne kufwa*. The twins must dress alike. When they are six years old a rod of *tulunguti* is cut, they are struck with it that they may not become angry. By the taking of the stalks of grass from each roof, the twins are integrated into the village. They are prevented from becoming angry.

In another prescription, *mufungula* (*Kigelia pinnata*) the bark, is used. The big fruits of this tree are likened to children (cf. Chapter VI). *Mululu*, the bark. As explained above (*see* page 70) this tree gives strength to the whole compound. Before cutting the bark, an offering is made to the tree, one bead being laid at the foot of the tree to the east and another to the west. *Mabele* (*Euphorbia matabeliensis*), the bark; *mabele* also means nipples. The sap is milky. The roots are pounded and rubbed into incisions on each side of each breast. This is evidently a magical action which aims at the increase of milk. The mother washes herself in the water in which the roots of *mululu* and *mufungula* have been soaked. The twins are also washed and given the medicated water to drink.

The killing of a child whose upper teeth appear first (lutara)

'Long ago in this country this was the custom. If a man begat a child, people were saying this: "If it grows the upper teeth first,

CHILDHOOD AND PUBERTY

we throw it into a pool, because it is not a true human being." When the old women saw the upper teeth cutting first, they took that baby to the Lukusashi. There they looked for a big pool and tied stones to its arms and legs and threw it into the pool without looking, saying: "You go and wash yourself, do not follow us, because you grew the upper teeth first for which reason we have thrown you into the water". They returned to the village without crying, not even the mother cried. The reason they threw away any baby which had cut its upper teeth first was because they were afraid that if it were allowed to grow up and it came to the time to pull out teeth, they should die to the last man; after the loss of each tooth a person would die. *Lutala* means to cut the upper teeth first, whereas we cut the lower teeth first.'

The address to the child, giving the reason for the action taken against it, is to make sure that its shade will not become revengeful for being wronged.

Some medicine men and women claim that they are able to reverse the order of the appearance of the teeth.

Birth out of wedlock

Birth out of wedlock hardly entails any stigma on the child, which is referred to as 'child of the village place', *mwana wa lubansa*. The unmarried mother also suffers very little disrepute, though she will be the object of an occasional disparaging remark made in her absence. The reason for this tolerance is that there is no sharp social difference between a married and unmarried mother, and there are few situations where the mother should be looked upon socially as unmarried. Marriage, as will be seen in Chapter V, is informally progressive and divorce is easy. The lonely woman readily accepts a suitor and is just as easily abandoned by him. The marriage was simply unsuccessful. Thus very few children would be classified as born out of wedlock. The woman usually accepts a man openly and publicly, thus avoiding the stigma of having indulged in fornication. Secondly, the child, irrespective of who fathered him or her, socially has always a matrilineal status. In spite of these easy-going social rules, it should not be thought that the Ambo are dissolute. They are discerning in the use of these rules of freedom. A married man rarely makes advances to a married woman, and it is even less common for an unmarried man to flirt with such a woman.

80   SOCIAL AND RITUAL LIFE OF THE AMBO

Typically the married woman merits hostility from her husband only if she conceives during his absence at work. Then compensation is due to him and usually also divorce follows. The woman would also fall into disrepute if she were persistently fickle. The Ambo, through their upbringing, have a simple and ingrained respect for the rights of others.

First touch of the child by the father

This rite is performed one or two weeks after birth. By this time the child has become physically stronger. This physical condition entitles the child to change its status of 'foetus', *kapopo*, to that of a human being. It is now considered that the child has 'ripened', *mwana wapia*. The status is conferred on the child by the father by a ritual touching of the child. The father chews *musambafwa* leaves, rubs his hands with the pulp, and then takes the child, holding it under the armpits. The child is smeared with the same medicine. After this rite the mother may handle salt, putting it into food which any male may eat without coming to any harm. *Wusambamfwa* means 'the washing of death'. The new-born child is thought to be very delicate, not strong or resistant to strong dynamic influences. The marital act of the midwife, and the touching of salt, honey or fire by the mother, release strong forces of a magical kind which injure such a fragile being as a new-born child. Some medicines act by making these forces 'slide away'. If the child dies after this rite of touching, it is buried in the manner and in the graveyard of the adults. If it dies before being medicated, it is buried in the manner of a still-born foetus.

The rite of 'nursing the child on the mat' (kulela kwa mwana pa mpasa)[1]

This rite marks the end of the natal period. It is performed preferably when the child is able to sit up. The father and the mother of the child lie on the mat. The child lies between them. After copu-

---

[1] Father Merolla describes a similar custom among the people of Loanda, in the 17th century. 'Great abuses: the fifth is that being to wean any of their children. The father and the mother lay him on the ground; and whilst they do that which modesty will not permit me to name, the father lifts him by the arm, and so holds him for some time hanging in the air, falsely believing that by those means he will become more strong and robust. This ceremony they call the lifting of a child and is in my opinion the most impudent and superstitious.' Jerome Merolla, 1704. Vol. I, p. 688.

CHILDHOOD AND PUBERTY 81

lation—which is their first since the birth of their child—if the child is male, the father wakes him up and binds round the child's chest a bark string into which are intertwined many little sticks of *kasansubwanga* tree. (*Kasansubwanga* means to sieve out the magical medicine of the sorcerer.) If the child is a girl, the mother wakes her up, and then the father does the same in the case of a boy. Should the parents not observe this rite, their child would suffer from a chest disease. Having observed it, the mother is allowed to handle honey which males may then eat without harm. She is not dangerous any more. She has returned to normal life.

The morning the parents have slept together, the child is washed in a basin into which is put a sixpence, a shilling or a string of beads as a reward for the midwife. The midwife comes to take the water, which is left for her, and under the eaves of the house washes her face and hands. If she neglects this the child would develop a chest disease which some say would be fatal. Until she washes, the midwife is 'black in the eyes', *kufita ku menso*. From now on she is free to resume her marital relations.

Until the child passes through the rite of 'the nursing on the mat', no woman who has had sexual connection may hold the child on the same day. Regular marital relations, about four times a week, start again when the child begins to stand, usually at the age of about a year.

The child is called by the midwife, *musela wanji*, 'my ward'. Girls when they grow older stamp grain for the midwife from time to time. The boy *musela*, may trap doves for her. Then the mother will say to the midwife: 'This is your present, which they picked up on the ground for you when born'. The midwife on her part will entertain her wards with food.

When the child begins to smile, people stop calling the mother 'the bearer', *mufyasi*, and call her 'the mother of the little boy', *banakalumbwana*, or 'the mother of the little girl', *banakasimbi*.

Aftercare of 'the child of sprouting'

It is believed that 'a child of sprouting' or 'of leaves' is brought into the world through the power of medicines overcoming the power of a revengeful shade. Such a child may not eat first fruits without special precautions being taken, although the whole population is allowed to do so after consecration and thanksgiving rites.

For such a child the first fruits must be doctored to take away

82   SOCIAL AND RITUAL LIFE OF THE AMBO

their, for him, baneful force. This is done simply by a fresh application of the original medicines by virtue of which the child was brought into this world. If the 'child of leaves' or 'child of sprouting' should eat newly sprouted leaves, the first fruits, the act would destroy the power of the first leaves which gave it life. By eating the first fruits, the child destroys, 'eats' in Ambo idiom, sprouting itself, which is symbolized by the first fruits. It would destroy itself as well, because this child sprouted like a leaf and because of the leaves of medicines.

Provided that powers are brought into play which neutralize the dynamism of eating, these children may eat first fruits. They are brought to the headman who chews some of the fresh grain with medicines, then spits this on the back, chest and the forehead of the child saying 'Go about in health, you my children, you shall not fall ill, you my namesake, you my father who have come back to your grandchild, by folding yourself in my womb, you the child of grandparent', *kamuyendele amakosa mwe bana banji, mulikulwalalwala, iyu, mwe, mboswa yanji, mwe batata mwabwelele ku musikulu wenu kwisa kulipeta mu mala anji, mwe mwana mbuya.*

An example of a prescription is as follows. The leaves of *ndale* and *musambamfwa* are used. *Ndale* means 'let me lie, let me sleep', here to make the malevolent shade lie down and sleep and not kill: *musambamfwa* 'washes the death away'. The same medicines were used before and at the birth of the child. This point is essential, as it involves the same strengthening of the life force, which is endangered by committing an act countering it.

If such children ate first fruits without precautions being taken first, they would become thin and sickly. If the child eats such crops through inadvertence it must be doctored afterwards. The bigger children perform the rite themselves but discontinue it after they become parents.

The naming rite (kuilike 'sina)

Every child is given a name of an 'ancestor' on either the mother's or father's side, whose shade will then take care of his or her ward, thus becoming a guardian shade, *mboswa*. A child has only one shade name, given to him irrespective of sex.

The choosing of the name is a complicated process. In some cases it is believed the shade, by causing a difficult labour, itself announces its wish to provide a name. Another possibility is the giving of a tentative name on the day of the birth. Numerous statements show

CHILDHOOD AND PUBERTY

that the common practice is to await the manifestation of the shade's will, for example in the sending of sickness or causing the child to weep excessively. Then recourse must be had to a diviner to discover its identity.

An informant's description runs as follows: 'When it [the child] begins to be sick at times, then the elders say: "Go to the diviner that you may see if it wants a name". First the diviner is greeted and told the purpose of the visit. A present of a string of beads is made to him. The diviner addresses the axe handle: "Tell the truth, look at the things they brought that you may tell the matter as it is. To steal the payment from the owner leaves me with shame". Then he asks: "Have you given respect to all of your clansmen and clanswomen?" [The meaning is: were all your dead kin honoured by naming children after them?] All visitors answer: "Yes." "Those of the father's clan, have you given them all due respect?" Again they agree: "Yes." Then the diviner asks if the father or the mother has gone wrong [by having an illicit intercourse, and thus harming the child]. When he asks: "Perhaps it wants a name to be given?" the answer [of the divining apparatus] is "Yes". "Enumerate, let us hear. Those of the father's clan: perhaps So-and-so?" The axe-handle refuses. "Enumerate those of its own (child's) clan? Perhaps the brother So-and-so?" It denies. "Perhaps its grandparent?" It hears and says: "Yes. I have come to say: Let me come to my grandchild. Have you heard?" "Yes we have heard." "Now it is your grandparent who has come back that you give her some respect. Let her speak. Let her hold us by the arms, let her free our legs. We are going." At home the clients say: "It is its grandparent we have seen. She said: Let me come back into my grandchild".'

The rite of naming the child is performed by the mother of the child's mother. She spits water on the child's chest and pronounces a prayer to the shade: 'If your father has come back, there on this world, do not come back with bad luck, you will live in good health. I implore our Kunda, you will walk in good health, without sickness.' Then a representative of the child's father's clan ties a string of white beads round the child's neck or right wrist.

The rite is performed in other instances also, when the shade had indicated its name before birth or when the name is given tentatively.

If the child continues to be sick or becomes sick again or cries more than is usual, the diviner is approached once more. He may announce that another shade wants its name to be given to the child.

84   SOCIAL AND RITUAL LIFE OF THE AMBO

The old name then has to be withdrawn. The maternal grandmother picks a small piece of grass stalk from the thatch and breaks it in two; one piece she sticks back into the thatch and the other piece she fixes vertically with saliva to the forehead of the child, or sticks it into the child's hair, addressing the shade: 'Look, we have withdrawn today this name and we stick it here, you, So-and-so. Thus today if you are agreeable to this name, sleep well, without crying, that we know that you have agreed. Now you are So-and-so.' When the prayer is finished, the mother spits water on the chest of the child. The old beads are exchanged for new ones.

It may be that a child does not fall ill till the age of six or seven and is thus without a shade name. Such a child is termed *cibulesina*, 'lacking a name'. If it is a boy he is called *kalumbwana*, the little boy, and if a girl *kasimbi*, the little girl.

If a child is ill, the diviner may discover that the child has been cursed. If the child had been struck only, its guardian shade would not be offended. The diviner's pronouncement may run as follows: 'Your maternal uncle is angry, you are cursing him; just when I have been born in their womb, they have cursed me'. Now he is angry saying: 'I shall kill myself that you may suffer.' The parents must apologize to the shade. White beads are put round the neck of the child and the shade is addressed: 'We implore you, my uncle, you will walk with good health; we shall not repeat it again, we have given you satisfaction.'

At other times when a child falls ill, the diviner may find that the child's guardian shade is the cause, being in need of beer. At home, when soaking the grain, the shade is addressed 'This beer we have soaked for you, may you feel well, may you sleep well that we may be thankful'. A string of white beads is put round the child's neck and water is spurted on its chest and back.

The meaning of the naming rites

Many writers including Melland (1923: 150, 53), Doke (1931: 241), Smith (1920; II: 152), Munday (1948: 1) and Colson (1951: 148) speak of naming and reincarnation among the Central African peoples they have investigated. Having spent many years among the Ambo, I am of the opinion that it is not simple reincarnation that is involved.[1] I once found a diviner of repute who

[1] The Konde do not believe in reincarnation. 'The idea, common in some parts of Bantu Africa, that a child who resembles his dead grandfather is that grandfather come back to life is scoffed at by the Konde. The child is like his grandfather and that is all.' Mackenzie, 1925: 195.

CHILDHOOD AND PUBERTY

defended reincarnation pure and simple. 'Look', he said, 'the dead people come back to this world again, one after another, and this is how the villages are filled again with new people.' When wanting a photograph of a shade calabash shrine (of a 'reincarnated' guardian shade) I was unable to find one. But at last a headman volunteered to show me one. He did so, and ridiculed the old diviner for holding an idea of reincarnation pure and simple. An interview of a woman with a diviner in a somewhat abbreviated form has been given above. The diviner asks whether all ancestors of the mother's and father's clans have been honoured by having children named after them.

In the prayer offered while a mother has painful labour, a shade is invited to have its name given and thus to be reborn. In many prayers, 'to be named in the child' and 'to be reborn' are equivalent phrases. A shade ought to be remembered and thus honoured. In the same way the spirit makes the child sick as an expression of a wish for a name or for beer. The crux of the matter is that there is on the one side a guardian, and on the other, a ward. The former acts upon the latter making him sick. Again, in the prayer of removing the name it is a simple apology which is offered and the trying of another name. There is no reincarnation involved. Such a change in a reincarnated person would be a metamorphosis into another personality or shade. I have also noted that individuals may live for years yet lacking a shade name. In the case of nameless children, the Ambo simply say that they have not yet received a shade.

Rebirth or reincarnation is, then, only a figure of speech. The ward of a shade is called *cibwela*, 'the come back'. A name has been revived and inherited. As has been mentioned above, ancestors have only one desire—not to be forgotten. There are only two means of being remembered: in the names of children and in an occasional beer offering.

Once a child is dedicated to an ancestor by being given its name, it falls under the full protection of the shade and becomes identified with it.

The child can take its name from the father's or the mother's side. However, every Ambo at his death has only one shade to be remembered, from his mother's clan.

Although, then, there is a plurality of entities, there is nevertheless a mystical identity of the guardian and the ward in the sharing of the common name and the community of interests, though the interests are not reciprocally identical. This mystical identity tends

86 SOCIAL AND RITUAL LIFE OF THE AMBO

to be looked upon by the Ambo as being close or equivalent to physical identity. My concluding remark must be that at least the Ambo concept of reincarnation is not that understood in Western society. And there appear to be contradictions in Ambo ideas, and some aspects of naming difficult to reconcile with others. Thus sometimes the patron or guardian is from the father's side and is of a different clan from that to which the ward belongs, yet this does not hinder the persistent identification of guardian and ward.

Infancy

A mother with a baby will try to enlist the services of a girl relative to help her to look after the child, if she has no suitable daughter. The child spends most of its time on its mother's back, when she goes to hoe or to fetch firewood, water or vegetables. Children are given the breast, whenever they want it and especially when they cry. The Ambo mother does not allow her baby to cry, in order not to offend the guardian shade who could make the child sick. Ambo mothers prefer to give their child to a nurse for care wherever possible, after weaning as well. The child is given light porridge after half a year. When it is able to stand, its diet includes the normal thick porridge.

Children wear a string of beads round the neck. Two medicine sticks, *nsita*, are strung between the beads as a protection against convulsions. Round the waist of the baby is another string of beads but worn as an ornament, *muncinda*. Otherwise the baby is naked. The carrying cloth (*cipapo* or *cipapilo*) protects the child against cold.

Hair clippings are buried, not burnt, lest the child should also be burnt. Nail parings are thrown into the grass.

A child who does not walk by the proper time is a *cite* and it must be doctored with the wood of the *cinyaku* tree. The wood is soaked, water is warmed and the child is washed with it for many days. *Cinyaku* is used, because it sprouts and grows quickly. So shall the child stand up soon like the tree and become tall.

Weaning

When the child can stand, it is weaned. It is believed that if this were delayed, and the mother conceived again before her child could stand up, her milk would turn to blood and her child would

CHILDHOOD AND PUBERTY

live to be a cripple without the ability to stand or to walk. To wean the child, chillies are rubbed on the nipples. A child is given a fowl to eat with *kakote* roots, which is used because old people make walking sticks from it, so that the child may go about as an old person. In Bemba *kakote* means an old person.

Cutting teeth and losing them

If teeth are slow to appear, a medicine is used. When a tooth comes out, the child takes the tooth and a cinder and throws the tooth to the east saying: 'You, my tooth, come out in this way as the sun comes out,' *we lino lyanji ufume fyenka fino mfilokufume kasuba*. The cinder is thrown to the west, with the words 'You cinder, you will come out in the same way as the moon comes out', *we, musimbe wanji, ulokufuma fyenka fino mfilokufuma mwensi*. Then the new tooth will grow quickly.

Childhood

Children of both sexes up to about six years old keep company together, mostly in the village itself or in the garden shelter with their parents during half of the year. Older girls sleep two or three together in a hut which is described as 'owned by' the eldest girl. Some girls of marriageable age sleep with a grandmother. The greatest pastime of adolescent and adult girls is dancing, organized by boys. Girls on the whole are better provided with clothes than boys. Those of four to five years old often have a skirt cloth round the waist or a cloth wrapped round the body above the breasts down to knees. The older girls of school age have blouses and a skirt cloth round the waist.

A boy's childhood runs on different lines. Up to five years of age he continues to pass the whole day with his mother, or in playing with children of similar age. From the time he is about six years old, he drifts more and more into men's company. He stays in the men's shelter watching their activities of basket- and mat-making and sharpening of iron tools in the fire, and observes the building of grain bins. He is continually being sent on errands, to fetch tools and materials or drinking water for guests or for men working and chatting in the village shelter. He brings embers for lighting cigarettes. Between the ages of four and eight he sleeps with a grandmother or grandparents. Then he joins up with one or more boys

88 SOCIAL AND RITUAL LIFE OF THE AMBO

who are relatives to sleep together in a boys' dormitory, *ngobelo*.
He will sleep in the boys' hut till he is of marriageable age. From
two to five boys sleep in one hut, most of them closely related as
'brothers' in one sense or another, or as cross-cousins.

The boys themselves build these huts which are low, small and
of weak construction. This has educational value, giving them
practice in hut-building and testing their abilities. Their women
relatives help in smearing. From the age of about six, a boy learns
from his older companions how to trap birds, mice and fish. Such
activities will become his main occupation, until he is about fifteen
years old. Trapping is encouraged, especially by his mother, for
utilitarian reasons.

Boys as well as girls, beginning at about the age of twelve, are
prevailed on to do some hoeing, mostly weeding. Orders, especially
to boys, are sharp and accompanied with shouts if they show reluctance 'because they eat also'. The establishment of schools upsets
this traditional training, opportunities for hoeing except in the
holidays and on Saturdays being greatly curtailed. Another major
agricultural duty which falls to children is bird-scaring, for several
weeks in April and May. The Native Authorities ask to have school
holidays at this time. Many children, even before the age of ten,
receive a hen for keeping and breeding as a present for their labour,
so that they may become accustomed to thrift and responsibility.

The duty of a young boy in his early teens is to accompany older
male relatives (especially his father) on journeys and other expedi-
tions such as hunting, fishing or collecting. He may sometimes carry
meal or blankets for his father on visits to a town or for hunting.
It is through such companionship that a boy develops a strong
attachment to his father.

It is customary to give a small loincloth to a boy from about his
sixth year. Soon the boy longs for shorts which he gets at the latest
in a few years' time. When he is about thirteen, he plans to go to
work to acquire clothes. Only the threat of heavy fines keep boys in
the last years of elementary schooling from running away to town.
Where the chief is lenient, the last class of standard two breaks up
in the middle of the school year because of the emigration of boys
to towns. Then, for several years, these boys grow up in towns.

Boys and girls may be beaten by their parents. An older girl,
when her breasts have begun to develop, will not be beaten by her
father because of 'compassion' or 'shame', as she is then of the rank
of 'mothers'.

CHILDHOOD AND PUBERTY

Girl's maturation

When a girl begins her menses she tries to hide the fact; her companions talk about it. Early in the morning, before people come out of their houses, an old woman 'instructress', *nacimbela* or *nakasya*, takes the girl—who has perhaps run into the bush—and leads her to the veranda of her mother's house. There the girl stands, head bowed and facing the wall. Then the instructress shouts: 'I have taken my girl' (literally 'the girl of initiation'), *natola cisungu canji*. The instructress ululates. The other women gather for singing and dancing. Usually a small drum is brought, to be beaten by a boy, and the *cimbwasa* dance begins. Among the Ambo, the women did not like to undress for this occasion. The crowd surrounds one or two old women dancing; onlookers clap hands. The songs are mostly of obscene content:

Kali kumpukusu ya bukala ee, — *Testicula membri virilis*
Nacimpokongwa walya limo, — Nacimpokongwa has eaten once,
Kanya masobe. — *Excrevit pubes.*
(*Kumpukusu* (ili class), testicles. *Bukala*, penis, *Cimpokongwa, partes mulieris*; *na*, mother of. *Masobe*, hair of pubes, *Kanyamasobe*, a proper name. *Nacimpokongwa* means here a woman who slept once with her husband and was then deserted by him.)

Cisungu kuwa nduno, — The girl has begun her periods now.
Kusyukila mbuto kulaba, — She is lucky, *semen desideratur.*
(*Kulaba*, common: *kukumbwa*, to desire.)

Mwaice wantanine sabi — The little child refused me fish.
Lelo waikala muli bomba — Today she stands in the crowd.
(Old folk become resentful, when a youngster refuses them what they ask for, especially some delicacy.)

After the dance, a woman comes who has borne her first child alive. She carries the girl on her shoulders into her mother's hut. The girl does not eat this day till the evening, when there is dancing at the door. Some of the songs sung then are:

Ni wani wapanda — Who made the medicine
Kalabana. — of *kalabana.*
(*Ni wani*, Nsenga form: Ambo, *mbani*, who. *Kalemalema, kalabana,* sorcery medicines.)

Mu calo ca sile baukana, — In the land of peace,
Mwaka wafwile batata, — In the year when my father died,
Kamfuma, kanjipaya inkulo, — I came out, I killed a waterbuck,

90   SOCIAL AND RITUAL LIFE OF THE AMBO

Uyu mwana wakula ne matwi.	This child has grown with ears.
	('with ears' means obedient.)
Baciwila balasyana,	*Ciwila* dancers dance,
Tekupala mwana	Not like a child,
Mundobwe kutetema,	Mundobwe trembles,
Kwati litete.	Like a reed.

(*Mundobwe* is a proper name. Trembling (as here) in the whole body belongs to the finest dancing. *Ciwila* is a possessed dancer.)

Cilundu ca mfuti	The butt of the gun
Calikonwene,	Was broken,
Pakutabata	When aiming to and fro
Ne mapewa.	At the roan.

(Probably there is a reference to the sexual act in this song. Why else should women sing a hunter's song in this situation?)

The course of initiation is called *cisungu*; the girl in initiation is also called by the same term. A *cisungu* girl may not be seen by anyone. If people saw her, they would be scandalized. She stays in the hut of an unmarried girl and comes out only at dusk, bowed, leaning on a younger sister and covering her head with a cloth or blanket. She anoints herself every day with powdered red *nkula* tree mixed with castor oil. It is feared that if she did not anoint herself, her skin would peel off. She is given new calico and a new mat. When her relatives want to see her, they must give her presents. Her playmates may come to see her if she goes to the fields at dusk.

The girl in seclusion never speaks aloud but whispers. If she did speak aloud, she would 'exhume her mother', *kusikula banyina*. She must not cry since this would be an extraordinarily bad phenomenon, *mbiko*. The instructress pinches her, if she does something wrong, but she must bear it patiently.

She may not scratch herself with her fingers but only with a stick. If she did scratch herself, her womb would come out, it would grow so big. This prohibition is based on word resemblance; *mala*, finger nails and *maala*, the womb or the belly. Finger nails may not be broken off, or she would lose her reproductive powers, *angaposa lufyalo*. Hair should not be shaven. To be shaven is tantamount to losing a part of the body; then she would lose her reproductive powers as well. She may not wash herself, because her reproductive powers would go into the water together with the dirt. If she cut the hair of her friends, she would also 'exhume her mother' unless the instructress begins the cutting.

The initiate also learns and accustoms herself to the prohibitions

CHILDHOOD AND PUBERTY 91

in the time of menses, which she will have to observe throughout her life. So she does not touch cooking pots at that time, neither does she cook. She may touch an empty cooking pot but not one containing relish. The *cisungu* girl eats salted relish, but she may not salt it herself, because she may affect a male with chest disease should he take some of it. A clan sister or instructress must put the salt into her relish.

She is also prohibited from handling honey, tobacco, fermented liquor and porridge, lest males should consume them and thus contract chest disease. She may eat honey when fed by the instructress. If she took honey herself, she would contract the chest disease. Women will accept all these things from a menstruating girl or woman, provided they can consume them at once so that males shall not take them.

The initiate anoints herself with wild spinach, *mulembwe*. This group of plants is slimy. The girl wants to acquire this property *ut coitus facilior fiat*. She scrapes the root of *cilingwe* and puts it into her private parts *ut membrum virile imitatur*. She stretches her vagina.

Instructions are given repeatedly by the instructress to the girl in seclusion. They are called 'the wisdom of the house', *mano a ŋanda*. They prepare the girl for wifehood. I give some examples. *Si post mestruationem coieris cum viro, noli abstergere penem ne forte controversiam inferas quod eum morbo pectoris afficeris. Cum quater coieris, in fine terga membrum. Kani waleka kuseesa, kani walala ne mwanalume libili, tekusumuna mwanalume, iyu, ungaleta mulandu; umgamukowesya mubili. Line walala, pakusila kulala, kumusumuna.* If a woman does not do so to the man, she is thought to be a fool who does not know her duties.

'When you have menstruated, you may not enter a hut, where a man is inside, you may enter only when the man comes out,' *kani waseesa, tekuinjila mu ŋanda, kani mwanalume ali mukati sombi kafuma panse mwanalume, epakuinjira mwanakasi.* This is *fyaku-tondela*, taboo (but see next example). The man would become deaf. Here there seems to be a play of ideas based on sympathetic magic. 'To enter a house' connotes the wedding and the marital act; to inherit a widow is 'to enter the house'. Entering a house where there is a menstruating woman magically resembles intercourse with her in that state.

'When menstruating, do not sleep with a man but only when you stop menstruating,' *kani wasesa, tekulalapo ne mwanalume, sombi*

8

92 SOCIAL AND RITUAL LIFE OF THE AMBO

kaleka kuseesa. This is a strict taboo, *mitondelo,* which if ignored would risk affecting the man with a chest disease.

'If a man takes you into the bush, come and tell it in the village, it is an offence,' *kani mwanalume akutwala mu mpanga kuti koisa kolabila ku musi, mulandu.* A marital act in the bush is an offence against the shades who would kill the woman's children.

'*Si vir mulierem lamberit, ducatur coram principe ut chusa instituatur.*' *Kani mwanalume walya mwanakasi, kamutwala ku mfumu kumupela mulandu. Quid significat edere mulierem? Si vir non habet condimentum, coit cum muliere atque tergit vulvam morsu pulmenti quod est in loco condimenti. Alius modus est lambere simpliciter.* The wife must report such behaviour 'to the village', to the matrilineage. It is said that a bad spirit had entered into the chest of the man, *ati cibanda camwimina, kuisa kuntibi.* The matter is further reported to the chief who then enslaves the man to the injured woman. The man might redeem himself by paying a gun. The woman brings up the case only if she wishes to—perhaps the man produced no semen and therefore no satisfaction.

'If your husband copulates with you while you are asleep, come and tell us, the people, why he has not awakened you,' *kani mwanalume akulala ku tulo, uise ulabile kuli fwe bantu, nindo tamubukisye.* The matter should be reported to the chief. 'Such a man is a sorcerer, because he would lie even with a corpse.' In the old times a gun was paid as compensation.

'Do not refuse your husband, he may become angry', *tekukana mwanalume, angakalipa.*

'When your man passes wind, do not spit (you offend the man)', *kani wanya bususi, tekusipapo mate (wasula mwanalume).*

'When you see that the pubic hair has grown on your man shave him', *kani wabona mwanalume misisi (maso) ya fula, ubeye.*

'Harlotry is no good, it is not seen where she will die', *bumensomenso tabuwemepo, tababonapo mpowafwila.* Through a dissolute life a woman may contract venereal disease and the span of her life may be shortened.

'If another man strikes you with his hand, do not tell that to your husband', *kani akupamapo lupi umbi mwanalume, tabalavila ku mulume.* Such behaviour is a sign of flirtation.

'If you are married to a lazy husband, do not say: "I do not want him", because a man has varied interests. Just watch and see, where he makes a gain.' *Kani waupwa mwanalume mufila, tekweeba ati: 'Namukana', iyu. Mwanalume ne cipobe, kubona kwa pobele.*

CHILDHOOD AND PUBERTY

Woman knows only housekeeping and hoeing. Man has many outlets. He may be good at finding relish, bringing wealth, he may be a good agriculturalist, he may be fortunate in begetting children.

'If he has killed a guinea fowl, do not talk saying: "My husband has killed a guinea fowl today", because the sorcerers in the village may hear of it.' *Kani waipayapo cuni, takulabilapo ati 'Balume banji baipaya cuni lelo', iyu, pantu mfwiti mu musi singoumfwapo.* Sorcerers are credited with demoniac envy, which alone accounts for the acts of bewitching the lucky person.

'If your man wants porridge at night, wake up and cook it for him. When you have cooked it for him, do not go and noise it abroad, saying: "My husband eats porridge at night". No, do not say it.' *Kani mwanalume wafwaya nsima busiku, kobuka, komunayila; kani wamunayila tekuyapo kulabila panse ku babyobe ati: 'Balume banji balokulya nsima busiku iyu.'* As there was a custom that men took their meals together, it might easily happen either because of a great number of guests or because not all the wives sent their meals to the village shelter, that a man might feel hungry at night. Some women may have been sick, others drunk or away. The making of porridge, when flour is at hand, should not present much difficulty; the cooking of relish takes a much longer time. Therefore a woman in seclusion at puberty was taught to set aside always some portion of cooked relish for such an emergency. Such a reserved relish has a special term: *mansendekela.* Teaching such foresight was to many informants the typical item of initiation instructions of 'the wisdom of the house'.

'In the morning heat water for your man (he will wash himself)', *mu lucelo kupisya menda a nwanalume (mwine asambe).*

'In the hot season mould a new jar to keep water cold for your man', *mu tusuba kobumfya nongo ya mukanga ya kunwamo menda atontwele a balume.*

'If your man wants beer, brew it for him, let him drink,' *kani mwanalume alokufwaya bwalwa, kokumbilapo, kanwa.*

'Give food to the relatives of your man', *kutebeta bakwabo ba mwanalume.*

'When your man beats you, do not refuse to cook porridge for him', *kani akupama mulume, tekukana kumunayila nsima.*

'When your husband beats you at night, do not cry aloud, (but cry secretly),' *kani akupama mulume, busiku, tekulilapo (sombi kulila cinsinsi).* He should not be ashamed before the villagers.

'When your mother goes out, you should not steal relish from the

94   SOCIAL AND RITUAL LIFE OF THE AMBO

pot on the fireplace,' *kani banoko bafumako tekusobola bucisa pamu-lilo*. This is thought improper. Such a woman would be looked upon as childish.

'If the mother-in-law scolds you, do not answer back, but simply keep silent', *banokofyala kani balokweba, tekuapukapo we, iyu, kuti kokutumene likoso*.

'When an elder orders you to do something, and you do not obey, you offend the elder', *kani akuluma mukulu, tabakana, kuisula bakulu*. An older woman is meant here. It is also feared that an offended old person may bewitch the girl.

'If you come across somebody stealing, do not speak about it. If you talk, they may kill him. If they kill him, then this is your fault. His bad shade may come to you', *kani wasangana muntu alokwiba, tabalabila iyu. Kani walabila, bangamuipaya. Abamuipaya mulandu wobe, cibanda cingesa kulimwe*. The saying goes: 'The witness is a bad thing', *bumboni bubipile*. The thief may bewitch the girl or may be killed because of her. Then she will be perse-cuted by his or her revengeful shade. Her children will die.

'If you meet an elderly person, do not refuse him fish; if you refuse him, he or she may bewitch you—if he bewitches you, you are dead,' *kani mukulu wakumana nakwe, tekumutana sabi, iyu. Awatana pambi wakulowa; kani wakulowa, kufwa*. Repeated acts of stinginess are often given as a reason for bewitching. Sorcerers are spoken of as very persistent and arrogant in asking for gifts. The Ambo are often carrying fish either caught or bartered or received as a gift.

The début of the initiated girl is known as *kufumya cisungu*. The *cisungu* girl is 'taken out' (of the hut) after the harvest, *pa cibwela-musi*, when the people come back to the village to stay there. She will have been living in seclusion perhaps from December to July. If a girl happens to start her periods earlier, her initiation course will be delayed. Now is the time of rest and plentiful food. The maternal uncle or the parents brew beer in honour of the girl. To more important headmen, a fowl is sent as an invitation. They in turn notify their villagers and announce the event. A rich headman may come to the beer-drink bringing a goat to be killed at the feast. The beer of the initiated girl is called *pa mubala* 'at the beginning'. This is an occasion for a great festival, celebrated by the whole country-side.

In the morning the women alone take the girl outside the village, dress her in beads and anoint her all over with red *nkula*, powdered

CHILDHOOD AND PUBERTY

camwood, mixed with castor oil. She wears *insangwa* rattles on the legs, and *buyombo* a kind of string skirt. Then a procession is formed, and heads towards the village. Two women lead the way. One of them throws an unrolled sleeping mat to another who catches it and throws it back playfully during the whole journey. The girl walks with her body bent; the instructress lays her hand on the girl's forehead, covering her eyes and touching both temples with her fingers. The procession comes to the hut of the maternal uncle. During the procession the women sing continuously and clap their hands, *cilombe-lombe iyo, calomba nsambo ku bena uisi*, a beggar begs ankle-rings from the people of the girl's father.

In front of the uncle's hut a mat is spread. A younger sister sits down, legs outstretched. Behind her the *cisungu* girl is seated, holding the head of her sister between her knees. The initiate keeps her eyes cast down. The maternal uncle comes, takes in his mouth some beer, some of which he swallows and spits the rest on to the breasts and shoulders of his niece saying: 'When I am dead come and take my name, my name is Cisenga', *kani nkafwa, uise ambwesye, nailika Cisenga*. This is a reference to naming a child of a niece after her maternal uncle.

Now the people give presents of small coins, putting them on the head of the initiate. These are collected into a basket, *kasele*. When the giving of presents has come to an end, the uncle takes an axe and at places round the edge of the mat on which the girl is sitting cuts the ground and puts beads into the openings. The girl's father then does the same.

The instructress now leads the girl before the drums, where the *cisungu* girl dances for a few minutes, facing them. A few women accompany her. When I witnessed this rite, there were three drums. Men stood behind the drums facing east, women stood opposite. After the dance a cross-cousin, *mufyala* (it may be a brother-in-law) seizes the girl round the waist and carries her away to a hut.

The dance which the girl performs on this occasion is *mutembe-tembe*. Here are some of the songs of this dance.

Kabongabonga kamwale,	A girl with a bent head
Iyaya iyayayele,	*Iyaya iyayayere*
Yaye sumbelongo.	*Yaye*, the row of locusts.

(*Kabongabonga*, means to bend the head and to sway it to the right and left like the movements of this dance. *Sumbelongo*, corrupt

96 SOCIAL AND RITUAL LIFE OF THE AMBO

from *masombe* (plur,) locusts. *Longo*, usually *mulongo*, a line, a row. Here is meant a line of locusts, the allusion being to the numerous progeny the girl is hoped to have.)

Mabala, mabala, kuwati ni ngo ;   Spots, spots like a leopard
Kansi ni citondo.   But it's the big mtondo (tree).
(*Ngo*, leopard, from Nsenga.)

Finally a gun is fired and women ululate. The rest of the day is devoted to drinking.

The girl at her puberty rites uses the following medicines: sap of the wild rubber tree, castor oil and the wings of a bat roasted on a potsherd and mixed together. She puts them into her private parts. The sap of the wild rubber is used to make the private parts elastic like rubber. Castor oil seems to be only a medium for applying medicines, and is generally used to anoint the body. The wings of a bat are meant to make the private parts open like the wings of a bat. Other medicines are also used.

Nowadays girls pound maize and perform other services for old women to obtain occasional further instructions on the 'wisdom of the house'. The stretching of the vagina continues.

Till the early nineteen forties girls' initiation was practised. The author witnessed a début about 1940. Though it is generally believed that initiation has stopped, at least one instance came to the notice of the author, showing that after 1950 some sort of initiation had been performed.

In the above description of a girl's initiation, the three stages of a *rite de passage* are easily discernible. The first stage is that of separation. The girl withdraws into seclusion from community life. The *rite de passage* is associated with and connotes a symbolic death. The only features of the symbolic death at this stage are the carrying of the initiate on the back of another person, which reminds one of a dead person, and whispering being the only manner of speech allowed. The initiate is 'dead', she is in the world of the shades, and therefore she may not speak aloud. At this stage, mystical death is also reflected in the hiding of the girl from the sight of the public. In other respects this stage, as an introduction to the rite, is marked jubilantly with a special dance and appropriate songs.

The second stage, the preparation, is differentiated from the first stage, though it is also a continuation of the first in that the

CHILDHOOD AND PUBERTY

first as well as the second stage involves separation. Whispering is common also to both stages. It may be argued that the dead do not wash, neither do they shave or cry from pain.

The second stage, apart from many common traits with the first, is marked off from the others by its length and the instructions given.

The third stage is that of incorporation or integration into a new status in society. This integration is symbolized by the uncovering of the initiate and her introduction into communal life. She appears with uncovered face in public, performs a token dance, and is seated when she is offered presents. Her new status is that of a marriageable person, which is shown by publicly carrying an open sleeping mat, the symbol of married life. The songs refer to the numerous progeny. The fertility theme is evidenced in the symbolic planting of beads round the sleeping mat. The characteristic feature of re-incorporation, the communal meal, appears as a large beer party.

The interplay of dynamic magical powers in the *cisungu* girl is apparent. To the Ambo she is not unlike a charged electric battery.[1] She is not isolated in her state, but is surrounded by and subject to other magical forces. Thus her reproductive powers must be safeguarded against other forces which may clash with and enfeeble or destroy them. They must also be prevented from adversely affecting other human beings. For these reasons, nothing may come off the body, neither dirt, hair clippings nor nail parings. Comparable is the safeguarding of a new-born baby whose vitality is not yet established.

It may be noted that transgression of initiation rules is under the pain of losing reproductive power, *angaposa lufyalo*.

There is another sphere of prohibitions, namely, those which aim at avoiding the clash of dynamically operating magical forces, which could harm either the subject herself or others. It is noteworthy that this relation extends only to males besides the girl herself. The reproductive power of the initiate, as well as that of menstruating women, likewise affects only the male. Other dynamic forces radiating with effectiveness are from objects considered to be 'strong', *cikali* (probably an Arabic word; e.g. *kali* = fierce, sharp, savage), which also has the meanings 'angry' and 'dangerous'. These objects are 'strong' for the senses. If they are combined with the

---

[1] I have heard Nsenga explicitly refer to girls dancing at their maturation ceremony as 'batteries'—in one case of a poor dancer as a 'flat battery'.—R.A.

98 SOCIAL AND RITUAL LIFE OF THE AMBO

radiating reproductive powers, their effect is overwhelming and injurious to the male.

Boy's maturation

Ambo boys observe no rites at puberty. It is stated that there is no need for it. A boy, however, uses medicines, probably physiologically effective, to increase his sexual activity and to strengthen his sexual organs and powers. After he has seen the effect of the medicines on his body, he seeks a girl to try her. Ambo are convinced that he could not beget children or even perform the marital act if he omitted this doctoring.

Boys drink an infusion of *munyamenda* roots, the purpose being to make the genitals grow big. *Munyamenda* means 'what excretes water'. Some may drink *ngwelulu* (*Zizyphus jubajuba*) roots, which may act as an aphrodisiac. Infusions of *ndale* roots (*ndale* means 'let me lie') may also be taken. Another medicine for boys is an infusion of *mubanga* (*Afrormosia angolensis*) roots, which is drunk. Three incisions are made on the belly and on the back and a compound inserted made of burnt wool of he-goat, burnt penis of *kabundi* lemur, scraped roots of *katenge* (*Dichrostachys mutans*), and *lwenje*. The he-goat is a symbol of strong sexual powers; the lemur is believed to have a strong penis; the core of *katenge* is exceptionally hard, and *lwenje* has whitish sap resembling human semen. *Mubanga* is a hard wood, signifying erectness.

V. MARRIAGE

IMPORTANT principles of sexual behaviour are presented to the girl during her maturation rites. They are concerned with the behaviour of a married woman, especially towards her husband. It is very important for a married or engaged woman to conceal any unfaithful flirtation or misconduct. The minor matrilineage of such a woman would never betray her, but she is bound to conceal any misbehaviour towards her by any man who is not her husband, even though she herself is innocent. Any feud between the woman's husband and other men could bring a supernatural sanction into operation. Some initiation rules dealt with what were regarded as major transgressions. These included prohibitions on intercourse with a sleeping wife or coitus in the bush. The first of these breaches is thought to be committed under the influence of a supernatural agency, the second is suspected of being connected with sorcery, the first is inevitably followed by supernatural punishment.

Premarital chastity is not insisted upon. But children and adolescents gain their sexual experience only occasionally and furtively. The prolonged absence of young males at labour centres seems to be the main contributory cause of the comparative 'sexual peace' in the country. When they return to the village they do not stay long enough to take root in village life. If they come back at a marriageable age, they at once scour the countryside for a suitable mate. When a youth comes back to the village, he may feel rather shy and lonely. Being somewhat isolated and not staying long at home, he has little time to develop with others of like kind a group behaviour which would tend to be disruptive of the accepted norms. On the whole, he tends to conform with the behaviour of the conservative, dignified, law-abiding majority of elders.

Girls are told by their mothers and other clanswomen to appear painstaking at their work and thus to attract and impress roaming suitors, the boys back from the labour centres. The extent to which this traditional attitude prevails is borne out by the fact that school teachers complain of having difficulty in obtaining wives, because they are unable to fulfil the essential prerequisites, i.e. to work for the mothers-in-law and to reside matrilocally.

100 SOCIAL AND RITUAL LIFE OF THE AMBO

The divorced, deserted and widowed women of riper age are more independent and can please themselves in accepting suitors. It is astonishing how men, particularly complete strangers and travellers, are readily accepted by these women. A strange man may come to a village and tell the headman that he is looking for a wife. The headman will extend hospitality to him for a few days, until the suitor has found a single woman whose family will provide further hospitality for him. They cohabit at once. Often these men, after a fortnight or even less, desert the woman, sometimes leaving her pregnant. Some of these men are tobacco middle-men, others are travellers who say that they have no money for journeying further. There is no stigma attached to these unions, which are not regarded as fornication, but as a usual way in which to start marital life with an adult woman. Everything has been done publicly which distinguishes Ambo marriage from fornication. Young girls are not usually given to such wanderers, but follow the more traditional procedure, winning the attention of local boys coming back from towns.

Girls used to marry early, just after puberty, because it was believed that it is dangerous for a young man to make his first marriage with a fully grown woman. Even a fully grown youth was afraid of a big and powerful *moye* (a grown up girl after initiation) lest she overcome him and he fail in coitus, with the magical consequences explained below (page 105). First the young man should fortify himself with medicines to improve his sexual organs. Then he should marry preferably a young, physically underdeveloped girl. Thus a fully developed girl does not have a chance of meeting an equal partner other than a widower or a polygamist or a divorced man. It has been mentioned by informants that there was a scarcity of marriageable girls in olden times. The boys, according to this tradition, married rather late, probably at about twenty-five years of age, to be able to satisfy the demand for the exacting work of the mother-in-law. Nowadays the age of marriage for boys is lowered and that for girls has risen. My sample shows a strong preponderance of females (144: 100) over males, no doubt owing at least in part to emigration of male labour. Many males stay at labour centres practically for good and their places are not filled by alien immigrant settlers. For girls nearly twenty years of age to be married to boys a few years younger is a complete reversal of traditional practice.

Quite a large number of young girls marry middle-aged polygamists. They all state that they do so because of the lack of a better

MARRIAGE 101

choice. Then fairly frequently these girls tire of such uncongenial
marriages and break them off after only short marital experience,
even though in many cases they have borne a child. They excuse
their instability by the plea of incompatibility of age. In other
instances, very young girls, for the lack of better choice, willingly
marry middle-aged local emigrants, domiciled in towns, thus foregoing matrilocal residence.

Middle-aged women, whether widowed or divorced, often defy
customary law by going to towns and marrying there, as many
court cases show. Others of this type eke out an existence living
in their home villages, with their maternal uncles, grand-uncles and
brothers.

The majority of boys return to their home villages in order to
marry. They often express their low opinion of the town girls and
women. What they seek in the country women of the tribe is stability
and reliability in marriage. Another factor determining their choice
is the possibility that they should return together to a village on
holidays or for good.

Something has already been said about the status of children
born out of wedlock. An explanation has been given why there are
few such children and why they are not despised as such. Young
boys however are averse to marrying a girl with a child born out of
wedlock.

In general Ambo have no accepted sexual custom which a missionary at least might regard as moral laxity. They do not enjoin
even a ritual cleansing copulation of the bereft spouse, contrary to
the practice of related tribes. Indecent or even vulgar talk in the
presence of the other sex is a serious breach of manners, and an
offence termed cursing, *matuka*. Here should be recalled the convention of giving a warning, and in fact asking permission, before
approaching a ford lest the traveller encounter a naked person of the
opposite sex bathing. Ambo morality in this respect is far stricter
than that of the Plateau Tonga. As children, the Tonga and the
Ambo behave similarly in sexual matters. The change in behaviour
comes after puberty, and lasts till marriage and after. The laxity
of the Tonga after puberty in many instances passes into dissolute-
ness. Rape and particularly elopement are common. Among the
Ambo rape is hardly known, and elopement unheard of. As for the
married woman, it is a common saying among the Tonga that a
woman after the second or third child must have a lover and seek
satisfaction outside wedlock. If there is such infidelity among the

102 SOCIAL AND RITUAL LIFE OF THE AMBO

Ambo, it is exceptional and not widespread. Almost half of Ambo polygamists trust to the fidelity of their junior wives, leaving them in their own matrilineal villages. The Tonga, apart from economic reasons leading them to need all their wives at one farm, would never on moral grounds allow such an arrangement.

Ambo men seldom interfere with the wives of others. Men would be ashamed to do so in their own village among their own brothers and if they are matrilocal strangers they must behave strictly. Men who went to other villages for illicit courtship would be noticed, because the villages are some distance from each other and compact in themselves. Men might indulge in unlawful courtships in the middle or late rainy season, when the population is scattered in gardens which are covered with high sorghum, or in gardens adjoining the neighbouring villages. But this is rarely done. A Tonga, however, who has never had an adultery court case in his life, would be a strange person in Tonga eyes.

Courtship

It is maintained that in the old days because of the dearth of marriageable girls, young men used to give their services to married women to work for their yet unborn daughters whom they hoped to marry. Before the birth of such a child, a young boy offered bark cloth to the woman 'to cover the womb'. If the child born was a boy, he became a friend of the would-be suitor.

Nowadays girls do not seem to be scarce. The boy asks a girl if she wants him. She may not commit herself in answering him at once, but she may say in the village that she is pleased. The boy now goes to the *balamu*, brothers and sisters of the girl, and talks the matter over with them. They mediate between him and the prospective mother-in-law.

If the boy is accepted by the mother of the girl, he begins to work for her. He comes on the first day with his relatives, his 'brothers' and 'sisters', and they hoe hard right into the late afternoon without a rest to show their eagerness. A relative of the 'mother-in-law' as she is termed already, in anticipation, is sent to call the workers to a meal. They eat porridge with a fowl for relish, which the mother of the girl has prepared, and are given a present of a string of beads. The suitor eats with his prospective brothers-in-law, but avoids his future mother-in-law. Sometimes he refuses porridge offered to him, so as not to arouse the suspicion that he

MARRIAGE 103

looks rather for porridge than for a wife. Then his portion of food is eaten by his companions or his parents, if they live in the same village.

When the suitor first brings firewood, he chooses about six big logs, takes off their bark and lays them down gently to show his respect for his future mother-in-law. He hoes in the garden, builds a hut or a grain bin, makes a mat and, in the old days, provided bark cloth. Nowadays he sends clothes for his fiancée from where he is working. He goes on working for his future mother-in-law for about a year.

If his mother does not make her appearance, the mother of the girl after some time asks why her future son-in-law always comes alone, and whether he is serious about the marriage. The boy then asks his mother to settle the marriage between the two families. The mother and the father of the boy go to the mother of the girl. The boy's mother brings a broad *lubango* basket: most accounts do not mention the father in this connection. She sits down and is commonly greeted with 'Peace. What do you look for?' 'We have come to give the marriage dues, we have come to enslave ourselves. Our child wants to marry your child.' *Nindo mwalonda? Twaisa mukufwaya bufi, twaisa kuliteka. Mwana wesu akofwaya mwana wenu.* The mother of the boy may simply say in more picturesque language: 'We have come to look for a cooking pot', *twalonde ntalo*. The cooking pot symbolizes the woman, whose main duty will be to cook for her husband.

Formerly, the mother of the boy presented a basket, and in it a sixpence, or a wristlet of beads. Today some pay five to six shillings instead of a goat which was sometimes given formerly. In the 1940s some paid as much as fifteen shillings. Ambo opposed the attempt of the Administration to fix a higher marriage price of some two pounds sterling. When they were compelled to pay by regulation, they afterwards returned the money privately rather than appear to be buying the girl.

This reluctance to accept a larger payment has an ulterior motive as well. It is feared that the marriage may break down and then the family of the girl will be liable to refund the payment. This reason is openly stated. Some old men maintain that the transaction of a goat or of five shillings instead of a goat, is an innovation, and that they themselves had paid nothing at their marriages. The beads in the string were of a large kind, called *kampekete*. Nowadays a small kind of bead is used. The marriage payment and beads given

104 SOCIAL AND RITUAL LIFE OF THE AMBO

on that occasion are called *nsalamu* or *ntengo*. *Ntengo*[1] refers usually
to the larger payment. The *nsalamu* beads are always meticulously
kept by the girl's mother. In case of bad conduct of a son-in-law,
the *nsalamu* is returned to him, and that means divorce. Return of
nsalamu is especially easy before the first child is born.

Now the time has come when the future mother-in-law thinks
fit to invite her prospective son-in-law to take meals from her. She
will send him meals to the village shelter, a custom called 'the eating
of porridge', *maliansima*, or 'to show the hearth', *kulanga mulilo*.
The mother of the girl goes to the mother of the boy with a broad
lubango basket of meal, a fowl or a sixpence or a shilling, formerly
with two strings of beads. This she carries uncovered: covered meal
is carried to a funeral.

The girl's mother is given the ordinary porridge. When leaving,
a shilling and sixpence or a similar sum is put into the empty basket
by the boy's relatives. The gifts which the mother of the girl had
brought are divided between the boy's mother and his maternal
uncle. The maternal uncle is called, shown the gifts, and may then
take a part of the flour or the fowl. From then onwards the mother
of the girl sends food to the village shelter for the suitor.

The wedding

When the boy feels he has sufficient means to start married life,
he chooses a woman instructress, *nacimbela* also called *nakasya*. She
may be his paternal grandmother or his father's sister. The bridegroom gives the instructress a shilling, formerly a string of beads,
and she in turn gives it to the mother of the bride. The instructress
teaches or perhaps rather reminds the bride in the evening how she
should behave with her groom. In the evening she carries the bride
on her back to the threshold of the boy's hut; if she is an old and
feeble woman, and the bride too heavy, she leads her by the hand.
The boy prepares the bed himself and the instructress spreads the
mat. The instructress smears the mat with leaves of *ngwelulu* tree
(*Zizyphus jubajuba*) so that the boy may not 'break his back',
kukonona musana, in case he has not taken the medicine of manhood.
She may also put two *ngwelulu* leaves under the mat at the head, and
two at the feet. It is stated that *ngwelulu* causes excitement, and that
the two leaves strengthen both testicles. *Ngwelulu* roots taste bitter.

[1] In Nsenga, *ntengo* refers to the token tiny circlet of white beads that is given to
the girl's guardian by the suitor's people when there is no tradition of inter-marriage
between the two groups of kin concerned.—R.A.

MARRIAGE   105

It is said that *ngwelulu* is simply medicine, *muyanda likoso.* I know of no symbolic explanation to advance here.

When all villagers turn in, the boy goes to his hut and finds his bride there. *Prima nocte nuptiali post actum mulier non abstergit membrum viri neque eum capit sed se habet ut cadaver velut sine vita.*

In the morning the instructress knocks at the door. The bridegroom says aloud: 'It is my home here', *mwanji muno.* He may add boastfully: 'Come, I shall put you together with my wife, your friend', *isa nkubike pa mukasi mubyobe.* Then the instructress ululates to announce the joyous news that the marriage act has been successfully performed. On the other hand if the boy were impotent, he would not have the right to call it his home, but would remain silent, and there would be no joyous shrill cry of ululation. The mother-in-law awaits the ululation most anxiously of all. If there is failure in the marriage act, and the bridegroom hides it and does not take a medicine, it is feared he will contact sleeping sickness.

In olden times, some thirty years ago, the instructress used in the morning to be given a hen and a cock, the cock being given by the family of the groom, the hen by the family of the bride. She laid them at the door. Then she gave a bow and an arrow to the bridegroom who shot at the hen from inside the hut. Sometimes he may have used a fish spear. If he missed, it was a sign that he had told a lie and had not performed the marriage act. Nowadays this shooting has been discontinued.

Also in olden times the instructress used to collect beads which the bridegroom had tied to the bed or to the poles supporting the mat.

Then the instructress brings hot water in which the couple wash themselves. Some deny that she sprinkles the pair. This may be a Lwano custom. At the present time the man washes himself; thereafter his wife will wash him. The bridegroom puts a shilling in the pot for the instructress and the bride is given new clothes, the instructress receiving the discarded ones. After the washing the old woman smears the floor to show the bride how to do so every day so that splashed water may dry up quickly. Then the instructress gives a cigarette to the bridegroom, and to the bride, to release them from the taboo of not being allowed to offer tobacco to anybody. If this rite were not performed, the couple would infect with a chest disease anybody to whom they offered tobacco. *Nsungwe* roots are mixed with the tobacco to ward off sleeping sickness in the

106   SOCIAL AND RITUAL LIFE OF THE AMBO

bridegroom just in case he was concealing his failure in the marriage act.

Now follows the wedding communal festival meal, *maliansima*. The instructress puts a pot of water for the porridge on the fire. At the same time the bride holds the left hand of the instructress at the wrist with her right hand, and the bridegroom grasps the right wrist of the bride with his own right hand. This purifies the bride, who otherwise would cause chest illness in men when giving them food. The same holding of hands is repeated when the instructress puts salt into the fowl relish which she brought, as mentioned above.

Porridge is cooked for the bridal couple, who eat it together for the first time. Other porridge is also cooked and passed to the villagers. After eating, people put strings of beads into the empty plates which are collected by the mother of the bride. The couple stay that day in the hut.

'The bones (of the fowl) are the womb of the bride', *mafupa ni mala a cisungu*. Therefore the bones of fowls are neither chewed nor thrown away, but are gathered by the instructress and brought to the mother of the bride. She hides them in the bush, where they are eaten up by small ants, *tunyelele*. If the bones were scattered, so the reproductive power of the bride would also be 'scattered'. Also a sorcerer may work on the bones.

Avoidance rules

The first meeting between a son-in-law and his mother-in-law takes place at the presentation of his first-born child to her. When the mother of the child goes to draw water and the father is left with the child, he approaches his mother-in-law asking her 'to nurse it, the child is crying, and I am tired'. She takes her grandchild, and after nursing it a while will say: 'Your child is difficult, it does not become quiet.'

There is a further and a more formal introduction of the son-in-law to his mother-in-law. A rite is performed usually after the birth of the first child. It is 'the beer of introducing the son-in-law', *bwalwa bwa kuinjisya mukweni*. A beer party is arranged. At the beginning of drinking, the mother-in-law fills the drinking calabash, *cipanda*, comes to her son-in-law, kneels down and says: 'Father, let him see your beer we have brewed,' *tata ngabone bwalwa bwabo twakumba*. The son-in-law accepts the beer and drinks it. A sister or a brother-in-law ushers him into the hut of the mother-in-law where he distributes beer. His father and his mother's brother are

MARRIAGE 107

invited to this beer drink. They leave ten or fifteen shillings in the beer pot when they depart the next day. From now on the son-in-law and his mother-in-law may speak and chat together, but must observe avoidance rules in other respects. The rite of introducing him into the hut of the mother-in-law does not mean that he may enter her house at will. If his wife ever seeks refuge in her mother's hut, he cannot go beyond the door, on pain of being beaten by his brothers-in-law, for example.

The son-in-law, before the birth of his child, makes a present of a shilling or a fowl to his father-in-law. He may then have conversation with him. The daughter-in-law can speak to her mother-in-law as soon as she has given her senior a present of a fowl.

After the burying of the navel cord, about two weeks after the birth of the child, the child's mother goes with her child to her father-in-law. By another account, she presents the child as soon as it begins to smile. She must also give her father-in-law a fowl; then she may address him. A daughter-in-law may not pronounce the name of her father-in-law until some three years have gone by, and then only privately.

When a daughter-in-law has drawn water for her father-in-law, she does not approach him but sends a child with the water. When she has made him a present of a fowl, she may approach him, but may still not address him before the presentation of his first grandchild.

The wife honours the elder brother of her husband. The elder brother may be real or classificatory as when the brothers are born from a maternal aunt of the husband senior to his mother. So these elder 'brothers' may be in fact much younger than the woman in question.

The husband does not honour his wife's elder brother as if he were a father-in-law.

A man does not flirt with the elder sister of his wife, real or classificatory, but shows her marked respect. When the real mother-in-law is dead, the elder sister of the wife takes her place.

The husband has special respect (*kutina*, to fear) for his wife's sister's daughters, who are among his classificatory children, though he addresses such a 'daughter' as 'mother'. By the same etiquette a man addresses also his own daughter as 'mother'.

The father may not sit on the bed of his children, though their mother may do so while they are still minors. Sitting on someone's bed means intimacy, which is to be avoided between succeeding generations.

9

108   SOCIAL AND RITUAL LIFE OF THE AMBO

Sisters of the father (*wisinkasi*, sing.) may not 'play' with the children of their brothers. These paternal aunts are classificatory fathers to the children of their brothers.

Special avoidances of married couples

During her menses a wife does not cook, because any male who ate her food would become sick in the chest, *kukowela*. A man or a boy may be injured by such food, even if he takes it for himself without it being given to him. She is barred from cooking for five days. After she has washed herself on the sixth day, she may cook again. She is also prohibited from putting salt into relish at this time until she resumes sleeping with her husband.

It should be recalled that neither the husband nor the wife may have extramarital relations while the wife is pregnant.

Neither the father nor the mother of the child may have sexual intercourse, whether intra- or extra-marital, before the rite of 'nursing the child'. If they do not observe these prohibitions, the child will die.

Ambo do not offer any explanation for these taboos. They call the avoidance of a menstruating woman 'to taboo the fire', *kutondela mulilo*. From the taboos and practices associated with menstruation and sexual intercourse, it may be inferred that the persons concerned in these conditions are believed to be in a dangerous state. A person when his or her sexual power is active may, in certain cases, be himself affected. In other cases he may affect others who come in contact with this power.

The girl menstruating for the first time has this power still unsettled, therefore she must protect it by avoiding actions and substances which would act contrary to it; she must not wash herself as this would wash away the power. The sexual act also saps the resistance of men during small-pox, war and the smelting of iron.

This power, diverted through failure in the marital act, recoils and kills the bridegroom with sleeping sickness. The adulterous act through its dynamism magically reacts on the pregnant woman, because she and her child are in an unstabilized state, 'unripe', and delicate. Even a child already born and fully developed would be injured by the dynamic power of the sexual act of the parent or the child's midwife, unless the child had become first physically and then magically 'ripe', through the performance of a rite and the application of a medicine.

MARRIAGE
109

Final emancipation of the young couple

The married Ambo male is gradually emancipated from the restrictions, social and economic, which matrilocal marriage imposes upon him. As has been seen, many of these fall away after the birth of the first child. The young couple have no garden, no grain bin and no hearth of their own for cooking. They have only a hut of their own. After the bridegroom has become a father, he may be allowed to make his own garden and to build his own granary, provided his parents-in-law have somebody else to work for them. If they have not, the son-in-law will work for them for many years, even though he becomes a grandfather himself. This is a traditional and a somewhat theoretical view. Nowadays no man would agree to such an arrangement, and perhaps never would have.

The making of a hearth

After the birth of the first child, the wife acquires the right to have her own kitchen, having been until now a mere helper of her mother. From now on she will receive unthreshed grain, about a carrying basket, *citundu*, for three days. The rite of allowing the young couple their hearth for cooking is called *kufisya muliro*, 'to put up the hearth'. After the birth of the first child a fowl is cooked. The father-in-law takes hold of the right wrist of his son-in-law who grasps the relish pot, *cinkombe*. The father-in-law then says: 'You have grown up, you have your own house', *mwakula, mwaba ne nanda yenu.*

The wife picks up the stirring ladle, *mwinko*, and when she holds it within the pot, her mother holds her by the right hand at the wrist and addresses her: 'Now you have grown up, do as you like, cook special relish for your husband', *pano mwakula kocita mfi mwafwaya, koipika mansendekela ku balume bobe.*

Marriage rules

If an Ambo is asked whether he can marry So-and-so, if she is a relative he at once calculates in what genealogical position he stands to her. First, he finds out whether she is in the same generation, or one generation above or below him, or whether she is distant from him by two generations. Marriages linking adjacent generations must be avoided.

One's own generation in regard to marriage is more diversified. This whole generation falls into two classes, into *bakwabo* (sing. *mukwabo*), 'brothers' or 'sisters' and *bafyala* (sing. *mufyala*), 'cross-cousins' of both types. Ortho-cousins and the children of polygamists are classed as 'brothers' and 'sisters'. Cross-cousin marriage is usual.

Many marriages link alternate generations. In such cases it is usually the wife who comes from the second descending generation. It should not be thought that generational difference necessarily implies a large discrepancy of age. It is asserted that a grandfather could not marry his granddaughter in direct line, even though by agnatic descent she is of a different clan. All one's grandchildren of matrilineal descent must also be excluded as possible marriage partners.

Though the rules are simple and clear-cut, doubtful cases do occur. Some few instances have come to my notice. In one case the relationship was very distant but the man had to address his wife, who was younger than himself, as 'mother'. She was of a different clan, because clan endogamy would not be tolerated. The elders were opposed to the marriage; they maintained that it was unlawful and would not have been allowed formerly. The man concerned in this case was young and took advantage of the distant relationship. The distant relations, especially on the father's side, are easily classed as strangers and not *bakwabo*. Thus father's father's father's father's brother and his descendants are strangers to one another.

There are some borderline cases where a man may not marry a woman if she had been intimate with one of his first ascendant generation, that is, with his 'father'.

Polygamy

From several instances which were reported by eye-witnesses, the important men of old, the chiefs and headmen related to the chiefs and the owners of strongholds, had fairly numerous harems of five to seven or even more wives. Perhaps the last polygamist with a large harem was Chief Mambwe Mboshya who had twelve wives. At the present time women are met with in villages who left their husbands because 'their wives abound', *banakasi bafula*. This expression has two meanings. Either the husband seduces many women, not marrying them, and his wife is advised by her matrilineal relatives to divorce him, or else the husband is a polygynist. I have met at least three women who left their husbands because of their polygamy. Sometimes the first wife, sometimes the last, revolts. However, very few women go to the extreme of divorce on account of polygyny; most, especially the younger ones, resist it in other ways. Another indication of women's objection to polygyny is the high percentage of polygamous wives living uxorilocally. The reason for such an arrangement is always given as marital jealousy, *bukwa*. This reason is at the bottom of all objections by women to polygyny. Men never accept polygyny as a reason for divorce, but they readily acknowledge the women's objection to polygyny.

The second wife is also married in most cases uxorilocally, at least in the initial stage. Often the man has to walk half a day or more to his new wife. Sometimes this second wife lives across a big river, so the polygynist is inconvenienced for a large part of the year, when the water is high, and he must own or have a share in a canoe. Men bent on polygyny must undergo these hardships rather than risk strife between two wives brought together in the same village.

Of the second wife it is said that she 'begs a favour from the husband', *akosenga mulume* (lit. begs the husband). The first wife is called true wife, *mukasi wa cinenesye*. The heating of water in the morning for the husband to wash in is a duty, but also the exclusive privilege, of the first wife. Therefore the first wife either herself heats the water or puts the junior wife's pot on the fire. This practice is 'the honour (due) to the owner of the husband', *mucinsi kuli bene ba mulume*. The second wife, if she lives in the same village as the first, may not heat the water for her husband until some years have elapsed. The polygynist distributes his favours equally to both or all his wives, sleeping with each alternately half a week or so at a time. During the pregnancy of one wife, when he is debarred from access to other women, the taboo does not extend to his other wives. When he is sick and dies, he must die in the house of his first wife, *mukasi mukulu*.

Men give as the reason for polygyny the need to provide food for guests, alleging that having only one wife creates difficulty in this regard. The real reason, never stated, suggests itself, when it is known that for at least a year after the birth of a child a husband is debarred from access to his wife. Some oldish men have said that they married younger women to bear children, when the first wife reached her climacteric.

Those who disapprove of polygamy point out that it creates difficulties in agricultural work; a polygamist has to assist both wives in making a separate garden for each and in cultivation. A polygamist also finds it difficult to provide clothes for a double household.

As may be seen from Table V, the tendency is for polygyny

112 SOCIAL AND RITUAL LIFE OF THE AMBO

to be prevalent among middle-aged men. In old age many polygynists return to monogamy owing to the decrease in their physical strength. However, a fairly large number of young men have accepted polygyny. In such cases these men do not go to labour centres as migrant labourers accompanied by both their wives. The young migrant polygynist finds that economically he cannot afford to keep two wives in a labour centre. So he leaves one behind.

TABLE V

Incidence of polygyny

Age	*Monog.*		*Past polyg.*		*2 wives*		*3 wives*		*Per cent.*	
	Pag.	*Chr.*	*Pag.*	*Chr.*	*Pag.*	*Chr.*	*Pag.*	*Chr.*	*Pag.*	*Chr.*
20–29	51	23	1		2	3			7·2	8·0
30–39	28	18	2	2	13	6	1		36·3	31·6
40–49	25	18	1	5	6	6	2	1	26·4	40·0
50–59	17	7	6	2	4	1	1		39·2	30·0
60–69	15	5	1		3				21·0	
70–	3	1	2							
	139	72	13	9	28	16	4	1		

In Table V are given both past polygamists and actual polygamists, otherwise a number of men who favour and practise polygyny would be listed as monogamists. Some of these men are too old or too weak for actual polygyny, they are with regret forced by their condition into monogamy; others are only temporarily monogamists, because one wife has died or they have parted with one without going through a divorce procedure; again, others are divorced polygamists living in monogamy for the present. The actual and past polygynists may be distinguished from convinced monogamists.

Pagan polygynists are distinguished from lapsed Christian polygynists if the tenets of Christianity exert some check on their adherents in this regard.

TABLE VI

Percentage of polygyny

Total pagans married	*Total Christians married*	*Actual pagans polygynists*	*Actual Christians polygynists*	*Factual pagan polygynists*	*Factual Christians polygynists*
184	97	32: 17·3%	16: 16·4%	45:24·4%	25:25·8%

Table VI shows that recently introduced Christianity has not yet made Christians as a group resistant to polygyny.

In Tables V and VI taken together, there are 48 polygynists listed, of whom 43 have two wives. Of these, 21 kept both wives in the same village and 22 kept their wives separately in two villages. Polygynists with three wives are rare. In the villages investigated, five such polygynists were found. Only one of them succeeded in managing all three wives in one village.

Divorce

The general pattern of Ambo marriage has been shown above. It has been seen that men do not make any substantial marriage payment. They may give presents to, and do some work for, the in-laws, which is equivalent in some ways to bridewealth and is returnable. On the other hand, a man may easily acquire another wife without being forced to amass a new large marriage payment.

Ambo have some ideal of marriage stability and seem to value it, as is shown by the way they try to keep to their wives. As mentioned already, they do not steal other men's wives, and wives, while married, do not readily accept lovers. Men respect the wives of others 'to fear the spouse of man', *kutina muka muntu*. Women openly state that they marry for life.

What men feel most through the cessation of marriage, is the loss of their children. Apart from their wives, they can never have control over their children. Fathers hold a position of honour, respect, gratitude and friendship among the matrilineage of their in-laws during the existence of wedlock. And after the cessation of marriage, they try to keep that position and provide for it to continue. The death of the wife may just as well jeopardize this position as divorce. But whereas death jeopardizes it only in particular situations, divorce is on the whole more liable to undermine the exalted position of the 'father of the clan'. This is the reason why men, in spite of divorce, generally try to part on good terms with the in-law matrilineage in order to be free from the strain of hostility. Divorced and unmarried men are much dependent on communal life.

Another motive for retaining the good will of the in-law matrilineage is the desire to retain the contact, friendship and gratitude of the children which takes the place of custody. Therefore sensible men will reduce their claims at divorce as much as possible to show themselves generous to the in-law matrilineage, who in any case would have to provide compensation. The future relationship of the divorced man with the in-law matrilineage depends much upon which party was to blame for the divorce, the amount of service the man rendered to the in-laws, and upon his character.

Women seldom initiate divorce; rather they provoke their husbands to do so. The woman's behaviour is explained by the fear of having to pay compensation to the husband, if it is proved that she is responsible for the breakup without adequate grounds. Very young women and the very old seem to be the most prone to divorce. The former feel they have a good chance of another marriage, the latter do not care for it.

The incidence of divorce

TABLE VII

Divorce Rate

Age	Number of men	Number of marriages	Number of divorces	Deaths	Number of extant marriages
20–29	62	70	6	3	61
30–39	44	78	16	8	54
40–49	34	69	13	9	47
50–59	28	63	19	9	35
60–69	19	42	8	13	21
70–	4	10	1	5	4
Total	191	332	63	37	222

Table VII shows that 18·9% of all marriages end in divorce. The number of extant marriages is larger than the number of men, because some men were polygynists.

Grounds for divorce

Each individual case of divorce is the outcome of a manifold interplay of factors and causes. Therefore the mere listing of divorce causes is unsatisfactory. Often in court cases the couple or one of the spouses asks for a divorce, giving no specific grounds but only a simple refusal to continue the marriage. The reasons listed below were not just taken from court records, but were obtained by inter-

MARRIAGE 115

view. Sometimes the inquiry touched only one spouse, which is an unsatisfactory procedure. Gaps in the information were filled in by inquiries among neighbours or relatives. Often there are several grounds for divorce, but it would be difficult to compile a list of them in such complicated cases. When a woman says privately that she has left her husband because of his polygyny, she may be believed. Yet such a ground for divorce may not even be mentioned in court, because the assessors would blame the woman, and she may not obtain even the support of her matrilineage in paying the heavy compensation demanded from the parties initiating the divorce. So the husband or even the wife will plead in court utter incompatibility 'not understanding each other', *tatukoumfwanapo*, 'we don't understand each other'.

TABLE VIII

Grounds for divorce

	Grounds	On the part of man	On the part of woman
1.	Desertion	15	
2.	Disease	6	2
3.	Lack of children	1	2
4.	Adultery		7
5.	Incompatibility		9
6.	Sorcery	2	1
7.	Cruelty	1	
8.	Refusal to follow husband		7
9.	Laziness		6
10.	Incompatibility of age	3	
11.	Polygyny	5	
12.	Old age parting		11
13.	Religious motives	3	1
14.	Various motives	3	
		39	46

The cases in Table VIII were collected within the years 1938–43 and 1950–53. Many divorces were noticed and inquired into though they happened before 1938 or between 1943 and 1950. With the reservations already given, the grounds for divorces may usefully

116 SOCIAL AND RITUAL LIFE OF THE AMBO

indicate general trends in Ambo marriage. My table does not indicate who started the divorce suit.

Many women may be met in the villages who assert that they have been deserted by their husbands. They are found in their matrilineal villages, or if their matrilineage does not own a village, they live with one of their closest relatives—such as brother, sister, mother or mother's brother.

There are genuine cases of desertion. It was not possible to interview the men involved, but my information is that in most cases these men acted out of sheer irresponsibility. A woman may desert her husband through her adultery or by a refusal either to follow him to live virilocally, whether the move is near or far, or to follow him to town. Women depart from their husbands in their old age, owing to polygyny or even to disease. A man is freer of movement, can more easily maintain himself through work and is freer to find a spouse. Therefore it is little wonder that some men regard desertion lightly.

The diseases mentioned were blindness or chronic eye infections either in the man or in the woman, leprosy, madness, venereal disease and, in two cases, general debility and the sickly constitution of the man.

In a typical case of divorce because of lack of children the mother-in-law accused the son-in-law of being followed by a revengeful shade, which killed the children. The man was forced to sue for divorce, and to try another woman. In another instance, a couple lost eight children out of nine but never parted, nor had the man ever tried polygyny.

As has been said, adultery is not very common. It is not easy to bring a case of adultery to court because it is difficult to prove it. Two witnesses are needed, or the obvious pregnancy of a woman when her husband was away at work. Circumstantial evidence suffices as where a man and a woman go into a hut and fasten the door. Witnesses must find a man and a woman together in the bush in this eventuality to have sufficient evidence of guilt. If somebody notices the offence and wants to proceed with the case, he calls somebody else as a witness and they surprise the couple. A woman guiltily pregnant often accuses someone other than the true accomplice. If the accused denies the guilt, the woman is pressed further to reveal the real adulterer. She may be scared into confession by the mystical sanction that the aggrieved man's shade may kill her children. The slaying of adulterers may have been common, and though the practice has been discontinued, the belief persists that the aggrieved shade of a living man, and especially that of a dead one, could harm the woman accomplice. These difficulties arise only when a confession is forced on the pregnant woman while the husband is away, because then the adultery is obvious.

In rape these conditions are absent. The culprit has done wrong and if he is killed it is a just punishment. His shade does not become revengeful, like that of a sorcerer who has been killed after trial and confession of guilt. What is abhorred is the perfidy of agreeing to intercourse and then turning against the partner.

'Mwape of Mboshya was sued because he committed adultery with Bwanga, the wife of another man. The chief ordered Mwape to pay two pounds to "the owner of the wife". To the treasury the defendant had to pay ten shillings.'

This is a short account put down in the court book, but the story is much longer. The woman had difficult labour, a sign that she had had intercourse with other men. The chief told her: 'If you take these two pounds unjustly, you will see misfortune', i.e. if the woman lied, the accused man would curse her with 'imprecations', *mafinge*. He may say, 'If I committed adultery, the money will be yours, if not, the money will return to me.' A woman is afraid that the aggrieved shade of her paramour will cause her death.

Men may complain of a wife's 'mouth', *kanwa* or *mulomo*, giving it as the cause of divorce. Had the women concerned been interviewed, it might be found that they had good reason to complain. In court the reason of incompatibility may be given: 'We do not understand each other.' Incompatibility may be the sole grounds for a divorce.

It is not common for one spouse to accuse another spouse of sorcery, unless he or she gives good reasons for such suspicion. This ground would not be pleaded in court nowadays as the accusation is forbidden under the Witchcraft Ordinance. The cases in my list come from private investigations. In one case a husband insisted that the door of his hut must be always open at night. This strange idiosyncrasy was interpreted as a sign of sorcery, and the husband was sent away. In another case the wife kept going to her mother and staying there. As well as failing in wifely duty, the woman was suspected of meddling in sorcery, but more simply she probably found the burden of virilocality hard to bear. In a third case an old woman refused to live with her old husband, though they had been living together for many years. In court the only reason she gave

118   SOCIAL AND RITUAL LIFE OF THE AMBO

was dislike of her husband. As her husband was a reputed diviner, it was whispered that she was afraid of his uncanny powers.

One case of cruelty was found where there was a complaint by a woman who left her husband. The husband, though not interviewed, may have had some reason for frequently chastising her, since she was driven by her own sister from her homestead, where she had taken refuge after divorce. The sister objected to the woman's laziness and lack of help. Much cruelty is prevented by the possibility of the wife suing her husband for harsh treatment. In such cases, the husband is ordered by the court to pay his wife a few shillings in compensation. These cases are not uncommon and do not necessarily lead to divorce unless they are repeated. Cruelty, of course, might have been a contributory cause or consequence of other grounds.

There are various grounds for a wife's refusal to live virilocally and various situations in which it occurs. Some women refuse to follow their husbands to towns; others will not follow their husbands to their villages. A young wife in love with a young boy would hardly ever refuse to follow him. It is the mother of the bride who, needing the help and companionship of her daughter, may oppose the move. In one case, a young girl married virilocally. Virilocal marriage of a young girl occurs very exceptionally, and it was explained that the girl had no mother and 'nobody' in her village, which meant that she had no close matrilineal relations on whom she could rely for help.

The ground of laziness is accepted in court and is mostly laziness in hoeing. Women may use the same reason to divorce their husbands.

The three cases of incompatibility of age in the list were of young girls, who had married polygamously.

A woman, dissatisfied with the polygyny of her husband, will go back to her village and stay there. Formal divorce will not be sought by either party, but the woman will sue for divorce first, if she finds a suitor able and willing to pay compensation to her former husband. In court she may say simply that she does not want to live with her husband any more.

A marriage may end by the couple parting in old age on the initiative of the woman, after living contentedly with her husband for many years, often throughout the whole of her married life and having borne children. Several cases within my observations were not peaceful partings at all. Some women, when asked why they

MARRIAGE 119

left their old husbands, said they were tired. One woman stated in court that she had no more strength to cook for her husband. There were cases where a woman simply left her husband and stayed in her village or with her relatives or her children without trying for a formal divorce. The old husband still considered her as his wife, but she no longer had anything to do with him. The man, more often than not, had a second wife.

There are instances of breaking up a polygynous marriage on account of conversion to, or return to, Christianity. In one case it was the woman who left her polygynous husband on religious grounds. There are other instances, where a Christian returns to the practice of Christianity after his junior wife has left him. A purely religious motive for breaking up an established polygynous marriage either on the part of the junior wife or the husband is extremely rare.

The supernatural aspect of the termination of marriage through death is presented in the following chapter.

Widows

Ambo acknowledge some kind of levirate and sororate. The bereft spouse does not pass through the releasing rite if he, as a widower, marries his dead wife's 'sister', or if the widow allows herself to be inherited by a 'brother' of her late husband. When a widower marries a 'sister' of his dead wife, the 'sister' is termed a successor of the deceased, *mupyani*. This kind of arrangement cannot be termed a proper levirate or sororate, because it is optional, not obligatory; it is very little practised and is not favoured. More often than not, the prospective heir will be already in possession of at least one wife and will not contemplate inheriting another. The inheritance of widows has the same advantages and drawbacks as simple polygyny. It is stated that in a case of a refusal to inherit the widow, someone else will profit (*kulya*, 'to eat') from the children who were begotten by a clansman. The boys will give clothes to a 'new' father and the daughters will increase other villages with their matrilocal husbands. Sometimes the surviving 'brother' may be constrained by a pronouncement of a diviner to inherit the widow from his deceased 'brother'.

There is no shortage of women; the possible heir has a wide choice. And further, a woman in this matrilineal society is not a profitable investment, so to speak, as is the case in tribes with bridewealth; she is to a large extent a liability. A woman who has been married already is easily acquired, and with gratitude for her part; the suitor does not need to spend months in submissive toil as he does for a girl straight from puberty.

VI. DEATH, SUCCESSION AND INHERITANCE

SORCERY is generally suspected as a cause of death if somebody dies in the prime of life after a short illness. Panic is aroused should several people die in a short time, no matter in what circumstances and at what age. 'How could Lesa, who created man, kill him? Lesa kills nobody.' Some deaths are believed to occur as a result of breaking a taboo. The commonest case is when a husband or a wife has extramarital intercourse, while she is pregnant. Another cause of death is said to be the felling of big trees (such as *mululu*, *mofwe* and *musangu*) for making canoes, without first doctoring both them and the workmen. The children of the fellers will die. However, hardly anyone would be foolhardy enough to fell such a tree without taking precautionary measures, and in practice scarcely any deaths are attributed to this cause. Aggrieved shades cause death, their victims being usually new-born children.

Smallpox is sent by Lesa, not by sorcerers because, it is argued, sorcerers themselves fall victims to this disease. During smallpox epidemics there was a strict prohibition against any sexual intercourse, so men had to be herded together at night in huts separate from the women. Those who did not observe this taboo, died. He who ate of first fruits without a first-fruit offering was killed by a lion. If a person is killed by lightning, it is not taken as an accident. It is argued that he must have been stealing crops and the owner cursed him. Death due to natural causes in the case of the death of an old decrepit person, is accepted by the Ambo. And the killing of an adulterer, for instance, is taken at its face value without any supernatural causes being attributed.

Graveyards are chosen with an eye to practical considerations. Sandy ground is sought in order to dig the grave easily; land near water so that the grave diggers may wash themselves before re-entering the village. If the village moves far away from the old graveyard, a new graveyard is chosen.

Death

When a person is seriously ill, especially in the hot season, he is carried to the bank of the river to seek a cool place. In grave illness, a sick person should by all means try to reach his own matrilineal village or his closest matrilineal relatives, his mother or his siblings. When someone is seriously ill, in the condition called *mukunda*, his or her closest matrilineal relatives are notified in the first place. They go to him quickly and squat round the sick person in silence.

A funeral friend, *munungwe*, of either sex must close the eyes and the mouth of the deceased. At once a gun is fired to let the people know that a death has occurred. The female relatives lament: 'Our man has left us,' *watusiya mubyesu*. 'What has killed him?' *kansi nindo yaipaya*? 'Perhaps a sorcerer,' *pambi ni mfwiti*. 'They killed our fellow out of envy,' *mubyesu balipaya litima*.

The exclamations of a mother may be: 'Mama, mother, my child, where shall I see him, my child, to be left alone,' *mama, mwana wanji, kansi ni kwisa nakumbwena mwana wanji, mama, kusyala nenka*. 'Had my child not come and died at once, I would not have seen him,' *kansi ngataisilepo likoso mwana wanji ne kumubonapo iai*. 'Sorcerers are here, they killed my child,' *mfwiti sili kuno. Syanjipayila mwana wanji*. 'It is because of his youth that my child has passed away. Were I a man, I would go far away [to diviners] to see what has killed my child,' *ni pa bulombe apita mwana wanji. Nga ndi mwanalume, nganayako kutali kuya kubona caipaya mwana wanji*.

A sister may lament: 'Oh, my brother [or sister] we walked both together, answer my call; with whom shall I walk, it were better had I died,' *mama, mukwasu, twenda babili, nkumbule we mukwasu, mwansya nenka mba nyende na bani, kansi nga ni nebo nafwile*. A Christian girl lamented her grandmother's death: 'Today, my mother, you (listen), today mummy, she is gone, my mother, today she is gone to Mass, today my mother, my mother, today, my mother,' *lelo, mama wanji, wewo, lelo mama, waya mama wanji lelo, waya ku Misa, lelo mama wanji, mama e mama*. The metaphor 'to go to Mass' means to die.

The lamentations are sung in plaintive recitation. At the moment of death, loud lamentations and women's wailing burst out. The nearest matrilineal relative of the deceased acts now as the 'owner' of the dead body, *mwine wa mfwa*. He sends messages to the

DEATH, SUCCESSION AND INHERITANCE 123

relatives, the nearest headmen and the funeral friends. The headmen announce the news to the villagers. Girls and women carry the broad *lubango* baskets of flour, covered, as a sign of mourning.

The funeral friends of the same sex as the deceased wash the dead body, anoint it with castor oil and tie a string of white beads round the neck. The beads are a present from a funeral friend. When a funeral friend enters the hut of the deceased, he or she feigns anger that the people, even clan relatives, *bakwabo*, are murderers. He may shout 'You brothers (and sisters) you have bewitched your relative,' *mwe bakwabo, mwalowa mubyenu.* The corpse may be cursed with obscene language, *matuka. Bukala bwenu bukeni. (Pro tuo pene surge.)* 'The sorcery of your mother kills me,' *bufwiti bwa banyinenwe bwanjiapaya.* 'You will not sleep with your wife: others will marry her,' *abakasi benu teti mubopepo, bambi bakuupa.* He or she may try to give the deceased some water to drink. Then the funeral friend bursts into tears and lamentations.

Other typical outbursts are: 'You people, you bad spirits, why do you cry here over him whom you have killed?' *mwe bantu, mwe fibanda, nindo mulokulira kuno, umwipeye?* 'You sorcerers, it is you who killed him [her], take him, eat him. You have not killed him to throw him away for nothing, because you have got your meat,' *mwe mfwiti, ni mwe mwamuipeye, mubuleni, mukamulye. Tamwamwipayile kumuposa rikoso, pantu mwaba ne nama yenu.*

In old times, the mourners, before burying the deceased, waited a few days until the nearest relatives could arrive and see the body for themselves. Now such a delay is not usual.

While these outbursts of sorrow and mourning go on, the preparation of the body for burial is carried out. After the washing, the anointing and the decoration, the body was folded into a position resembling the foetal one. The legs were bent, the fists clenched, and the arms bent so that the fists touched the cheeks. When I asked why the body was folded, I was told it was done to make it smaller. A smaller grave required less digging. Nowadays the body is stretched at full length, wrapped in calico and then in a mat, *mpasa.*

At night the mourning goes on. People come and sleep in the open air on mats, fires being lit here and there. The young people dance to the accompaniment of drums. The older people sing funeral songs to the accompaniment of gourd drums. Drumming and dancing are continuous and tireless throughout the night. Should the dancers be remiss in mourning, they would offend the

124   SOCIAL AND RITUAL LIFE OF THE AMBO

shade of the deceased by withholding from him his due honour. Then his shade would avenge the slight by afflicting especially the 'owner' of the dead with ailments.

In the morning the body was tied to a carrying-pole. Formerly a part of the wall of the hut was pulled down and the corpse brought out through it. This was done as a precaution, lest the children see the corpse and be frightened, think of it and then die, people say. The corpse is laid down outside the hut. A little child, a clan relative or a child of the deceased, spills some flour on the ground by the head of the dead body saying: 'Go and sleep; who killed you, they will not sleep for a long time, may you come to divine against him,' *koya ukalale, wakuipeye tabalalila ubwele kumubukila*. Another version of this imprecation is: 'Go and sleep; remember who killed you that you may return to come and kill him,' *koya ukalale, uibukishye wakuipeye, ubwele uise umuipaye*. This is a threat to the supposed sorcerer who has caused the death. When the burial party sets off, the widow throws herself on the ground as if she wanted to hurt herself out of sorrow. After the third fall or so she is stopped by the deceased's 'sisters'.

The bier is now taken and carried by men to the grave. Any man may carry the corpse. Apart from men, only old women, *mpelafyala*, 'who have stopped bearing children', go to the burial grounds. It is said that young women may 'catch' a bad shade there. It is also said that they have 'soft' hearts, so they may think of the deceased and die.

Wherever outside the village the bier is to be rested, a few square yards of ground are scraped. Flour is scattered on every such resting place, *citusisyo*. Travellers used to throw some tobacco on these spots for as long as they were visible and say a prayer to ensure a safe arrival or to have a successful hunt.

When the burial party has arrived at the graveyard, the eldest of those present makes an offering of flour on the first grave saying: 'Do not make trouble, a new friend has come, we shall obey all laws.' First the body is measured to see how long the grave ought to be. It is then dug with a hoe and the soil is taken out with a basket, *kasele*. The customary depth of a grave is a man's height, sunk deep lest an animal or a sorcerer be able to interfere with the corpse. Should the diggers come across a big stone while digging, it is a bad omen. They must stop and divine. If it should appear that the newcomer does not want to lie there, they placate him to make him change his mind and stay.

DEATH, SUCCESSION AND INHERITANCE 125

Formerly a recessed chamber, *cipembwe* or *pembwe*, was hollowed out at the bottom of the grave in the side wall. Nowadays, short poles are laid at the bottom across the grave at a few inches interval. Upon them a mat is spread. The body is entirely unfolded, and the corpse is lowered, suspended on two strong bark ropes held by four men. Everybody tries to hold the ropes or the mat, at least ceremonially. One man, a clan relative, but preferably a grandson or a funeral friend, climbs down into the grave and adjusts the corpse. Formerly the body was placed in the side chamber so that it looked towards the village. Thus the shade would be able to return there to have his name revived in a new-born child. The head is turned westwards 'where the dead go', *kuciyabafu*. The recess chamber used to be blocked with upright, short poles put together closely and supporting a mat which prevented the soil entering and touching the body.

Then all present would go on their knees and push the soil into the grave with their elbows. It was done this way for fear of touching the grave soil with the fingers or hands. The soil was also stamped down with the feet. Now the soil is scraped in with hoes. When a grave is nearly filled, about one foot from the top, the carrying-pole is cut up and thrown into the grave as well as the ropes. The basket which had been used for excavating the earth, may be cut up and thrown in, or may be taken by a funeral friend. The hoe is knocked out of the handle, which is cut up and thrown in also. The hoe blade is taken by the man who entered into the grave. A brother or a sister of the dead makes an offering of tobacco, throwing some at the head of the body and saying: 'This tobacco which you grew, we give to you, you will smoke in the grave, when you shall sleep, and we also shall smoke that which was left,' *fwako uyo, walilimine, twamupela, mulokupepa mu manda, kumwalala, nafwebo nayo wasyala twalikupepa.*

When the grave is at last filled and swept a line is drawn down the centre along the whole length of the grave and then three lines crosswise. Some flour is scattered over the mound. These precautions are taken, it is said, so that if sorcerers come and interfere with the grave their footprints may be clearly seen. The calabash which the deceased used in washing himself is upturned and placed on the grave to let the shade know that he must not come to the village to look for food. The calabash is pierced so that no one will steal it.

The party now sets out on the return journey. Nobody looks

126 SOCIAL AND RITUAL LIFE OF THE AMBO

back lest he bring home with him a bad shade. If somebody were to look back, he might even see one. The 'owner' of the dead comes out, meets the party on the outskirts of the village and if the village has it, gives them the medicine of *coni* to drink. Only the 'owner' of the dead can touch the gourd of *coni*. If someone else coming from the graveyard touches it, the medicine would be affected by bad shades brought back from the graveyard.

The 'owner' of the dead takes feathers from the fowls brought and killed for the mourners, wraps them in grass from the thatch of the deceased's hut, lights the bundle and fumigates the buriers' feet, moving the firebrand over them. He also fumigates the heads of the buriers, encircling them with the firebrand. Fumigating is done with the left hand. According to the explanation given to me, the right hand is the symbol of strength and contains more strength. Thus to use the right hand would increase the sorrow for the deceased. The pungent smell of the feathers is said to drive away bad shades, as well as the smell of the corpse. The grave-diggers, called *fimbwi* (plur.) 'hyenas', do not go about the village but go straight to the hut of the deceased to leave there any bad shades that may have accompanied them. During the burial this hut has been swept clean and smeared by a woman funeral friend. The grave diggers and all the mourners eat, the relish being the fowls (and formerly goats) brought by some of them.

In the meantime, the bereft spouse, with the upper part of the body uncovered, has been lying disconsolate on the bare floor for several hours. Neither widow nor widower goes to the burial. Neither he nor she may perform any action, until ceremonially re-introduced into the actions of daily life by clan brothers or sisters of the deceased, who should be of the same sex. The bereft spouse is then given a cigarette, water, and porridge. He or she is shaven, given a fire-brand, water to wash, and an axe with which, grasping it together with a relative of the deceased, he or she feigns cutting wood. A similar performance is carried out with a hoe—and a pestle in the case of a widow.

The reason given for this ritual reintroduction into the activities of daily life is that such a person is overwhelmed by sorrow and is like one paralysed. Reintroduction breaks the apathy of sorrow. Another account has it that the neglect of this reintroduction would cause a chest disease in the surviving spouse.

After the funeral and the final meal, the female funeral friends sweep up the ashes where the mourners were sleeping outside at

DEATH, SUCCESSION AND INHERITANCE 127

numerous fires. The hut of the deceased is now called *cituuka*. It may be inhabited for some time by the remaining spouse if necessary, but later on it will be pulled down. Two reasons for this are given. People fear that it may harbour a shade or that its continued existence may make the clan relatives think of the deceased.

Funerary inversions

Funerary inversions are acts performed during funeral rites which are in reverse if compared with normal life. Among the Ambo, the mourners are shaven, especially the bereft spouse; all ornaments are taken off; the mourning spouse must lie on the bare ground and not on a mat. The bereft has the upper part of his or her body uncovered for some time. Mourners must sleep or rather watch outside by the fires during the whole night; the baskets of meal carried to the funeral must be covered, whereas the basket carried in connection with marriage is uncovered; the bier is taken through a hole made for that purpose in the wall at the back of the hut instead of carrying it out through the door; to fill the grave, the soil is pushed with the elbows and not with the hands; the funeral friend curses the corpse; the 'owner' of the dead, the closest matrilineal kinsman of the deceased, fumigates the buriers with his left hand; the mourners put on old clothes; at the funeral of the chief his wives (the widows) are locked up and receive very harsh treatment; they come out covered. At the release of the bereft spouse, white beads are tied round the left wrist.

Death and burial of a leper

The burial of a leper was conducted in a special manner. The lot of a leper is miserable and used to be even more so. In an advanced stage of the disease, he was excluded from the village community and lived at some distance in the bush. When he became very ill so that the end was in sight, he (or she) was transferred a mile or so away, and placed in a shelter, *mutanda* (*zaleba*, made of branches). When the leper died, the doorway was closed and the body was left there to decay. The ground round the shelter was scraped clean to prevent bushfires from reaching and destroying it. If a leper died near the village, he would be carried away and placed on a tree to be eaten by birds.

The prohibition against burying a leper rests on magical grounds.

128 SOCIAL AND RITUAL LIFE OF THE AMBO

It is believed that if the leper were buried, his leprosy would reappear in the matrilineage. The body must therefore be thrown away. Conventional burial conveys taking care of or preserving of the body. Leaving a leper's body to decay conveys the idea of wilful rejection.

Death and burial of a pregnant woman

When a pregnant woman undergoes a difficult delivery, and when in spite of all remedies and counteractions she dies, her relatives believe her husband to have killed their 'sister'. He is punished and rudely treated. No one hastens to reintroduce him into daily actions as described above. The matrilineage of the dead woman may be so angry that a pot is brought and the husband is insulted: 'You killed our "sister", take out the entrails, cook them and eat them' (eating a corpse is considered to be a sorcery practice).

The husband is prevailed upon to pierce the womb of his dead wife and thus to kill the unborn child. He does so with a rafter which is sharp-pointed. Widowers may even be required to cut the womb with a knife and to pierce the child. In 1947, a Christian refused to perform this act on the grounds of his religion, possibly as an excuse for evading a distasteful action. It is a harrowing ordeal for young men, very often completely innocent, and they recoil from it. A moderated rite is to drive a rafter into the grave mound and leave it there. The man, while driving the rafter into the grave mound, says: 'I have killed two cattle.' The brother of the widower may drive the rafter into the ground, when the widower is absent. The people present scatter out of horror.

I have not been able to obtain a satisfactory and clear explanation of the belief behind this rite. It is said that the husband has killed two people and so he must go through the ceremony of killing the child as well, though in a different way. It looks as though the rite is a punishment of the widower and secondarily a duty to the child so that it should not be buried alive. If it were, the wronged shade would take revenge.

Burial of a still-born child (kapopo)

The Ambo concept of *kapopo* has been discussed already (pages 77–8). When such a child dies, it is buried by a few old women, *mperafyala*. They carry the body to the burrow of an antbear, a

DEATH, SUCCESSION AND INHERITANCE 129

hollow in a tree or a hole in an anthill. They push in the corpse and block the opening with stones, sticks and earth. When coming back, they doctor themselves against 'the bad wind', *kabesya*, or, as others class it, 'a bad shade', the *cibanda*, of the foetus or the child. The shade is thought to infect those who come in contact with the dead body with a disease that causes a bursting of the soles of the feet or sores on them (pelagra?). This disease is also called *kapopo*.

There are various prescriptions to ward off the disease. For example, wood of *mwanya* and *iposo* trees is put into water, and the buriers and other villagers pulp it by treading. The infusion is slimy. Such medicine makes the feet slimy so that the shade and all bad forces cannot grip them but must let them slip away. This is the medicine of immunity, *miyanda ya ntesi*.

Husband and wife do not resume marital relations until after two months. After the first intercourse together they eat thick ordinary porridge without relish, but into which the above mentioned medicines have been put. Every villager touches a lump of this porridge.

The mother of the dead child has to observe the same prohibitions as after the ordinary birth of a child. The prohibitions refer to honey, fermented liquids, salt and tobacco which she may not pass to men and women. Here the prohibition is stricter than at menstruation and childbirth, because it refers even to women lest they bear similar children. She may not cook for men. The woman who breaks these taboos affects others, but she is immune herself from any bad effects of her actions. These prohibitions cease after the first marital act and subsequent doctoring.

Women capable of bearing children do not attend the burial of a still-born child lest they be affected magically and might themselves bear still-born children.

Burial of a childless woman

The woman who dies without bearing a child is buried with a sausage tree fruit tied on her back with the words: 'You have not left a child on earth (outside), this is your child,' *tawasyapo mwana panse, mwana wobe ngu*. This is to placate her shade and show it that her childlessness was not because she had been wronged.

Suicides and people struck by lightning are buried in the ordinary way.

130 SOCIAL AND RITUAL LIFE OF THE AMBO

Funeral beer

Funeral beer is soon arranged if food supplies are ample. Otherwise up to a year may pass before the relatives of the deceased can afford a beer festival. A funeral friend or the man who went into the grave puts grain into water. Then a woman funeral friend ululates. After a few days when the big beer pot, *citalo*, is taken off the fire again a woman ululates. The 'owner' of the dead takes the pot off the fire.

After a few days of brewing, the beer is in the stage of sweet beer, *fipele*. The man who buried the dead and who entered the grave takes some of it to the first resting place, *citusisyo*, and pours it there, saying: 'This beer, drink,' *bwalwa mbu, nweniko*.

In the evening, on the eve of the beer feast, the 'owner' of the dead is given a drinking calabash of beer to taste. In the morning he makes a dedication with the funeral beer. He takes some beer in the drinking calabash, spills some of it on the ground in the deceased's hut, saying: 'May this beer be good, may what is bad be good, let us come and amuse ourselves well, may people drink well'. He drinks the rest of the beer. Usually there is a great gathering of people. The atmosphere is festive. Guests sleep outside at fires. Dancing proceeds the whole night long just as was done during the funeral, but only the young people dance. The elders, inside a hut, play gourd drums and sing funeral songs.

One pot, the biggest beer pot, *nyina ya bwalwa, nacinya*, 'the mother of beer', is brought to the deceased's hut and there is drunk by the buriers, the grave diggers and those who carried the corpse. Prominent among these mourners are the funeral friends of the deceased, the *banungwe*. This pot is also called 'the pot of offering', *nongo ya cipupwilo*. These mourners drink the beer, dance and sing funeral songs in the hut. A woman funeral friend, who has swept and tidied the hut of the deceased and who swept away the ashes after the mourners on the day of the funeral, may also receive a pot of beer. The 'owner' of the dead gives small presents to those guests who have brought their gourd drums to the festival. The funeral friends who formerly were paid with beads and today with sixpences put them into the empty beer pot. The woman who brewed the beer collects the money.

At the end of the beer feast the weapons of the deceased are brought out and smeared with the dregs of beer to wash away the dirt of their former owner.

DEATH, SUCCESSION AND INHERITANCE 131

Redemption of the bereft

The beer feast always starts in the evening. It is only the funeral beer which requires the mourners to stay up overnight, *kucesya*. The next day in the morning the drums are silent and the guests are drunk. The whole day is given up to drinking. About three o'clock in the afternoon the beer feast is publicly closed for the guests.

The third day is the day of the left-over-beer, *bwalwa bwa mulala*. On this day after the funeral beer, inheritance and succession affairs are settled. Two or three beer pots from the previous day are left over for this occasion. Two clans, or, rather, two matrilineages of different clans, that of the deceased and of the bereft, squat in a circle, *kuikala citenge*, i.e. sit as in the village shelter. The question of death dues is fixed by negotiation, if there is no inheritance of the widow or succession by another 'sister' in place of the deceased. Nowadays the sororate or levirate is rarely carried out.

The bereft spouse with the help of his or her matrilineage pays death dues in order to be released from the shade of his or her former spouse, to whom he or she still belongs. For the Ambo the marriage bond endures beyond the grave. Therefore the bereft spouse must remain continent or sexually faithful to his or her dead spouse under pain of being afflicted with madness by the shade of the dead spouse. This taboo lasts up to the inheritance or redemption day. It is not a simple delivery of payment. The payment must be ritually clean and acceptable, acceptability being tested through divination. Death dues must take account of the number of children surviving, and so on. If a woman died and the man leaves many children, the children themselves will be a portion of the payment and he may have to pay as little as five shillings. A death after two months of married life does not entitle any dues to be received.

The death dues should be paid preferably at once. Then the 'owner' of the dead sleeps with the death dues. If he has no bad omens or bad dreams, the death dues are accepted, and thereafter the bereft spouse is free to marry again. With the dues a string of white beads is offered, which is especially exposed to divination. If they are damaged by rats, or if the basket in which they are laid is attacked by termites, it is a sign of refusal on the part of the shade. The bereaved person is then believed to have been unfaithful after the death of the spouse and payment may be increased. Dreams are also decisive. After the acceptance of death dues a 'sister' of the deceased ties white beads on the left wrist of the widow or widower

132 SOCIAL AND RITUAL LIFE OF THE AMBO

with the words: 'We release you (chase you), may you look for another spouse, you may put on a wristlet yourself and marry', *twanutanda ufwaye mwanalume umbi ufwike rusambo mwine upwe.* Should the matrilineage of the dead woman harbour great grievance against the widower, the child of the latter is used as an intermediary to bind the beads. This is usually done after a death in childbirth.

Inheritance of the widow

After the death of a man, his 'brother' may inherit the widow if he is willing and she agrees. On the first day of the funeral beer, i.e. on the eve of the drinking day, the widow is led to the hut to sleep with the heir. After the couple have slept they remain in the hut for the day. Porridge is cooked by *nacimbela*, the puberty ceremony instructress. On the third day a fowl is killed. The instructress grasps the relish pot in which the fowl is put, the man touches the hand of the instructress and the woman touches the hand of the man. The same is done with salt and porridge. The porridge and fowl is served to both matrilineages, that of the heir and that of the widow.

In the porridge are mixed medicines (e.g. one made from the *cisoko* tree) against madness. The widow, as a sign of mourning, was prohibited until this moment from going to the kitchen. By this ritual touching of the relish pot, she is allowed to start cooking again without being exposed to developing a chest disease. If she had once sworn that she would never agree to be inherited, she drinks the medicine of *coni* against swearing.

When the widow or widower enter upon a new marriage after being redeemed, they are also doctored against madness. The man or woman marrying a widow or widower need not be doctored.

Succession to headmanship

The funeral of a headman is more ostentatious, and many people also come for the funeral beer. The choosing and installation of the headman takes place on the third day of the funeral beer. He is seated on a mat spread in the village. The weapons, *fyensyo*, 'which the dead had used', his spear, fish-spear, axe and gun are handed to the heir. A woman representative of the matrilineage hands the gun to the heir, saying: 'You have been given, this is your gun. Guard it as the owner guarded it, and use it as your guardian had used it'.

DEATH, SUCCESSION AND INHERITANCE 133

The various 'brothers' of the deceased used to lay claims to his wives. One would say: 'I would like to inherit this wife.' Then someone says: 'This is the owner of the village.' All present say: 'Wait, let him agree.' The candidate accepts the choice. The elders of the village and friends lay down presents, tobacco, axes, money. They say: 'You are So-and-so, thus giving to him the name of the deceased headman, which is that also of the village. The elders and neighbouring headmen instruct the new headman, while giving presents, to conduct himself with dignity, *kuikala ne buntu*, and to have 'the heart of humanity', *kuba ne mtima wa buntu*. 'They [the headmen] do not listen to the gossiping of the young people in the village,' *tabakutika-kutika mu musi ku banice*. 'They do not listen to the gossiping of the women,' *taboumfwa fya banakasi*. He is told 'to have one heart only, the same which your brother had', *kuikala ne mutima umo umo wenka wapintile mukwanu*. ('One heart' means to keep one's word: 'two hearts' means to be of changeable, deceitful and unsteady character.)

After the offering of presents accompanied by these instructions, the headman is led to a hut to be hidden from the public. Whoever wants to see him is expected to give a small present.

Final funeral beer

After some time another beer feast is arranged in order to bring back the shade of the dead to the village, *kubwesya mupasi ku musi*. This rite does not differ from that of the funeral beer except for the address to the shade, said at the libation: 'You who have died, we give you this beer, that you may come and dwell with us in the village', *mwebo mwalifwile tukomupela bwalwa ubo mwise kuikala nafwe pa musi*.

VII. RELIGION AND DIVINATION

The supreme being

THE Ambo believe in the existence of a Supreme Being, whom they call *Lesa*. He is the creator, *Mulenga*, of everything, and master of atmospheric phenomena, particularly those connected with rain. Hence he is the lifegiver, since food cultivation and growth in general are made possible only by rain. In speech *Lesa* is identified with these phenomena. Thus 'it rains' may be expressed, *yaloka* (*mfula*), '(rain) has fallen' or *waloka* (*Lesa*) 'he has fallen'. Often Lesa is directly expressed as lightning, *Lesa wapena*, 'Lesa is lightning'. One also hears the expressions 'Lesa has thundered', *Lesa wabuluma*, or 'Lesa has struck', *Lesa waseluka* or *wasika* referring to a thunderbolt. Lesa is visualized by the Ambo as having an enormous tail loaded with fire. When he wants to strike with a thunderbolt, he swings his tail like a crocodile. It is believed that this tail is also in appearance not unlike that of the crocodile. It is also believed that a thunderbolt once struck a bamboo, split it, and that some of Lesa's tail was left in the bamboo. People who steal are thought to be struck by lightning in punishment.[1] The emphasis is, however, not because of an idea that Lesa's work is identified with lightning but rather that the strength of the curse of the wronged person magically or automatically causes lightning to strike the wrongdoer. This is consonant with Ambo ideas of Lesa having created the universe, but then having ceased taking any specific interest in it. Despite this indifference to the world's wants in general, however, one more reference is made to him in everyday affairs. People who would dare to laugh at cripples are warned: 'Lesa changes fortune,' *Lesa ni malumalu*.[2] Lastly, it must also be noted that animal pests by which many animals were

---

[1] The stars are thought to be fires in Lesa's village. The few Ambo names for stars are *kapompwe*, Orion, from its resemblance to a battle-axe; *ntanda*, Venus, and *mulalafuti*, the milky way. *Tulimi* are the pleiads, the gardeners, because they appear when it is time to plant crops. It may also be noted that the moon is held to be a living being (though with no supernatural functions) who is both born and dies every month. The sun only faints and then rises again, and it has legs because it walks.

[2] *Malu*, ideophone, recognizable in *kualuka*, to change.

RELIGION AND DIVINATION

135

wiped out are ascribed to Mulenga, as well as human epidemics of smallpox.

According to Ambo standards there is aloofness, distrust and suspicion bordering on hostility, between clan-strangers, this being especially true in the past; a similar attitude of aloofness is therefore held to exist between the shade of a deceased member of an alien clan and a living person. The same relationship exists between man and Lesa. Hence a direct prayer or offering to him was not possible because, as an old informant appropriately expressed it, 'nobody is of Lesa's clan'. On the other hand, offerings were made to the chiefs' shades by sons—but more particularly grandsons of the chiefs—which is in harmony with the familiarity in the social relations of people of alternate generations. Though Lesa controlled the most important thing in the life of the Ambo, rain, he could not be approached directly. Offerings and prayers for rain were addressed to the shades of chiefs, even as if, it is clear from the wording of prayer, they controlled rain. This seeming contradiction is explained by the Ambo saying that as the chiefs' shades 'are with Lesa' so they are able to intervene with him. Moreover, chiefs' shades are invoked also in their capacity as 'the owners of the bush', *bene ba mpanga*, or 'the owners of the country', *bene ba calo*.

Another name given to the Ambo Supreme Being is *Cuuta*, for he 'embraces the whole world', *kukumana calo conse*. The name is derived from *kuuta = kufwika ku calo*, 'to be heard in the world' (cf. *buta*, the bow) according to one informant. Others, however, consider this name to be of foreign origin.

As the Ambo deity, under the name of *Cuuta*, is thought of as omnipresent, he is invoked in oaths: 'Though the case is apparently against me, I am not guilty; Cuuta has seen me; it will come out, if I am guilty, let me die,' *nangu kakosele nebo sikwetepo cebo; alimbwene Cuuta, kulibwenesya nga nali na cebo ningafwa.* 'By Cuuta, I have not taken that little thing,' *Cuuta, nsibulilepo ako kantu.* More often, especially with school children, just *Lesa* or *na Lesa* is used in swearing.

Lucele is another name for Lesa, but some say that *Lucele* is not the Supreme Being but another supernatural being. *Lucele* is the Lord of Life. 'When a grown up person or a child is ill, and nearly dies but recovers, it is said: nobody is killed for the sake of Lucele. Lesa does not kill', *muntu mukulu nangwati mwaice akolwala, uli pepi kufwa, kabuka, kapuluka, pano ati Lucele tepailwa, Lesa tepaya.*

136   SOCIAL AND RITUAL LIFE OF THE AMBO

Similarly, a failure of sorcery is ascribed to the work of Lucele.
Though a sorcerer comes, and arranges that a person should die yet
Lesa may refuse: do not kill that person', *nangwati mfwiti yaisa,
yabona muntu ati afwe, Lesa akana: wipaya muntu uyu*. But from
these quotations we see that the names Lucele and Lesa may be
used indiscriminately and equivalently. It is also said of Lucele as
of Lesa that nothing is difficult for him. 'Whatever he wishes he
says: let me do it.'

A different view is that Lucele does not live with Lesa, but on
earth, a great being, invisible, keeping close to water. Should great
rains come, and the streams be flooded, people speak of the water
of Lucele: *ndunduma, icama* (*yamba* = flood). And in this connection the version preferred by some is that their heaven is not
beyond the sky, but in the depths of the earth: 'Is it not in the
grave dug in the earth that man is buried?'

The Ambo say that their knowledge of the world hereafter was
brought by an intrepid and very fortunate antbear hunter, who
crept down into the antbear's burrow and reached the abode of the
departed. He saw there a big village and gardens, where these
underground dwellers who marry like people on earth live in great
bliss. There is no game but only antbears, *mpendwa*. Does not this
animal live in the depths of the earth? A relish is fish. Again the
proof is simple: rivers flow deep and fish live in rivers. Other
information about the life hereafter was brought by a person who
died but who was not admitted into Lesa's abode, so he returned to
earth. He then related that he had seen a great village. Yet another
version begins that this is only a story. A man was hunting antbears.
He speared one but it ran off with the spear still plunged into it.
The spear having been a borrowed one, the hunter was forced by
its owner to fetch it back to him. In this way the hunter reached the
underground world; what he found out there is described in the
preceding account. None of these stories, however, is generally
believed.

Some beliefs about Lesa and heaven may be gathered from old
funeral songs. For instance

Chinkonko kwa Lesa	There is bliss in Lesa's abode.
Balokutwa: kalimo (or *kabale*)	They are pounding a little meal.

When a traveller approaches a village and hears a little stamping of
grain, it is a sign that all is well there. Shots, drums and songs, on

RELIGION AND DIVINATION 137

the other hand, may announce a funeral. (*Cinkonko*, onomatopoeic of pounding, is an expression of bliss; *kalimo*, means a little work, and *kabale* a small dish [of meal].)

Mwayumfwa mitungu ya pansi	Have you heard the gourd drums
Yalila bwino;	They sound fine;
Kwa Lesa takuya	Who goes to Lesa
Babwela	Does not return
Kwa Bilinkita.	To the village of Bilinkita.

(*Mitungu* is a Lamba word, used here in poetry for the Ambo *malimba*. *Bilinkita* is a name, signifying a well-known person.)

Nine wabona Lesa.	It is on me Lesa has cast his eyes,
Nine wakupaila membya.	It is me Lesa has struck with his rods,
Kasinga ka mu'munda;	A little stump in the garden;
Napalanya ni mama.	I likened it to my mother,
Naye Lesa alasimbanya.	But even her, Lesa has smashed.

(*M'munda* is a foreign word [Nsenga] used here for the Ambo *mu mabala*. *Alasimbanya* is a poetical expression for the common *alalufyanya*.)

These songs are traditional, and do not seem to reflect Christian teaching. Older people do not sing Christian songs, especially at funerals, and it may be noted that Christians use the term *Mulungu* for God, borrowed from Nyanja. The songs imply that the shade of a deceased goes to Lesa. The Ambo state explicitly that the shades of departed chiefs are with Lesa. On the other hand, chiefs' shades are turned into lions which roam the bush, and offerings are made to them in their country.

Particularly at the inauguration of a new village site, the shades of people who formerly lived nearby (the Ambo move in an area they believe to have been long and extensively settled) are approached to see if they will allow the building of a new village. The shades persecute a woman who has had sexual intercourse in the bush because their graves are there, and thus in this case also the presence of the shades is accepted in some way at the place of their burials.

It is evidence therefore that although the Ambo belief about the place of the shades is anything but definite, there is some delimitation to be considered. Of the funeral songs cited above, the second

138   SOCIAL AND RITUAL LIFE OF THE AMBO

states that a shade goes to Lesa (and the two last ones convey a belief of death coming from Lesa, who acts harshly).

The Ambo differentiate between various shades, *mipashi* (plur.). The 'nearest' in which they are interested are the shades of the dead members of one's minor matrilineage and guardian shades, who may be from either one's matri- or patrikin. Relatives other than matrikin do not make offerings, they watch and 'only listen', *bakokutika likoso*, i.e. they are allowed to be present but do not actively participate. Approach to one's kin and guardian shades, which is private, is to be distinguished from that of a public kind to departed chiefs' shades.

Offerings and prayers to guardian shades may be made privately and done by individuals. There are also communal rituals, if we may include in these offerings to guardians made by a person on behalf of another member of his matrikin. Old women, *mpelafyala*, take part in both kinds of ceremony, to scrape the sacred spot of grass at the beginning, and to ululate at the end. Young women take active parts only in the former kind. There is no prohibition against their attending public offerings: but it is said they have nothing to do there.

Divination

Dedication both to guardian shades, whether confirmatory or because of afflictions caused by outside revengeful shades, and to chiefs' shades, is bound up with divination. Divination is necessary to ascertain the will of a shade, and to determine the type of propitiation required. The supernatural world with which the Ambo can deal through divination is composed of the shades of one's kin (and own clansmen), of members of alien clans, and of sorcerers. The scope of divination, however, is confined to death, illness, bad luck in hunting, the withholding of rain, difficult delivery, and the naming of a child. By sending these misfortunes a shade may show its anger at being neglected and its need of an offering. But equally misfortune may be caused by a living agent expressing resentment against the person affected. Divination may also reveal certain other specific demands of the shades: that tradition should be upheld, for instance, and that the well-being of the ancestors' general interests should be continued. Thus, a shade's name is bestowed on a new-born child, a shade's wife is inherited, the pottery-making done by a shade in her lifetime is continued, hunting is perpetuated,

RELIGION AND DIVINATION 139

sorcery practised by a shade is continued, and so on. Divination may show that affliction is caused by a shade of an alien clan, for example, avenging something by causing new born children to die. The placating of alien shades before building a proposed fish weir does not require divination.

From these remarks it is clear that Ambo attitudes to the world of the shades are non-ethical. A man is not punished by them for his own misdeeds, if they do not imply neglect of offerings to the shades. He may even be directed by a shade to practise sorcery, but this should not be misinterpreted since Ambo sorcery is anti-social only when it causes death in the matrikin. The social context of offerings to the shades is clear in that only matrilineally related people take part in dedications.

Diviners

Many people, men and women, divine by means of an axe handle, an art they learn from others and in which they gain additional confidence by being treated with an appropriate medicine. Axe handle diviners are called *bankonko* (plur.), rather disparagingly, from the onomatopeoic *nkonko*, the sound of striking the handle with the fingers at the start of divination. Diviners of this lowest type are very common: they are consulted over many minor ailments such as the cause of headache, simple chest trouble, or problems in connection with the naming of a child. They are not sufficiently expert to be consulted in matters where evil spirits (*fibanda*) are concerned, in the killing of new-born children or in death-dealing sorcery.

The higher grade of diviners is composed of professional medicine men called *ŋanga*, though the former kind may also be so called. Their honorific title for professional diviners is *balaye* (plur.). The *balaye* do not confine themselves to the axe handle, but use more complex divining apparatus and methods of various types, which have often been acquired from beyond the boundaries of the tribe, whence, indeed, the *ŋanga* themselves may have come. The *balaye* are competent to deal with bad shades and sorcerers; they can treat women so that they may bear 'children of leaves'. (*See* Chapter IV.) They have a vast knowledge of herbs, and are in possession of rare *fisimba*, ingredients mostly of animal origin which are added to various medicines. The essential character of the training of the *ŋanga* is its great practicality. An apprentice accompanies his

140   SOCIAL AND RITUAL LIFE OF THE AMBO

maître on his tours throughout the land as an assistant. From fees received for his diagnosis and medicines, the diviner doles out some remuneration to his pupil. When I first arrived in Ambo land, in 1938, the client paid a token fee, *lusomo*, a sixpence. If, despite divination and treatment, the patient dies, no fees are paid. Some *bankonko* do not accept even the first payment. Today, after a successful divining, the patient when he recovers will pay the diviner something in the order of ten shillings. For treating 'the children of leaves' *balaye* are paid a larger amount when the children are several years old.

Divination techniques

In divination by axe handle a diviner takes an axe, heats the head of its handle in a fire to make it 'hot' or 'active' (*kupia*), spits on the handle and touches its head with the two scars on his own fore-head—the scars which mark every diviner where medicines were applied to ensure his expertise. Before he lays down the axe, and knocks with his bent fingers against its handle, the diviner touches his chest with the axe and also his hand, between the finger and the thumbs, where incisions were made and medicine inserted in his apprenticeship. He then lays the axe down on the ground next to him, with its head pointing towards him, addressing it thus: 'You are the prow of the canoe, you do not forget the landing-place; you are the cutter which cuts one question.'[1] He puts the question: 'Does the grandmother want beer?' He moves the handle towards himself, head-end first. If the handle slides easily, the answer is in the negative. Next he puts questions about other relatives of his patient, eliminating first those of one sex, then those of the other. He may then ask whether the illness comes from a bad shade, or from the patient himself. When in answer to one of the questions, the handle sticks fast to the ground, the diviner pronounces: *Wasumina*, 'it has agreed'.

Although Ambo, when asked about the source of a diviner's pronouncement, reply that it is their (the diviner's) guardian shade, it may be inferred that, guided by the dynamism of the diviner's medicine, the apparatus gives the answer in its own right. In the technique just described, the imitative actions aim at the awakening

[1] A splinter of a canoe prow is used in the divining medicine so that the handle may have the same quality as the prow of the canoe, to find the right place of landing, meaning the right answer to a question. To cut a question means to give an unequivocal answer.

RELIGION AND DIVINATION

of the divining medicines, and the questions are addressed always to the apparatus and not to the diviner's guardian spirit. The symbolism of divining medicines also points to the conclusion that it is the divining apparatus, constrained by the properties of the divining medicine, that is the source of the diviner's pronouncement.

A diviner may address his questions to a calabash adorned with red beads which he calls 'the chief wife', (*mukolo*), in which it is believed there is a spirit of a murdered person who speaks. Ventriloquism is necessary for this. Equally important is the use of a gourd which has been smeared with medicinal leaves, contains medicines and is covered with a pot. Questions are addressed to the gourd during the smearing. If the juice of the smeared leaves dries quickly, the patient will die; if the juice dries slowly, the patient is doctored and there is hope that he will recover.

Ngulu is a small bead having edges, which is put into a pot. The diviner shakes a rattle and calls upon those present, one by one, to take out the bead. They do not find it but when the *ŋanga* looks for the bead himself he reveals it hidden in someone's cheek. This person is then declared to be a sorcerer. In another technique, a string two and a half feet long is stretched between two sticks three inches high, which are fixed in the ground. A small horn is threaded on the string. If, when asked a question, it moves as if dancing, the answer is in the affirmative. For a negative reply, the horn does not move. This method is a higher grade of divination than the other ones used, because it can answer questions about the work of bad shades and about sorcery.

Another divining method is by 'lots' (*fipa*). In the morning, a man goes to the bush and digs a hole roughly six inches in diameter and of the same depth. He places two sticks on either side of the hole. Beyond the sticks on the right hand side he spills some meal; on their left hand side, he spills some red powder. Should any of the red powder fall into the hole, death will occur. The diviner addresses the sticks: 'You *fipa*, show us whether you fall into the hole where you are with meal that we know there is no death. If you, *fipa* with the red powder, fall into the hole, tell us if there is death.'

Another method of divination involves finding the nest of the *lububi* spider. At the sides of the nest, the diviner places sticks, on the right a stick for health, on the left a stick for death. The spider is addressed as *musilimfumu*, 'the chief of earth'. If it moves the stick of death, death will occur. The address is: 'Now, O chief of

142 SOCIAL AND RITUAL LIFE OF THE AMBO

earth, we have come to you, tell us. At the village So-and-so is ill. If there is health for him, tell us!' This procedure may be used in connection with the naming of children, sickness, and for finding sorcerers. *Lububi* spiders are used in divination in other ways. Black ants are also important. A diviner chews medicine leaves into pulp, which he places at the entrance to a nest of black ants. He addresses them: 'You, chiefs of earth, show us, if there is health for So-and-so, if he will get up.' If the ants cover the pulp with earth, it is a sign of approaching death; if they push away the pulp from the hole, it is a sign that health will come.

Lastly, *kasimwengwe* divining must be mentioned. A very small gourd dipper is balanced on the ground. A duiker's horn containing medicines is placed in the dipper, resting on the edge of the opening. The diviner blows into a round *nsense* fruit shell with a pebble inside while he asks a question such as: 'Is it chiefs' shades who withhold the rain?' If the horn stands up in the dipper the answer is in the affirmative and the diviner calls out the names of the chiefs. To one name again the horn stands erect. 'Why does the chief withhold the rain? Is it the beer?' Perhaps the horn again stands erect. The question is answered, the oracle has spoken.

Divining medicines

The efficacy of divining apparatus is through medicines. In divining by *munyeŋu* ants, *musolo*, the leaves are used. This tree has many seeds, therefore it does not 'lie' but truly bears fruit. To the Ambo, a barren tree is a lying tree. Hence the fruitful *musolo* becomes the symbol of divining truth.

In divining by the axe handle, a medicine made from *musundu*, the leech, is used. As the leech sticks to the body so the handle may stick to the ground. A splinter from the prow of a canoe, *kasanga ka bwato*, is used also because the canoe never misses the landing spot. So the axe handle will always reach a true oracle. The wood and leaves of the tree *ndale* are used. *Ndale* means 'let me lie down'. The meaning is that the divining handle will stick tight to the ground at the right moment, thus indicating the oracle. The medicine is rubbed into incisions between the thumb and the finger.

The diviner is forbidden to eat the mushroom, *busepa*, which grows on a rotting fallen tree. If that were done, the medicine would resemble the mushroom, and the handle would lie down uselessly as the rotten tree does.

RELIGION AND DIVINATION 143

For divining by the *lububi* spider, another medicine containing the *ndale* tree, the wood and the leaves, is used so that the divining sticks will be laid by the *lububi* to indicate the truth.

Beer offerings (bwalwa bwa mupashi) *in private contexts*

Should a man or a woman fall ill, first the appropriate medicines are applied. If these have no effect a supernatural agency is suspected to be the cause and a diviner is consulted. He is either visited, or called to the patient's bedside. Very commonly he announces that the illness is due to a shade of a close matri-kinsman who is offended because beer has not been dedicated to him for a long time.

In this case, the sick person ritually puts the first handful of sorghum into a pot of water to begin the brew saying: 'This beer we soak, let us see if I shall walk in health, without being sick again,' *bwalwa tukosabika, tubone ŋende makosa te kulwala libili.* The sick person claps his hands and one of the clan women, or a female funeral friend present, ululates. A wristlet of white beads is tied round the left wrist of the sick person by a matrilineally related kinswoman as a sign of the dedication to be offered. There was also an old custom at this stage, which has been reported to me but apparently never witnessed even by the old people, that when the diviner had pronounced the cause a clanswoman of the sick person took some water in her mouth and spurted it (*kufubata*) on the chest and the back of the patient saying: 'If it is you, guardian shade, show it,' *kani ni mwe, mboswa, abwenesye.*

On the morning of the beer-drinking, a selected pot of beer is brought into the house of the sick man for the offering, *nongo ya cipupwilo.* Then a clan relative takes the shade calabash (*see* below) of the sick person, if he already has one, with his own and pours some of the dedicated beer into both of them, also giving some beer from the pot containing the offering to the invalid. The latter pours it into his or her shade calabash or—if he has none—at his bed head, saying: 'This is the beer you asked for, we have brewed it for you, we shall see if I shall be in good health and not be sick again,' *bwalwa mbu mwalifwaile, twalikumbile, tubone ayende makosa, tekulwalapo libili.*[1] The sick person drinks some beer from the shade calabash and claps his hands. His funeral friends then finish the beer in the dedication pot.

[1] If the offering is made to a shade other than of the guardian class, the beer should not be poured into the shade calabash.

144 SOCIAL AND RITUAL LIFE OF THE AMBO

A person must obtain a shade calabash if a diviner indicates that sickness or childlessness, for instance, is caused by a shade wanting a calabash to be dedicated to it, *cipesi* or *mutesi wa mupasi*. A person can have only one such calabash, which is dedicated only to a guardian shade, and not to any other, according to common opinion. The practice of maintaining calabash shrines, however, if they may be called such, seems almost to have died out. To the shade calabash belongs a dipper, a gourd-shell with a natural handle. An apparently typical calabash was some six inches in diameter with an opening say two and a half inches in diameter. It was adorned with a string of white beads put around the opening, or across or inside it, and kept under the bed of its owner, hung over his doorway, or in a *cisansa*, a three-forked pole set in the ground inside the hut.

The making of a spirit calabash is connected with an offering of beer such as has just been described. When the grain is being soaked in water in preparation for beer-making, the calabash is dipped into the mixture, to the accompaniment of deep *kukambila*, the clapping of hands of the gathered matrilineal kinspeople, by one of them who prays: 'If it is you, his guardian shade, who makes the child sick, may it get well, we brew beer for you.' After this, women ululate, and the calabash is lifted out. This rite is performed at the bedside of the sick person.

When the brewing of the beer to be offered to the shade has reached the last stage, one pot is brought to the bedside of the patient. His shade calabash has been placed near his bed, and some beer is drawn from it with a dipper. The officiant at the ceremony, who must be a clansman of the patient, sits *bukunda*, on the ground with legs bent at the knee and crossed, or if a woman, kneels sitting on her heels. The officiant says a prayer similar to that at the soaking of the grain for brewing. Those present clap their hands and the women ululate. The beer is poured into the spirit calabash and some of it is drunk by the patient. The officiant then places a string of white beads in the calabash. The remaining beer is drunk by the attending clansmen, clanswomen and funeral friends.

On the occasion of any offering to a shade the sick person must be given a string of white beads which he or she ties round his left wrist. It is explained that, except apparently in cases of dire necessity, neither parent of the afflicted can offer to the shade because this would entail making this present to the patient, yet to do so would not be in accordance with the respective statuses in Ambo

RELIGION AND DIVINATION 145

society of parents and their children. If the sick person has a shade calabash, the present of beads goes to it rather than to the person himself, but it is against custom for parents to make a present even to their children's shade calabashes.

Should the owner of the shade calabash be far from home, for example in town in search of work, he alone may make an offering to his guardian shade. He squats *bukunda*, and claps his hands, saying 'give us strength on our journey', *batupe makosa mu bulwendo bwesu*. He drops a string of white beads into the calabash. Afterwards, as in his own village, his sister or brother may wear them round the left wrist. In another private or individual ceremony, first fruits are offered to the shade of the calabash. The procedure, particularly among the more pious, if they have a shade calabash shrine, includes the chewing of new grain and then the spitting of it into the calabash, praying: 'This food, eat your shades and likewise we shall also eat,' *filyo mfi mipasi lyeniko, nafwe tulyeko*. He claps his hands, some clap before prayer also.

Approaches which may be either communal or individual to the shades in connection with hunting, I have already described elsewhere (Stefaniszyn, 1951). A hunter has a hunting guardian shade in addition to his namesake guardian shade. Formerly hunting offerings were made at the 'pole of trophies', *cinsanda*, a three-forked pole driven into the ground in front of the hunter's hut. On the pole, which was adorned with trophy heads and horns, a calabash with hunting medicines was kept, lodged between the three prongs.

Here it must suffice to give a brief summary of this hunter's ritual. But first it should be said that a hunter's guardian shade is either the relative from whom he inherited his gun or simply any dead relative who was a successful hunter himself, his father, a maternal uncle, a brother or a maternal grand-uncle.

Dedications to the shades connected with hunting are both communal and individual. Communal rituals are made by a village through two or three elders to a matrilineal ancestor, who was a hunter of renown. The elders offer flour with an ordinary prayer at a sacred spot, such as under a big tree, where there may have been shade huts in olden times. The headman may say 'If it is you who lie in this bush, we have come to seek relish'. Such a communal offering is arranged before a communal hunt or a fishing expedition.

Before joining the expedition, in addition each hunter makes an individual sacrifice to his own hunting guardian shade at his pole of trophies. He spills some flour at his bed-head and places there a

146   SOCIAL AND RITUAL LIFE OF THE AMBO

string of white beads, with the same prayer he uses before going to hunt on his own. If he receives no adverse sign during sleep, and the offerings are found intact in the morning, he joins the expedition, for his shade approves of it. Immediately before setting out to hunt, the hunter prays to his hunting guardian shade: 'Light up my eyes that I may see well where I am going.'

If a hunter repeatedly fails to kill game, he must consult a diviner, who may discover that some of the dead clan relatives, the hunter's namesake guardian shade or the hunter's father's shade is demanding a beer offering. Beer may be brewed to placate any dead clan relative who died suddenly or mysteriously without having recourse to divination first. Sometimes divination may show that bad fortune is caused by a living person. Perhaps the sister or the mother-in-law of the hunter bears him a grudge, because she had received too little meat from his last expedition. She is then told of her sin, whereupon she must confess and stop grumbling. However, for the shade, beer is brewed. When the hunter comes home from the diviner, his mother or his sister throws meal on the trigger of his gun, saying: 'If it is you, So-and-so, please show us the red thing' (viz.: flesh, meat). Grain is soaked for the beer. The hunter throws the first handful of grain into the pot of water saying: 'This is the beer we soak, show us if it is you that has become angry. Give us the red thing.' Rituals then follow as described for other offerings.

Dreams

While somebody is asleep, his or her shade (*mupasi*) may wander about and see many things which are hidden from him while awake. People use such expressions about dreams as: 'My head was playing, the shade was wandering,' *mutwi wanji wasala, musimu ukoyenda.* When a person dreams that he flies he is thought really to fly to God. A person who has his legs bent in sleep cannot fly in dreams, because a bent body is like one in fetters; it is not free.

If someone falls asleep and dies, it is proof that he went straight to God and has remained there.

In time of sleep the shade wanders and is in communication with other shades, of living and deceased relatives. Sorcerers at work may be recognized easily and be told of medicines by the shades.

Dreams are of the same significance as omens and divination. They are a bridge, a link with the supernatural world. Most dreams

RELIGION AND DIVINATION 147

are said to come from one's guardian shade. When awake, a man has to act as he has been taught to do in dreams.

Dreams are specially used to ascertain the will of the local shades in the case of building a new village, and to discover the will of the shade of a deceased spouse as to the acceptance of death dues from the bereft spouse.

To dream of beer means rain. To dream of a beer party means a funeral, because a beer party reminds one of funeral beer.

To dream of a bushbuck, *nkwiwa*, means a fall, from *kuwa*, to fall. The dream is interpreted as referring to death or sickness.

Dreaming of birds is a good omen. Birds seem to mean good shades.

To dream of a lion is a good sign, because the lion is the equivalent of a chief. Chief Mboloma is turned into a lion after his death.

The leopard is called a bad spirit, *cibanda*, therefore to dream of him is unpleasant.

To dream of meal or of porridge means a funeral, as people come to a funeral with meal, and there is a large amount of porridge cooked for guests.

To dream of game is a favour of one's guardian shade.

Duiker and hare are good omens in dreams. The duiker is called *insya*, which is reminiscent of *kusya*, to leave; therefore bad things will leave the dreamer alone.

To dream of fire means that sorcery is at work. Fire is connected with sorcery.

To dream of a great amount of tobacco means a funeral because much tobacco is distributed to people who dance *cinsengwe* at the funeral beer party. A small amount of tobacco is equal to a piece of meat. It is a good omen.

To dream of water or rain means tears or a funeral. To dream of a crowd of silent people means a funeral, people gathered together for burial. To dream of people digging a pit silently also means a funeral, as do dreams of falling into a pit.

To dream of a sick man in black calico with his head covered means that he will die.

To dream of your dead wife becoming angry means that you have killed her. The same holds good of a woman dreaming her dead husband is angry.

To dream of a dead man or people taking a corpse out of a house means that someone will die.

If on a journey one dreams that one's wife is fat, then she is very

148 SOCIAL AND RITUAL LIFE OF THE AMBO

ill and on the point of death. If one dreams that one's wife is thin and emaciated, then she is in good health.

To dream about a gun is *malyo*, and means good luck in hunting. To dream that you have killed a man means that, if you go in the bush, you will kill game.

If a man involved in a court case dreams that he is bound, the next day he should run away.

If you often dream that you converse with children, it means that somebody's familiars, *tuyowela*, are after you. Go and seek medicine from elders.

A dream while on a journey that one's wife is flirting with some-one else, means adultery has been committed.

To dream of honey means tears at a funeral. To dream that one has found young bees only without honey means good luck in hunting, *malyo*.

To dream of a mat means a funeral. A person dies lying on a mat; that mat is folded with him in it and carried to the grave. To dream of a shut or derelict house also means death. To see vultures in the village in a dream means death.

To dream of forked poles is a good omen, because their colour is either red or white; both colours are good. Red means meat, white means a good shade.

If you dream that you agree with your wife, you will divorce her; if you dream you quarrel with her, you will agree.

To dream about one's mother is to dream of an aggrieved shade. You should look for medicines against such a dream. To dream of one's father, on the other hand, is a good dream; your father has come to show you medicines. It is also auspicious to dream of a good-natured dead man.

To dream of a bad-tempered dead man means medicine has not succeeded in appeasing an aggrieved shade. The man who has such dreams has killed the dead man, and he will be killed by the shade.

To dream of an unknown man is a dream of sorcery. To dream that one lies on white ants means death. To dream one has been bitten by a snake or that one's brother was so bitten, is a bad omen.

To dream of crops standing in the fields is a good omen of food. Dreams about porridge while on a journey mean hunger. To dream of eating porridge amidst a crowd, on the other hand, means a funeral.

If you dream that you are hungry, you will eat. If you dream that you cut yourself, don't go to hoe that day.

RELIGION AND DIVINATION 149

When you dream of your dead brother, it is your good luck to see your dead brother. If he asked you for beer, you need not go to a diviner but may begin straightaway to brew beer for him.

Omens

An omen is an event, as the Ambo understand it, which is against the common run in nature. It may be a perfectly natural phenomenon but seldom observed. A big tree in the bush suddenly falls in sight of a passing Ambo. Then the Ambo asks himself: 'Why did this tree wait to fall until I came by?' These out-of-the-common events are arranged by the guardian shade of the person who sees the omen. A rule for interpreting bad omens is that the person who saw the omen will not die but his clansman or clanswoman will.

Good omens, *mupasi wa malyo*, are signs presumably coming from good shades; in hunting, from the hunting guardian shade. Though the good omen is a sign coming from a benevolent shade, the good omen is also termed *mupasi*, the good shade. This may be compared with *Lesa*, God, giving rain, but rain being also *Lesa*; in other words the effect is equated with the cause.

A chameleon digging a hole forebodes death. This animal is a symbol of death according to tradition; its digging a hole means the digging of a grave. It is a bad omen, *mbiko*. Others may be listed:

It is a bad omen to see chameleons copulating, or to see a puff adder running or a python moving fast. Such actions are against the natural habits of these animals. It is also ill-fated for a man to see a python for the first time when he is grown up, or to see the honey of *cipasi* bees for the first time.

A rabbit running away, then stopping and gazing is a strange event, because rabbits seldom behave in this way. It is also a bad omen to see a small, quick variety of lizard, *kabandami*, digging a hole to lay eggs. This quick lizard should be seen always running. Some, however, deny that to see *kabandami* laying eggs is a bad omen; they argue that *kabandami* laying eggs is not an uncommon event.

Seeing a rabbit dead but with its head intact is a bad omen. If the rabbit had been killed by an animal, the head should have been eaten. The same belief is held about the guinea fowl and the genet.

A lourie flying from the east, crossing one's path, and then flying to the west is a bad omen, because to the west go the dead. The lourie is chosen, probably because it is red, the symbol of blood

150 SOCIAL AND RITUAL LIFE OF THE AMBO

and flesh. Also manslayers were adorned with red feathers of the lourie.

A ground hornbill crossing one's path, going west and beginning to cry is a bad omen, because its cry is mournful.

A civet crying, when being killed, is a bad sign.

Maggots found in the excrement of a man forebode misfortune because it is natural for them to be in meat.

To hear a *masombwe* insect (the biggest praying mantis) buzzing is bad. Black mambas seen fighting is a bad omen, because they do not usually do so. A hyena excreting in the village is a bad omen. The hyena being regarded as the envoy of a sorcerer, the village will scatter or else be treated with medicines.

The twitching of eyebrows is a sign of coming tears.

To see a blind worm is bad, because it is seldom seen. And to see a jackal crying in the village is a bad sign, because it seldom happens.

A cockerel cackling like a hen is bad; it must be killed and eaten.

The wall of a grave falling in is a bad omen.

A new house falling down is a bad sign: if a grain bin, after it has been filled, falls down, the owner will not eat the grain but someone else may.

To see a duiker cross one's path is a bad omen, because duiker means *insya* which resembles *kusya* 'to leave'. The meaning is that real trouble has been left in the village.

Good omens include seeing a lourie, when hunting, for that is a sign of success. The lourie is partially red, thus signifying meat.

The twitching of eyelids foretells a gift of meat. A fly falling into the mouth means the same. The twitching of the back is a sign of carrying game or, some say, a corpse. The twitching of fingers because they can hold a spear means the killing of game.

To see big black ants, *mucebu*, is to see meat. A baby eating charcoal means one will receive a gift of meat.

Prognostications announcing the coming of guests include pins and needles in the feet, the *nsweswe* bird calling *cekeceke*, soot or burnt grass falling in the bush, and insomnia.

Alien shades

Thus far individual and communal approaches to the shades have been discussed, these being all of the matrilineage or the clan—or at most, certain of the father's matrikin—of the person on whose behalf the offering is made. On the horizon of Ambo religion there

RELIGION AND DIVINATION

appear other spirits which are outside the kin group, revengeful shades (*fibanda*, sing. *cibanda*). The shades of one's own kin may also become angry, but only very seldom are they referred to as *fibanda*. An occasion in question is when the hut of a dead relative is destroyed for fear that a *cibanda* may live there, presumably the shade of the deceased.

The Ambo believe that a shade of a person who dies with a feeling of injustice is bad and revengeful. This belief is held of shades of one's own kin as well as of those of strangers. That is why a child who is drowned because his upper teeth grew before the lower, is told the reason why, and is asked not to 'follow' its slayers. A sorcerer sentenced to death was expected to confess his crimes, so that the executioner had no fear of vengeance. A barren woman is given the fruit of a sausage tree as a substitute for a child to remind her that she has no reason for a grievance.

The most common activity of the unrelated, avenging shades is to cause the death of new-born children to afflict the mother, for presumably having conceived in the bush where graves are. The shades of people buried there avenge such an affront. But another reason given for shades killing new-born children is that their mother has revealed to her husband advances made by another man and that her husband has killed his rival (probably by sorcery) thus angering the shade of the dead man. Today, a husband would think twice before he killed his rival, but formerly marital jealousy was a sufficient justification.

A *cibanda* may sometimes persecute a man causing the death of his children. In this case, his wife's matrilineage may accuse him of having a 'bad shade'. But there is belief in a medicine strong enough to control such bad shades and to render them powerless to do further harm to the woman. An approach to alien shades before building a new village or fish weir for instance (as described above) is a rare instance of communication with them and asking their will and even their favour, by someone who is not related to them by descent. In the evening the headman sprinkles a handful of sorghum meal saying: 'Let us see whether here where we have come is a good place; may you show us: but if it is a bad place, the meal, please come and eat it,' *tukabone kuno nku twaisa kati kuweme, mutulangisye: mba kati kubipile bunga mwise, mulye*. A peg or a pole for building a hut will also be laid down on the ground with the words: 'Behold this tree, we have come here, if here where we have laid it is a good place, let us find that it has not been attacked by

152   SOCIAL AND RITUAL LIFE OF THE AMBO

termites,' *citi nci, twaisa kati nku twabika kuli kuweme tukasangane kuti tacibumbilwe muswa*. If the meal is scattered, or the pole attacked by termites, it is a sign of refusal on the part of the local shades, then another site is tried. In the case of the new village sites the gardens or the bush tracts chosen for gardens need not be abandoned.

Before any villager can move to the new site the headman must go to the new place to perform the marital act which is a part of the ritual of inaugurating a new village. Great significance is attached to his dreams on that night: should they be unfavourable, a new site will be sought. To rise in the morning after a marital act is said 'to rise with arms', *kubuka ne maboko*. With this condition fulfilled, the headman makes fire by friction, in the traditional way without the use of matches, saying: 'This day, it is that we have come to another bush, we make a new fire,' *nsiku ino mpanga twaisa imbi, tukosika mulilo wa bwangu*. The new fire in a new village is a symbol of a better and brighter future. All the villagers come to take glowing cinders from the headman's hearth, *kulapula mulilo*, 'to kindle their own fires'. The new ritual fire must not be allowed to go out until the first game has been killed. Then the burning log is splashed with water mixed with the blood of the slain animal. The best omen is the killing of a griesbuck and the use of its blood, for it excretes always on the same spot. Thus the people will also stay in that place for a long time.

To turn now to the construction of a new communal fish weir, permission must first be sought and blessings asked from the local shade, which may be that of a person drowned at the spot. The dedication rite is performed at the nearest, biggest tree on the bank where the fish weir is to be built. The headman comes with a companion or two, who are village elders or his affines. They sit in ritual manner, *bukunda*, and clap hands. The headman pours some meal into a small heap, praying: 'You who have died here in the water, we want our weir to be strong in order that we may eat fish; give us good health,' *mwe mwafwile kuno ku menda, tukofwaya cansa cesu cikose, tulyemo nsabi mutulimbikile bwino*.

Other alien shades are those of the bush, which are also called by the generic name *fibanda*. They are, however, sometimes differentiated as described below. They are spoken of as having only half a body, one arm, one leg, and living on flies. On the right bank of the lower Kampoko, in the Lukusashi valley, is a flat expanse of bush country called *Ciimbeimbe*, 'the singing bush'. It is an extensive tract, seldom visited and never inhabited. It was so named because

RELIGION AND DIVINATION 153

travellers can hear the singing and drumming of *fibanda* there, though should people attempt to follow the sounds, the sounds stop. Almost opposite, on the other side of the Lukusashi, is a high mountain, *Cililangoma* 'where the drum is beaten'. Men never go there. It is inhabited by *fibanda* called *tuoma*, 'the little drums'. As the name suggests, they engage in drumming. They breed doves. It is believed that on the top of Cililangoma is a pool of water with only one fish in it, but I have no further information for an analysis of this.

Chiefs' shades

Departed chiefs' shades must be honoured for the general good of the country. Thus approaches to them may be distinguished from approaches to all other spirits in that they are public not private, although it has already been shown that private dedications, for instance, may be offered by individuals or groups. Since people of the Ambo chiefs' clan, Nyendwa, are not permitted to make offerings themselves, and this is done by sons and—even more—the appropriate grandsons of the chiefs, we see that here the exclusiveness of a matrilineal ritual solidarity, which otherwise is general in Ambo society, is modified in favour of agnatic kin. The chiefs' shades are called upon in times of drought for rain and at the offering of first fruits.

Sometimes before propitiating for rain, elders go to a diviner to ascertain the cause of the drought. When sown grain has sprouted but is dying because of lack of rain, an offering is made without divination. On this occasion, a diviner may decide only where to make the offerings.

It is the shades of the chiefs who are supposed to be those most interested in the welfare of the particular district concerned which are invoked for rain. Chiefs' shades are approached in the places where the chiefs died. Such a place is often surrounded by a hedge of *miyamba* trees. Another place of dedication may be at the big tree where traditionally the chief's body was laid, a baobab or a *mululu*.

The spot chosen for the sacrifice is first scraped clean of grass by women; men build spirit huts. One is a miniature copy of a village shelter, a *citenge*, about one and a half feet high, with a conical grass roof resting on four forked poles. Another hut is put up nearby to represent that of the chief's principal wife. This latter is an imitation of the conical *nkunka* type of hut, about one foot high. To make it,

154   SOCIAL AND RITUAL LIFE OF THE AMBO

four forked sticks are leant against one another to form a pyramid. This skeleton is covered with bark round the bottom, the rest being covered with grass; an opening is left for the door. In the centre of the hut a hole is dug roughly three inches broad and half an inch deep. Should it be thought there is no time to build such huts, they are dispensed with, and the offerings made simply on the scraped ground beneath the big trees.

Only men, boys and old women go to pour meal for rain. The headman sits *bukunda* and makes the most humble prostration of *kulamba*, lying full length on the ground first on the right then the left side. Now sitting, the headman spills a handful of meal into the hole in the ground in the middle of the miniature hut saying: 'We have come, you our chief, to ask rain and food and relish for us from Lesa. Shall we live with honour without begging (food). No.' *Twaisako mwe mfumu yesu, kutulombela mfula ne cakulya ne bucisa kuli Lesa. Tulokwikele ne bulemu tupumbe. Iyo.* Traditionally only sorghum meal is used in dedications and not maize meal. Then the headman pours water on the floor. The usual clapping of hands and the ululation of the old women present follows; in former times the *lusonsolo* bells were rung. A white hen is killed. The roof of the shade hut is sprinkled with the hen's blood and its feathers are stuck in the roof. The children present cook porridge and eat it with the roasted fowl. The fowl is roasted to save time. White stands for a benevolent shade, for good luck and good omens.

On its return to the village, the procession beats with branches all whom meets it.

Sometimes a goat is given to the officiant *Chikwashya*, 'keeper of the graves', to be offered as well as meal. The goat is brought by a delegation of some three or four elders, to a shade hut built perhaps four or three feet high. Chikwashya spills meal on four places on a dish placed in the model hut, then pours water and stirs the meal into gruel. He says: 'This meal we give to you, for which you have craved, give us also rain, the sorghum has dried through the sun,' *bunga mbu twamupela, mwalikulila, mutupeleko mfula nafwe, masaka auma ku kasuba.* Next the goat is killed, and its blood sprinkled on the floor of the shade hut with the words: 'Look at this goat which you were craving, you should be giving us rain, sorghum has dried through the sun.' Another prayer, reflecting older conditions, ran: 'Let the country become quieter, you warriors may you govern the country so that war may lessen,' *calo cinake, mwe bankondo mulele calo ne nkondo inake.*

RELIGION AND DIVINATION 155

When the rains are late, resort must be had to divination. If the diviner declares that: 'It is chief So-and-so who wants beer,' grain is soaked at the chief's village in a fenced place and at the same time the shade is addressed: 'If it is you, today we shall soak the sorghum. We shall put out grain in the mortar, you yourself pour water on it, we refuse to draw water in our stream, you yourself soak it with rain,' *kani ni mwe lelo masaka twakukusula tubike panse mwipondo. Mwabike mwebene, fwe twakana kutapa ku nyika yesu, mwabike mwebene ku mfula.* After brewing the beer, one pot is brought to the place where the offering is to be made, *cifikilo.* The officiant prostrates himself (*kulamba*) and sits *bukunda*: he then draws out some beer with a dipper, some of which he pours on the ground and prays: 'This is the beer you have asked for, we have brought it for you, we also pray, may you bring long rains,' *bwalwa mbu mwalombele, twamuletele, nafwe twatota, mulete miloke.* He drinks the rest of the beer in the dipper. Those present finish off the remainder. In other respects, the ceremonial follows the accepted pattern of beer offerings. Logically connected with this offering is the harvest thanksgiving or first fruit dedication, which is made on the same spot as that for rain, but without divination. When the crops are ripening, the headman sends small children to the garden to pluck one ear of sorghum from each garden. In the morning, four or five elders go to a big tree or another sacred spot. They surround it in the expected posture. The more respectful will clap their hands not only after the prayer but before it, but the officiant does not prostrate himself, as he does not implore the shades. He merely puts down the grain on to the ground and says: 'This is your food, let us also eat fresh crops,' *filyo fyenu, nafwe tulyeko fya bukumo.* Clearly this rite is an acknowledgement of the chief as the 'owner of the bush'. First crops are offered to him, and his permission is asked to use them.

In the past, Ambo religious ritual centred on shade huts, as described above, constructed on sacred spots for the occasion of a particular offering and then abandoned. Other shade huts were of more permanent use and generally situated nearer the village. There were two kinds, those of commoners, *tumimbia* (plur.) and those dedicated to chiefs' *tusaba* (plur.). The two kinds differed in appearance. The *tumimbia* were some two feet high, the roof being supported by four forked sticks. The chiefly *tusaba* were three feet high or more, with five to seven poles supporting the roof. In a *kasaba* (sing.) there was a weapon stand on which the chief's bow rested.

156 SOCIAL AND RITUAL LIFE OF THE AMBO

A *kasaba* served also as a sanctuary where murderers would seek refuge. In the shade huts of both types war trophies were preserved, and the skulls of slain enemies. All shade huts contained shade calabashes.

Spirit possession

A person may meet in the bush a spirit *mukupe* (sing.) which strikes him. The man, or more often the woman, falls ill, and behaves in a strange way, swallowing uncooked flour, and singing at night. He says he 'wants to sleep at the river', and if not watched will run away. He eats raw eggs, imitates the bark of the jackal and whines like a zebra. He climbs trees, even very slender ones, and jumps from one to another. Women may be struck particularly when they go to draw water, and on returning to the village or even outside if they fall down, in a swoon or convulsively. They can be treated with medicines only by another person who has been possessed. Possession may be by three kinds of spirits, by *masyabe*, *bamoba* or *baciwila*. For each kind there is a different medicine, and it is the response to a particular treatment which offers a clue to the kind of spirit by which the person is possessed. This being ascertained, the possessed is made to dance, starting at night and lasting till dawn. For each kind of possession, a different dance is required, with its own figures, rhythm of drumming and special songs. The possessed dances alone but surrounded by a large chorus, *cimfinde*. She dances with raised hands, waving her palms, an action not performed in other Ambo dances. On her head the dancer wears a circlet made of zebra mane, *mubebe*, a grass skirt, *buyombo*, and leg rattles, *nsangwa*. She may have a small ornamental axe as well. The *bamoba* tour the villages, to exhibit their dancing and for which they receive presents in return: indeed, some only feign this kind of possession. The *masyabe* neither exhibit their condition, nor feign it. To end her possession the possessed person must ask for maize, dig a hole, and bury the maize in it pouring over water and medicine.

The possessed tend to have relapses every two months or so, at the new moon. It is emphatically stated that dancing 'cures' a case of possession and brings the person back to normal. It is maintained that if the possessed did not dance, she (or he) would die. There is no speculation among the Ambo about the possessing shades. It is not said that they are the shades of the departed. The general

RELIGION AND DIVINATION 157

theory of shades is applied to them; thus they have only half a body and live on flies. The only difference between the various kinds is in name, which may be traced in certain instances, discussed below, to foreign borrowing. It is said, however, that *masyabe* is the oldest form of possession, and that the other kinds were adopted later. According to Doke (1931: 256) *moba* possession among the Lamba was introduced in 1915. Also among the Lamba *syabe* is the oldest possession display.

Some songs may be given to illustrate the different kinds of possession.

(a) *Syabe songs*

Syabe means both the possessing spirit and the possessed. At a *masyabe* dance three drums are beaten; in other dances only two drums are used.

Mwalibona syabe?	Have you seen the *syobe*?
Lyawa na lelo.	She has been seized also today.
Lyawa na mukolongwa.	She has been seized at the *mukolongwa*.

Mukolongwa is the name of a tree. The Ambo designate places in the bush by big trees. The person in the song has become possessed; she lies unconscious at the *mukolongwa* tree.

Njiwa inkalila m,munda.	The dove stays in the garden.
Njiwa we,	Oh, you dove,
Njiwa yo.	Oh, that dove.

Informants explain this song as an allegory. The dove in the garden is the *syabe* spirit in the chest of the possessed. *Njiwa* is a Nsenga word for Ambo *ciba*, 'dove'. *Inkalila* is also Nsenga for the Ambo *yaikalila*, 'it sits in'. *M'munda* is a Nsenga word for the Ambo, *mu mabala*, 'in the garden'.

Waya mulelengo syabe,	The *syabe* is gone in rags,
Waya mulelengo syabe,	The *syabe* is gone in rags,
Eaye, mulelengo syabe,	And the *syabe* in rags,
Waya mulelengo syabe.	The *syabe* is gone in rags.

The possessed is looked upon as a person extraordinary. Hence he or she may go about half naked, especially in the fit of possession.

158 SOCIAL AND RITUAL LIFE OF THE AMBO

Syabe possessed persons are treated with medicines against madness.

Eaye mitenge,	Ah! the roofs,
Eaye yayaye yayayele,	Ah! Ah! Ah! Ah! Ah! Ah!
Katanta mitengo,	She climbs the roofs,
Bamama wesu.	Our mother.
Mwe baume?	My friends?
Mfi mwanjitira findo?	Why do you call me?
Cilale-lale kalumowane,	The boy sleeps in the bush,
Oyaye oyaya elele	Oh . . . Oh . . . Oh
Kali mutente.	This is like a swing.

The possessed likes to climb roofs and to wander in the bush. Her dancing is likened to a swing: *cilale-lale*, to sleep here and there.

(b) *Moba songs*

Bamoba kanjita mwinsya	
ng'ombe,	The *moba* calls me the guardian of herds,
Mwinsyanombe bwelele.	The guardian of herds I shall come back.

The belief in a guardian shade of herds, *mwinsyanombe*, is not common among the Ambo for they point out that in their hilly country, herds of game do not abound. The Lala and the Lamba believe in guardian shades of game, thus the theme of this song seems to show borrowed traits. The word *moba* is also borrowed from the Lamba. In this song the possessed person aspires to become a guardian of game.

Walisinkwile kulingula	He again marries me
batukobele,	Who struck me,
Kulamolu kasisyala,	Those with big feet are left away,
Wowe wowowo,	Ya . . . ya . . . ya . . .
Kulamolu kasisyala.	Those with big feet are left away.

Kasinkula is from *kusinka* 'to block', 'to stop'. *Kulamolu* are 'people with big legs', the ordinary people; the shades are credited with thin legs. *Kulingula* is an Nsenga word for the Ambo *kuupa* 'to marry'. *Kukobela* is poetical for 'to strike' and is not used in common speech.

Here is brought out the belief, recorded by Doke for the Lamba,

RELIGION AND DIVINATION

159

that the *moba* dancers are spouses of shades. The shade has married the possessed dancer in a relapse. The shade which struck the dancer had barred (*kusinkula*) the dancer from marrying ordinary people 'with big legs'.

Ku manyengwe tekulalapo,	In the play huts it is no good to sleep,
Napilayamba,	I am overcome,
Napilawila.	I am seized.

These are the reflections of the possessed with the prospect of sleeping in the bush, like children who play at mothers and fathers in small huts they build in the bush.

Bona kulaunda,	See how it circles,
Pa cibansa caiko ndeke.	The aeroplane on its aerodrome.

Kulaunda 'to go around', is derived from the English word 'around'. The dancing of the *moba* is likened to the circling of the aeroplane.

Kwa Mboloma kunaile,	At Mboloma whither I went,
Nalota bayambo,	I dreamt of the *bayambo*,
Bayempaula moba,	Who struck the possessed,
Nalota bayambo,	I dreamt of the *bayambo*,
Basyempaula mawewe.	Who struck the patient.

Bayambo are the *bayambo* shades. Doke (1931: 256) speaks of *bayambo* as the spirits of the Twa hunters. The Lamba are nearer to the Northern Rhodesian Twa, therefore have a better knowledge of them. The Ambo having borrowed the word *bayambo* use it as a synonym for the *moba*. The song expresses the belief in how possession begins. The song also confuses the *bayambo* shades with the *bamoba* shades.

Kamimbya lelala,	Oh swallow, *lelala*,
Mailo tulokuya.	Tomorrow we go.

The possessed likens himself or herself to a darting swallow. The shade will seize the possessed-to-be tomorrow when the possessed will run away into the bush (where shades dwell) unless stopped by the villagers.

Kubula nsangwe,	I have no rattles,
Naipengela moba.	I am shabby for the shades.

160 SOCIAL AND RITUAL LIFE OF THE AMBO

The possessed while dancing should wear rattles tied to the calves of the legs. The lack of rattles may displease the shade.

(c) *Cibila songs*

Nakuya kwa Cangacanga,	I shall go to Cangacanga,
Kubafwika mpande.	Where they wear *mpande* shells.
Kwa Sele msonko,	At Sele's tax is taken,
Mbweneko.	I shall see it.

Impressions are recorded of the arrival of the first Europeans: the selling of *mpande* shells at Cangacanga (to Mr Harrison-Clarke) and the collecting of tax by Mr 'Chirupula' Stephenson (here nicknamed Sele).

Kabafwala malaya,	They dressed in a shirt,
Kabalicebele,	Admiring themselves,
Ne babipile bonse,	Though somebody may be ugly,
Bawama.	He will be looking fine.

Cibila songs are of varied and rather irrelevant themes as the above examples show. The most common form of possession is still the *masyabe.*

Medicines of spirit possession

Namasyabe, otherwise called *cisoko* roots, are soaked and the infusion is drunk. With leaves of the tree, the patient is fumigated under a cloth. *Cisoko* is used for treating widows and widowers for madness. It is significant that this tree has another name from the *syabe* shade and is used for the same purpose of protecting against madness in the case of widowhood and of spirit possession.

In cases of *bamoba,* the *namwando* herb is used. The patient is struck with the root of the above tree without words. The roots are soaked and the infusion is given the patient to drink. The *bamoba* possession takes place when a person is struck in the bush by a shade. Now the patient is struck with the counteracting medicine. The patient is also given infusion with soaked *namwando* roots to drink. The sign of possession is that the patient, after being doctored, responds to the treatment by waking up and singing.

For *baciwila,* the roots of *cinamwela* are soaked and the infusion is

RELIGION AND DIVINATION 161

given to the patient to drink. The patient is also fumigated with *cinamwela* leaves boiled in water.

Spirits in animals and trees

The big game animals and other dangerous beasts are believed also to have some kind of bad shades, *fibanda*. The bigger and more dangerous the beast, the more powerful the bad shade it possesses. Lions and elephants of both sexes seem to possess them, but among other game animals only the big, powerful males have them. After having killed a lion or an elephant, for example, the hunter must be doctored. If he is not doctored, he will be affected by the bad shades of the animal, raving, and having bad dreams. Finally he will be driven mad. The shades of other big males, such as buffalo or an eland bull, do harm only to the guns. They enter the barrels of the guns by which they were killed and make them afterwards always miss their quarry.

Similar *fibanda* dwell in big trees such as are felled for canoe making. Some Ambo explain that really these tree shades are not proper shades but rather a 'force' or 'strength', *nkosa*, of these trees. If such a tree were not doctored before being felled, it would cause death in the families of the lumberers.

The Ambo, then, fear awe-inspiring objects whether they be big trees, the biggest and fiercest animals or big mountains, which they consider are peopled with bad shades. Every extensive forest is peopled in a special way with shades. An Ambo fears to be overwhelmed by the enormous strength of some of these objects. He is able to kill a lion, and cut the *mululu* tree, but he is afraid of their strength after his deed. The same principle holds for the killing of a man. The Ambo equates the killing of a man with the killing of a lion in terms of reward and taboo. There is also recognized a gradation of ill effects: the spirit of a lion, of a man or of an elephant may drive the killer mad: the spirits of other animals may bring him only bad luck in hunting by infesting the barrel of his gun. The female game animals, except the female elephant, do not impress the Ambo as having any fearsome shade. There is complete silence about the existence of shades in female large animals and in the small animals of both sexes.

To neutralize the shade (or power) of a big tree cut down for making a canoe, lest the feller's children should die, a medicine is made from *munsanga*, a creeping water plant (so that the canoe will

162   SOCIAL AND RITUAL LIFE OF THE AMBO

do likewise) and the *kabosya* tree, which will cause the shade of the tree to rot (*kubosya* means 'to make something rot'). The *kabosya* is made to work on the substitute for the canoe, *munsanga*. When the tree falls, the medicine man runs to the crown of the tree, plucks some leaves from it and puts them with the medicine on a fire which is lit on the stump. People are fumigated with its smoke and those working on the canoe wash their faces morning and evening in water which has had *munsanga* leaves soaked in it.

To render the shade of a male or female elephant harmless the hunter cuts a peg of the *musolo* tree and drives it into the ground near the head of the dead elephant. He then ties the trunk of the elephant to the peg to drive away the shade. *Musolo* recalls the verb *kusolola*, 'to drive away'. Next the hunter cuts a twig of *mwenje* and sticks three sticks from it into the nostrils and anus of the animal. Then he reverses the sticks, that from the anus going to the nostrils and vice versa, to deceive the shade. *Mwenje* means 'a torch' or 'a light'; by changing the light the shade is thought to be deceived. Next, with closed eyes, the hunter breaks off grass and leaves with his mouth, chews them, spits out the substance and smears the body of the elephant with it. This is also done to deceive the shade, the hunter with closed eyes not seeing the elephant or its shade, and thinking not to be recognized as a man but to be taken for the grazing animal he is imitating. When taking out the elephant's tusks, the nostrils of those present are blocked with *ngwelulu* leaves, the medicine of immunity, otherwise people would break their legs while crossing the tusks.

BIBLIOGRAPHY

BARNES, J. A. *Politics in a Changing Society*. London: Oxford University Press for Rhodes–Livingstone Institute, 1954.

BRELSFORD, W. V. 'Notes on some Northern Rhodesian bow stands or tridents.' *Man*, Vol. XL, No. 47, 1940.

COLSON, E. 'Modern political organization of the Plateau Tonga', *African Studies*, Vol. VII, Nos. 2–3, 1948.

COLSON, E., and GLUCKMAN, M. *Seven Tribes of British Central Africa*. London: Oxford University Press, 1951.

DOKE, C. M. *The Lambas of Northern Rhodesia*. London: Harrap, 1931.

HAILEY, LORD. *An African Survey*. London: Oxford University Press, 1938.

LANE POOLE, E. H. *The Native Tribes of the East Luangwa Province of Northern Rhodesia*. Livingstone: Government Printer, 1934.

MACKENZIE, D. R. *The Spirit Ridden Konde*. London: Seeley Service, 1925.

MELLAND, F. H. *In Witchbound Africa*. London: Seeley Service, 1923.

MEROLLA DA SORRENTO, JEROME. *A Voyage to Congo*. Churchill, 1704.

MUNDAY, J. T. 'Some traditions of the Nyendwa clan of Northern Rhodesia.' *Bantu Studies*, Vol. 14, No. 4, 1940.

MUNDAY, J. T. Inyendwa (W. Lala-Swaka traditions) Fiwi la. U.M.C.A., N. Rhodesia, 1941.

MUNDAY, J. T. 'Spirit names among the Central Bantu.' *African Studies*, Vol. VII, No. 1, 1948.

RICHARDS, A. I. *Land, Labour and Diet in Northern Rhodesia*. London: Oxford University Press, 1939.

RICHARDS, A. I. 'Bow stands or trident.' *Man*, Vol. XXXV, No. 32, 1935.

SMITH, E. W., and DALE, A. M. *The Ila-speaking Peoples of Northern Rhodesia*. London: Macmillan, 1920.

STEFANISZYN, B. 'Central African superstition.' *The South African Clergy Review*, Vol. I, No. 3, 1948.

STEFANISZYN, B. 'Mutivi.' *N.A.D.A.*, No. 27, 1950.

STEFANISZYN, B. 'Funeral friendship in Central Africa.' *Africa*, Vol. XX, No. 4, 1950.

STEFANISZYN, B. 'The Ambo', in *Bemba and Related Peoples of Northern Rhodesia*, by W. H. Whiteley and J. Slaski. Ethnographic Survey of Africa, West Central Africa, Part II. London: International African Institute, 1951.

BIBLIOGRAPHY

STEFANISZYN, B. 'The hunting songs of the Ambo.' *African Studies*, Vol. X, No. 1, 1951.

STEFANISZYN, B. 'Clan jest among the Ambo.' *N.A.D.A.* No. 28, 1951.

STEFANISZYN, B. 'African reincarnation re-examined.' *African Studies*, Vol. XIII, Nos. 3–4, 1954.

STEFANISZYN, B. 'The rise of the Chikunda "Condottieri".' *Northern Rhodesia Journal*, Vol. IV, No. 4, 1960.

STEFANISZYN, B. *The Material Culture of the Ambo of Northern Rhodesia* (In the Press).

STEPHENSON, J. E. *Chirupula's Tale*. London: Geoffrey Bles, 1937.

TEW, MARY. 'A further note on funeral friendship.' *Africa*, Vol. XXI, No. 2, 1951.

TEW, MARY. *Peoples of the Lake Nyasa Region*. Ethnographic Survey of Africa, East Central Africa, Part I. London: International African Institute, 1951.

TRAPNELL, G. C. *The Soils, Vegetation and Agriculture of North-Eastern Rhodesia*. Lusaka: Government Printer, 1943.

INDEX

Administration, xix, 50, 51, 66

Adulterer, 64; prohibition, 74; at child-birth, 76; case of, 116; killed, 121

Adultery, wife cannot sue for, 74; occasion to, 102; as reason for divorce, 116; dream of, 148; supernatural sanction, 108

Affinal relatives, 16–18; segments, 29; *see* mother-, father-, son- and daughter-in-law.

Agnate, 31; agnates in village, 42

Agnatic segments, 29; kin, 153

Ancestor, shrine, 64; to be remembered, 85

Ancestress of matrilineage, 78

Attitude, to clansmen, 4; to supernatural world, 139

Aushi, 57, 58

Avoidance rules, relaxation of, 16, 20; of son-in-law, 17; of married couple, 108; *see* prohibitions.

bakali (pl.), chief's henchmen, body-guard, 60, 63, 64

bako (pl.), *see muko, mukweni.*

bakwabo (pl.), *see mukwabo.*

balaye (pl.), diviner-herbalist, 139

bamapasa (pl.), twins of different sex, 78

bampundu (pl.), twins of same sex, 78

bambuya (pl.), grand-parent,

bamfumu (pl.), chief, 65

bamubala (pl.), Mboshya's court officials, 50

bana (pl.), *see mwana.*

banakalumbwana, mother of little boy, 81

bankonko, lesser diviners, 139

banugwe (pl.), *see munungwe.*

Bayambo (pl.), shades of Twa hunters, 159

Bayongo, Bemba, xxii

Beads, white for child, 83, 84, 86; at courtship, 102, 103, 104; at redemption, 131, 143, 144, 146; for hunting guardian shade, 145

Beer party, man looks for, 19; funeral, 60, 62; for guardian shade, 84, 85; for initiation, 94, 97; for chief, 63; for son-in-law, 106; funeral, 131; final, 133; offering, private, 143–4; to dream of, 147; offering, public, 155

Bemba, xxii, 59, 64, 65, 66; Bemba father, 21

Bembaland, xxi

bene, see mwine.

Bewitch, to, for offence, for accusation, for stinginess, 94

Birth, of child ends probation, 20, consequences, 109; mother at childbirth, 76; prohibitions at, 74, 76 seq.

Bisa, xix

Boy, behaviour watched, 20, 99; given clothes, 20; concerned with clothes, 18, 19; childhood of, 87; sex and, 100; maturation of, 98; in courtship, 102; goes to offering, 154; to dance, 66

Brelsford, W. V., 69

Bridegroom, fails, 109

British Administration, 56, 71

Brother, position of eldest, 10; brothers sleep together, 87; elder of husband, 107; woman lives with, 116; inherits woman, 119; offering to dead, 125; brothers lay claims, 133; at dedication, 145; hunting guardian shade, 145

Brother-in-law, 29; and his sister's husband, 10

Bukanda, xxi

bukunda, respectful squatting, 144, 145, 152, 155

bukwa, marital jealousy, 111

bunani, aversion, 77

bunungwe, see munungwe.

busepa, kind of mushroom, 142

busofu, prematurely born child, 77

Burial, of chief, 56; common, 123; seq.; of leper, 127; of pregnant woman, still-born, 128; childless woman, 129

buyombo, zebra mane, 95, 156

Bwashi, xxi, 63

calo, land, 66

cendo, marital exile, 31

Chembe, xxi, 64

Chief, authority of, 49, 50; bodyguard of, 60; -in-charge, 61; selection of, 62; rights and duties of, 63; land and, 66; polygynist, 116, *see* Burial.

Chiefship, succession to, sister's daughter's son, 12

Chibale, xix, 53

166 INDEX

Chibuye, xxi, 53
Child, lack of, 116, chap. IV; to be inherited with mother, 119; its part in funeral, 124; burial of still-born, *see* burial, as part of death dues, intermediary, 131; named, 138, 139
Chikunda, xxii, 27, 64, 68
Chikwashya, xxi, 30, 56–60, 154
Chilemba, 57, 58, 67
Chilimba Nondo, xx, 6, 7, xix
Chingombe Mission, xix
Chipepo, xx
Chisomo xxii, 53, 64, 72
cibanda (pl. fi-), bad spirit or shade, 61, 147, 151, 152
cibate, washing basin, 37
cibuli, a kind of carnivora, 70
cibwela, reincarnated ancestor, 85
cikole (pl. *fikole*), section of village, 27, 30, 44
cikolwe, founder of lineage, 7
cikoto, matrilineage, 8
cikutu, child born with caul, 77
cilema, cripple, 77
cilolo, captain, 63
cimbwasa, a kind of dance, 89
cimfinde, chorus, 156
cimo, one, 8
cinamwela, a herb, 160
cinguwa, glade, xviii
cinkombe, relish pot, 109
cinyaku, a herb, 81
cinsanda, a pole of trophies, 145
cinsengwe, a beer dance, 147
cipapo (*cipapilo*), cloth to carry a child, 86
cipasi, ground bees, 149
cipesi, calabash, 144
cipembwe (*pembwe*), grave chamber, 125
cisinte, *see* cikolwe.
cisoko, a herb, 160
cisungu, a girl at initiation, 90, 91
ciswango, a wild beast, 29, 46
citalo, big beer pot, 130
cite, a child retarded in walking, 86
citemwa, a good conscience medicine, 70
citenge, shelter, 153
citewa, a platform behind palisade, 68
citundu, a tall basket, 36, 109
citusisyo, resting place of bier, 124
ciwila, a kind of spirit, dance, 90, 156
Clan, chap I, solidarity, hospitality, 2, 3; names, 3; list of clans, 4, 5; alliance of, 6; clan of father, 1, 21; clan brothers building apart, 29; 'brother', 37; affiliation, splits, 39; alien, 41; clans in village, 43; endogamy, 110; not to think of clan relative when dead, 127; clan at inheritance, 131; strangers, 2, 4; Lesa has no clan, 135

Clansman, of chief, 63; to honour, 83, curse of, 3
Clanswoman, 3; at offering, 143
Compensation, avoided in clan disputes, 2; for adultery, 14, 64, 80; for adultery and divorce, 20; by mother's brother, 22; woman not compensated, 54; in divorce, 115
Conciliation, in disputes, 2
coni, medicine of swearing, 3, 126, 132
Court case, mother's brother spokesman, 22
Cross-cousin marriage, 31, 110; cousins sleep together, 87
Curse, of clansman (woman), *see* clansman, curse against stealing, 121; curse of death, 123
Cuuta, name of God, 135

Dance, war, 61; funeral, 123; at funeral beer, 130; initiation, 89; debut, 94; of prowess, 64; of the possessed, 156
Daughter, of sister, 9; mother and, 10; father and, 21; helps mother, 86; of wife's sister, 107
Daughter-in-law, 107
Death, of wife, 113; end of family, 13; of herdsman, 29; signal to move village, 28, chap. VI; of chief, 56, 61
Debt, 52
District Commissioner, 29
Divination, not at delivery, 76; at child's death, 74; to ascertain will of shades, 138; at sickness, 143, 144
Diviner, watched by father and mother's brother, 22; at chief's death, 61; at naming child, 76, 83, 84; consulted in bad luck in hunting, 146; diviners, 139; approached in draught, 153
Divining techniques, 140; medicines, 143
Divorce, end of family, 13; compensation in, 20; after, return home, 32, 40, 43; no right to, 54; easy, 79, 80; when husband dissolute, 110; meaning of, 113, 114; grounds for, 114, 115, 116; in polygyny, 110; effects of, 4, 113
Doke, C. M., 64

Endogamy, 2, 110
Enslavement, 2, 52, 92; of suitor, 92

Family, 13–18; expanded, autonomy, 13; supplied with clothes, 20
Father, legally stranger, 113; consequences of his death, 14; bequests to his son, receives gratitude, not informed of marriage, does not teach sorcery, his position, 21; and mother's brother, 22; of matrilineage, 42; physical role of, 74; takes medicine

INDEX

167

Father, (*cont.*)
77; touches child, 80; side of, 82, 83; gone wrong, his clan, accompanied by his son, 88; of bridegroom, 106; his children, 107, 113

Father-in-law, testing son-in-law, 19; visited by daughter-in-law, 18; leader in work, 20; daughter-in-law, 107

fibanda, see cibanda.

fikole, see cikole.

fimbwi (pl.), buriers, 126

fipa, lots, 141

fipele, sweet beer, 130

fisimba, animal parts, 4, 70

fiti, trees, 45

Funeral rites, 56; beer, 62, 130; final beer, 137; friendship, 6, 12, 21; based on clanship, 3; *see* dance.

Funerary inversions, 127

Garden, belongs to man, 19; villages split seeking, 39; headman provides, 49; right to vacate, 66; occasion to adultery, 102; separate, 111

Genealogical links, 49; position for marriage, 109

Generation(s), form matrilineage, 27; in village, 30, 42; adjacent, 11; senior of wife's kin, 20; marriage between alternate, 110; familiarity of alternate, 110

Girl, in courtship, 102; menstruating, 108; not beaten by father, 88; beer in her honour, 94; instructions to, 19; given clothes, 18, 20; looks after child, 86; childhood of, 87–8; initiation of, 89; behaviour of, 99–100; with child out of wedlock, 107

Grandchildren, matrilineal, 110; offer to chiefs' shades, 135; *see* grandparents.

Granddaughter, 62

Grandfather, to work for parents-in-law, 109

Grandmother, paternal, 104; maternal names child, 83

Grandparent, begging from, 12; behaviour, marriage possibility, 12; differences of affines, 16

Grandson, *see* grandchildren.

Gun, 21, 57, 59, 68; fired, 96; at death, 122; inherited, 132; shade harms, 161

Headman, administering medicine, 3; founder of matrilineage, 7; succession to, 12; collecting matrikin, 27, 32; death of, unpopular, brothers of, 29; emerging, 36; behaviour of, deputy, duties of, 4, 48; his councillor, heir of, 62; not appointed, 65; requests land, 66; invited, 94; and

Native Authority, 50; sister of, 30; agnates of, 31; office of, 40, 44; rights and privileges, 47–51

Husband, brother pays death dues for sister, 9; supernatural responsibility, of, 14; behaviour towards affines, 16, 19; watched, 26; escapes to town, 20; stranger, 32; provides garden, 48; injured, redeems wife, hereditary position, in matrilineage, 64; given land, 66; hostile, 80; not to refuse him, advice about, 92; polygynist, 110; of Nyendwa, 54; deserted, 116; jealousy, 99; debarred from wife, 111

Ibumba, group, 49

icama, flood, 136

Inheritance, in female line, 53; of widows, 119, 132

Incest, between in-laws, 17

indibu, bell, 61

insangwa, rattles, 95

insoni, golden mole, 70

insya, duiker, 147

Kabandami, lizard, 149

kabesya, tree, xviii

kabosya, tree, 46, 162

kabundi, lemur, 97

kabungwe, death place of chief, 57

kafungu, tree, 47

kakote, tree, 87

kalabana, sorcery medicine, 89

kalumbwana, little boy, 84

kamimbia (pl. *tumimbia*), commoners' shades' shrine, 155

kampekete, kind of beads, 103

kampenga, chief's mourner, 51

Kankomba, xx, 56

kansanda, chief's burier, 56

kanwa, mouth, 117

kapafu, womb, 8

kapondo (pl. *tupondo*), outlaw, 52

kapopo, foetus, 77

kaputu, plant, 46

kasaba (pl. *tusaba*), chiefs' shades' shrine, 155

kasansubwanga, tree, 81

kasele, eating basket, 63, 95, 124

kasembe, sweeper, 57

kasimbi, little girl, 84

kasimwengwe, divining apparatus, 42

katenge, tree, 98

Katukutuku, xxi

kaulu, captain, 63

kaundu, quail, 69

Kayetano, xii, 64

Kin group, 39

kubosya, make rot, 146

kubumba, mould, 58

kuciyabafu, west, 125

168 INDEX

kufisya (*mulilo*), arrange (*hearth*), 109
kufita (*ku Menso*), be black (in eyes)
kufubata, spurt, 143
kufumya (*cisungu*), the début of girl, 94
kufungula, to open, 77
kufwa, to die, 70
kuilike'sina, to name, 82
kuipanga, at chief's court, 58
kukaka, bind, 70, 54
kukonona (*musana*) break (back), 70
kukowela, grow thin, 77, 108
kulamba, prostrate, 154
kulanga (*mulilo*), invite to meal, 104
kulisya (*mapi*), clap (hands), 11
kulula, be bitter, 10
Kunda Mpanda, xix, 53, 56, 57
kukambila, clap hands, 144
kupapa, carry child on back, 77
kupia, be hot (and active), 140
kusangula (*nkalamu*), transform (into lion), 58
kusansika (*see musansiko*), make bed, 58
kusenga (*mapi*), beg from grandparent, 12
kusikula (*banyina*), exhume (mother), 90
kusopa (*musi*), watch (village), 48
kusolola, chase away, rearrange fire, 20
kusonkama, squat, 11, 17
kusweta, be red, 46
kusokola, see *kusolola*, 47
kusonta (*danda*), to give (hut), 48
kutaila, give ceremonial present, 63
kutina, fear and respect, 107
kutondela (*mulilo*), be barred from fire, 108
kutopa (*musi*), to grudge village, 43
kwabo, at home, 9
kwanga, execute war dance, 61
kwanji, at my home, 44
kwesu, at our home, 9, 44

Lamba, 64
Lala, xix, 53
Land, 19, 66
Lenje, xx
Leper (leprosy), 36, 56
Lesa, death and, 121; dream and, 121, 147, Supreme Being, 134, 149
likatesi, monster, 58
Lion, 16, 56, 58, 59, 64, 67
Lisebele, 50
lubango, broad basket, 103, 104
lububi, divining spider, 141, 143
Lucele, 135
Lukusashi, xvii, xix, xxi, 79
Lumbwe, husband of Nyendwa, 54
Lungo, xx
lunyena, child excreting at birth, 77
Lupanda, 44, 68
lupani, mopane woodland, xv, 14
lupapi, a plant, 77

lusato, python, 45
lusomo, token payment, 140
lusonsolo, double bell, 58, 60, 59, 154
lutala, grow upper teeth first, 54, 78, 79
luteta, medicine against lion, 45
lwabia, a plant, 76
Lwangwa, xix
Lwano, 54
lwanda, plant, 76
Lwembe, 42, 52, 53
lwenye, tree, 98

Maala (pl.), finger nails, 90
mabele, breasts, 78
mafinge, imprecations, 117
mainsa, rainy season, xviii
Makumba Chabala, xviii, xx
mala, stomach, 90
malenje, buffalo grass, xvii
malinga, palisade, 6
malyansima, wedding feast, 104, 106
Man, duties and rights, 19, 20; provides clothing, buildings, proteins, 19; exclusive sexual rights of, 20; right to economic services of wife, 20; procreator of matrilineage, 20; receives compensation, 20; gives names, 21; travelling of, 15; choice of residence, 32; marries away, 32; Nyendwa, 62; right hand, 63; accepted by woman, 79; married or otherwise, 79; not snatching others' wives, 102, 113; his children, 115
mandu, chief's war drum, 6
Mapunde (Ngoni), 67
Marital, jealousy, 15, 111; life, instructions to girl, 19; exile, against matrilineal solidarity, 27; boy in exile, 20; abandoning, exile to form village, 28; exile, 31; residence, Nyendwa, 54; infidelity, rare, 102; relations, suspended, 77
Marriage, economic position of, 13; accepting proposition of, 16; intra-village, reliable within the tribe, 101; cross-cousin, favoured, 31; residence, 32; in village, 42, 43, chap. V; failure in, 105; informally progressive, 79; payment for, 103, 113; restricts man, 109; stability of, 113
masaka, sorghum, 1
masombwe, praying mantis, 153
mata, bows (regalia), xxi
Maternal, uncle, see mother's brother.
Matrikin, tolerates wife beating, of father, 21; agnates of, 42; starts village, 27; Mwanso lost no members, 37; owning village, 42,; in exile, 43; bewitch, 48
Matrilineage, major, 7; not residential unit, 8; its village, 9; amalgamation of

INDEX

169

Matrilineage, (*cont.*)
families, 13; core of minor, 20; grateful to its father, 21, 113; forms village, 29; numerical strength of, loyalty to, minor, lost contact with, 31; minor, owns village, 41; headman's duties to, 48; its head, 50; chiefly, 53, 62; leaders of, 72; watches over its women, 32, 92, conceals her faults, 99

Matrilineal, centre, 31; unity, 32, 36 solidarity, 27; village, *see* village, interests, 36; groups in village, 42; clansmen, tension, 43; grandchildren not to marry within, 109; relatives, notified, 127

Matrilocal residence, 32, 101, 110

matuka, curses, 101

mbiko, bad omen, 142

Mboloma (Chontabunga), 63, 64

mboswa, guardian shade of ward, 82

Mbosya, xii, xix, 42, 50, 52, 54, 61, 64, 65, 110

Medicine, of swearing, 3; against crocodiles, 46; against lions, 45; against hyena, 47; of transformation, 58; chief's, 69; at child's birth, 77, 81; sexual, 98, 100, 104, 105; for child, 108; learnt in dream, 146

milende, sacred burial grounds, 58

Milonga, xxi

misamba (pl.), Brachystegia woodland, xviii

mitala, neighbourhood, xvii

mitende, peace, 18

mitete, reads, xvii

mitondero, prohibitions, 92

miyamba (pl.), trees, 57, 153

Mkushi, xvii

Mkwemba, xxii

moba (pl.) *bamoba*), a kind of spirit possession, 156

mofwe, tree, 170, 121

Mother, bestows clan, 1, chap. IV, takes medicine, 77; changes status, 81; gone wrong, 83; mother's mother names child, 83; gives breast, 86; daughter and, 10; son, responsibility for wife to, 16; consents to virilocality, 18; of chief, 62; of adulterer, 64; of wife, 74; at childbirth, 76; unmarried, 79; mother's side naming, 82; notified of death, 122

Mother-in-law, visiting, avoidance, 17; controls son-in-law, 107; controls uxorilocality, 20; to work for her, 99; decides in courtship, 102; behaviour to son-in-law, 106; daughter-in-law and, 107

Mother's brother, shares marriage payment, 104; of bridegroom, 106; of wife, rights, 131; his position, 13, 21,

22; reincarnated, 84; at initiation, 94, 95; married women live with, 101; maternal uncle, *see* mother's brother.

mpasa, mat, 123

mpelafyala, woman ceased to bear, 124, 138

mpemba, electors, councillors, 62

mpendwa, ant bear, 136

Mtondo, 50

Mubanga, xx, 67

mubanga, tree, 97

mucebu, kind of black ant, 150

mucenje (or *mucenja*), tree, xviii

mufungula, tree, xvii

mufyala, cross-cousin, 22, 95

mufyasi, parent, 81

muka (*muntu*), wife (of person), 14

mukasi, wife, 22

mukolo, chief wife, 141

mukomfwa, tree, 70

mukulu (*bantu*), eldest sibling, 10

mukunda, grave illness, 122

mukupe, kind of spirit, 156

mukwabo, sibling, clans-, man/woman, 12, 110

mukweni (*muko*), son-in-law, 16, 23, 43

mulaku, 53

mulamu, brother-, sister-in-law, 17, 22, 102

mulembe, tree, 70

Mulembo, xix, xxii, 57, 58, 59, 63, 67

mulembwe, wild spinach, 91

Mulenga, 134

mulokasi, daughter-in-law, 23

mulomo, lips, 117

mululu, tree, xvii, 70, 78, 120, 161

mulume, husband, 22

Mumba Chundu, 57

muncinda, baby's beads, 86

munsanga, creeper, 161

Munsunki, xxi, 64

munsyo, mother's brother, 22, 23

munungwe, funeral friend, 58, 122

munyamenda, tree, 98

munyenu, ants, 142

mupasi, shade, 138, 146, 149

mupyani, heir, 119

musamba, tree, xvii

musambamfwa, tree, 18

musangu, tree, 121

musansiko, sleeping mat, 58

musela, ward, 81

musikisi, tree, xvii

musikulu, grandchild, 22

Mushyalila, xxi

musolo, tree, 46, 162

musundu, leech, 142

mutanda, zaleba, 127

Mutanta, 50

mutembetembe, dance at début, 95

muteteka, tree, 76

170 INDEX

mutobe, tree, 70
mutondo (*mtondo'*, Nsenga pronunciation), tree, xviii
mutyoka, tree, 70
muyanda, medicine, 105
mwafi, poisonous creeper, 45
mwana (*wa lubansa*), child (of courtyard), 79
mwana (*wapia*), new-born child 79
mwanakasi, woman, 110
mwanalume (brave), man, 64
Mwanso clan, 36
Mwape, xix–xxii, 52, 62, 68
Mwape Katuta, 8, 29
mwela, cold, dry season, xviii
mwenje (Swahili: *mwenge*), a shrub, torch, 70
mweyama, tree, 45
mwika, child born with feet first, 77
mwinko, ladle, 109
mwipwa, sister's child, 110

Nacimbela, instructress, 75, 104
nakasya, *see* nacimbela.
Namupala, xxi
namwando, plant, 160
Native Authority, 50, 72, 88, and headman, 50
ncilu, medicine of difficult delivery, 76
nanga, 'witch-doctor', 139
ndale, tree, 82, 142, 143
ndubaluba, lourie, 65
ndume ('*ya bufi*'), (false), brother, 17, 23
ndunduma, flood, 135
Nephew, uterine, 30; *see* sister's son.
New-born child, 79
ngobelo, boys' hut, 88
Ngoni, xxi, 27, 67
ngwelulu, tree, 98, 104, 162
nkaka, pangolin, 70
nkalamu ya pansi, tree, 45
nkama, tree, 79
Nkana Yalobe, xx
nkata, head-ring, 75
nkole, hostage, 52
nkosa, strength, 161
nkula, red wood, 59, 94
nkunka, lean-to hut, 153
nkwiwa (Nsenga word), bushbuck, 147
nsalamu, marriage token, 104
nsangwa, rattles, 156
Nsangwe, xxii
Nsenga, xix
nseswe, kind of bird, 150
nsomwe, tree, 69
nsoni, golden mole, 70
ntele (pl.), bamboo
ntengo, marriage payment, 104
ntetemesi, the inside of elephant tusk, 71
Nyanja, 137

Nyendwa, xx, 50, 52, 53–4, 56, 57, 61, 62, 68
nyina (pl. *banyina*), mother, 2. 28
nyinafyala, mother-in-law, 23
nyinamfumu, mother of chief, 54

Orthocousin, 110

Petauke, xvii, xviii, 53
Plateau Tonga, *see* Tonga.
Polygamist, marries young girl, 100; trusts wives, 102
Polygamy, 110 seq.
Polygyny, opposed, 116
Poole, E. H. Lane, x, 68
Prohibitions, of chief, 66; of mother, 77; at childbirth, 77; *see* avoidances and marriage rules.
Provincial Commissioner, 72

Richards, Audrey, 66, 69

Sandwe, tree, xviii
Segment, of minor matrilineage, 8, 49; seniority of, 4; matured, 28; of Mwanso, 36
Segmentation of matrikin, 27
Self-help, 52
Seniority, genealogical, 8; senior generation of wife's kin, 20; in succession, 48
Serenje, xvii
Sexual, rights of husband, 14; lapse, 14 privilege, 63; activity, 98; peace, 99; organs improved, 100; custom objectionable, 101; acts sap resistance, 109; intercourse of midwife, 77
Shade, revengeful, 74, 81, 94; to name, 76; not to wrong, 79, 92; checked, 81; guardian, 82–4; aggrieved, 117; of stranger, 135; of chiefs, 153; dreams from shades, 146 seq.; worship, 143; *see* divination.
Sibling(s), do not bury each other, 6; designation of, 8; identity, of interests of, succession, inheritance, 8–9; starting village, 27; two groups, 27; positional, 53; behaviour, 49; sister, 64; notified, 122; in village, 43; sister of chief, 63
Sister, position of, 9; not to marry polygamously, 17; control of, 49; of chief, *see* sibling, sister's daughter, 64; father's, 104; clan, 5; laments, 122
sikulu, lord, 65
simananda, owner of house, 13
Slave, brother giving sister as, 9, 64; to bury chiefs, 54,; sent to work, 50; ritually killed, 58; of chief, 72
Slavery, for incest, 17; suppression, 50; *see* enslavement.

INDEX

Son, in-law, 30; position, 43; of chief, 50, 61; of Chikwashya, 59; avoidance rules, 106

Song, funeral, 136 seq.; birth, 75; initiation, 89; debut, 95; spirit, 157

Sorcerer, sleeps with wife asleep, 92; aroused, 93; behaviour of, 94; may harm bride, 106; shade of, 117; buried, 56; execution, 64

Sorcery, incest as, 17; not taught by father, *see* father, suspicion, 28; effect of, 48; human flesh used in, 57; chief and, 62

Sorghum, 1, 5, 71, 102, 105, 143, 155;

Spear, 21, 59; inherited, 132

Spirit, possession, 156; medicines of, 160; animistic beliefs in, 161

Succession, not children to father, 21; to chiefdom, 44, 56, 62; to headmanship, 48, 132; *see* widows.

Stranger, clan, attitude to, 3; integration of, in funeral friendship, 7; marrying, 38; in village, 41, 43, 49; relatives as, 110

syabe (pl. *masyabe*), a possessing spirit and dance, 156

Taboo, 108, *see* avoidances, prohibitions, marriage rules.

Tonga, 71, 101, 102

Town, taking wife to, 20; spending time in, 19; refusing to go to, 118

tunyelele, small ants, 106

tuoma, sprites, 153

tupanda, bow stand, 69

tupondo (sing. *kapondo*), *see kapondo*.

tusuba (pl.), hot, dry season, xviii

tuyowela, familiars, 148

Ululate, 105, 138, 143, 144, 154

Ululation, 76, 96

usi, father, 22

usifyala, father-in-law, 22

usinkasi, father's sister, 22, 108

Uxorilocal, residence, 15; as protection, 18; period as test, 19

Village, site, xvii, of founder, 8, 28; returning to, 19, 32, 100; working in strange, 20; co-operation, in, 20; formed by matrilineage, 23, 27, 28, 41, 43; widows stranded in strange, 27; scattering of, split and change, 28, 29, 39; plan and size, 29; shelter, 29, 87; eating in, 93, 104; composition, 42; section, 30, 44; doctored, 45-7; autonomous, 49; administration of, 50; stockaded, 68; delivers outside of, 75; live in, 101, ; two wives, in, 111

Wife, supernatural responsibility of, 14, 131; company with husband, travelling, 15; looking for, 19; beating, 19, 20; of chief, 56, 58, 61; wergild, 52; not compensated, 54; adulteress, 64; wife's mother, 74; seeking refuge, 107; of polygamist, 110; acquires kitchen, 109; second, 111; death of, 113

Witchcraft Ordinance, 117

Woman, birth honoured of, 18; travelling, marital rights, chastised by husband, economic duties of, 19; Nyendwa, 21, 54, 62; ancestress, 27; no right to select domicile, 28, 38; disposition of clanswomen, table V, stranger, 43; as headman, 48; as hostage, 52; as chief, 62; for chief, 63, pregnant, 74 seq.; attitude to marriage, 79; old and young prone to divorce, 114; deserts and deserted, lack of children, 116 and divorce, 117

Yamba, flood, 135

yalwela, war medicine, 69

ya nsangu, medicine of transformation, 58